SURVIVOR: Cadwallader Colden II

in Revolutionary America

by

Eugene R. Fingerhut

California State University, Los Angeles

Copyright © 1983 by

University Press of America, Inc.

P.O. Box 19101, Washington, D.C. 20036

Library of Congress Cataloging in Publication Data

Fingerhut, Eugene R.
Survivor, Cadwallader Colden II in Revolutionary
America.

Bibliography: p.
Includes index.
1. Colden, Cadwallader, 1722-1797. 2. New York
(State)--Politics and government--Revolution, 1775-1783.
3. American loyalists--New York (State)--Biography.
4. New York (State)--Biography. I. Title.
E278.C67F56 1982   973.3'14'0924 [B]   82-20092
ISBN 0-8191-2868-6
ISBN 0-8191-2869-4 (pbk.)

ACKNOWLEDGMENTS

Sources for this biography were obtained through the kind cooperation of the staffs at the Henry E. Huntington Library; Los Angeles Public Library's Genealogy Room; John F. Kennedy Memorial Library, California State University at Los Angeles—especially Ms. Chris Caldwell of interlibrary loan services; New-York Historical Society Library; William L. Clements Library; and Library of Congress.

Of outstanding value were recommendations of Paul Zall of California State University at Los Angeles, and the labors of Ms. Kate Mearns, sometime research technician at the Senate House Historic Site, Kingston, New York; Mr. Robert Eurich, administrator of Hill-Hold, in Montgomery, New York; Professor Leo Hershkowitz at the Historical Documents Collection of Queens College, and Mr. Roger Wood, my former student. I benefited greatly from the expertise of Professor Milton Klein, who critiqued an early version of this study and reinforced flagging spirits. Professor Richard Dean Burns was a gentleman, scholar, and friend when needed. Mrs. Bernice Lifton's timely advice avoided many possible errors. The secretaries of the Department of History at CSULA were invaluable in their aid.

Of a different type is my indebtedness to the persons to whom this book is dedicated. Lyn makes all things possible. Karin, Mindy and Terry, and now Steve assist her.

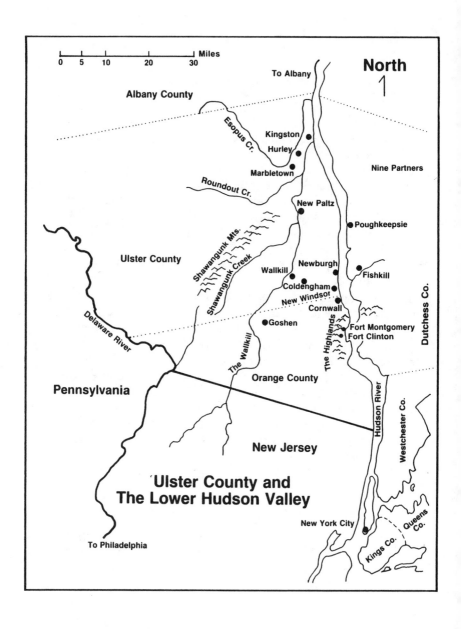

Miles
0 5 10 20 30

North

To Albany

Albany County

Esopus Cr.

Kingston
Hurley
Marbletown

Nine Partners

Roundout Cr.

New Paltz

Poughkeepsie

Shawangunk Mts.

Ulster County

Shawangunk Creek

Wallkill

Newburgh

Coldengham
New Windsor
Cornwall

Fishkill

Dutchess Co.

Delaware River

Goshen

The Wallkill

The Highlands

Fort Montgomery
Fort Clinton

Pennsylvania

Orange County

Hudson River

Westchester Co.

New Jersey

**Ulster County and
The Lower Hudson Valley**

New York City

Queens Co.

Kings Co.

To Philadelphia

Contents

   I. The World of His Youth............................ 1

  II. The Second Son..................................... 11

 III. Squire Colden II.................................... 23

 IV. The End of a Dream............................... 39

  V. Prisoner of the Revolution........................ 51

 VI. The Failure of Influence........................... 71

VII. Banished... 87

VIII. At Home in New York City....................... 99

 IX. Restoration 119

  X. "The Old Gentleman"...............................133

      Notes..153

      Bibliography..177

      Index..187

Chapter I
The World of His Youth

The old man reached for his quill and paper. He had a most pleasant task to perform, for he was going to describe his family and narrate its history. To a Scottish cousin he had never met, Cadwallader Colden II recalled his father's settlement in the colonies, and his career as a medical doctor, member of the governor's Council, royal New York's surveyor-general, several times acting governor, and ardent tory. He remembered his siblings who had all died, some of them leaving minor children whom he had taken into his household. He and his wife, Elizabeth, cared for them and later the children of his deceased daughter. As he wrote Elizabeth sat by him "as busy at her needle as if just beginning the world," although she had endured a dozen births. Seven children survived childhood, but only six lived to that year, 1796. They resided with their families on nearby farms; even the sole bachelor remained at home. As Elizabeth busied herself Cadwallader recalled that, "We have now lived together above fifty years, and I believe, no fifty years were spent happier by any other pair."[1]

If as he wrote his mind wandered from family concerns he must have realized that he had not been so constantly happy. True, his wife was a continual companion, partner, friend, loved one, yet their life together had suffered a revolution which he opposed and which had split the family. Oaks are majestic trees yet their rigidity is their undoing in a hurricane. Heroes die in battle, in jail, in exile, or in poverty. Colden's strength was as a willow's: he bent and rarely acted rashly. He had survived as a loyalist because of his personality, luck and the division in his family's allegiance.

Throughout his life he had aspired to prestige and sought the public status supposedly due him. That he failed to win them was partially because of psychological insecurities stemming from relations in his childhood. To see the Revolution through his eyes is to see it from a different perspective than that of such New York revolutionaries as George Clinton and John Jay, or such loyalists as Oliver DeLancey and William Smith, Jr. Colden endured prison, emotional crises, exile, and impending financial ruin in a Revolution he opposed. Observers who doubt his triumph should recall the tragedy of such men as the Massachusetts loyalist, Thomas Hutchinson, who died forlorn in a miserable exile.

The Colden family in America had been sired by Cadwallader, Sr., who moved to the southern part of New York's Ulster County in 1727, seven years after he obtained land for his estate, "Coldengham." When the site was ready he brought from New York City his wife Alice and six children: eleven-year-old Alexander, six-year-old Elizabeth, five-year-old Cadwallader II, three-year-old Jane, and one-year-old Alice. The infant Sarah was to die in two years, but at Coldengham were born John in 1729, Catherine in 1731, and David in 1733. This brood was settled in an area just emerging from the wilderness along the west bank of the Hudson River.

Society on the east side of the Hudson Valley was different. There life was dominated by the immensely large land patentees and manorial lords such as the Livingston, DeLancey and Beekman families, whose domains with tens of thousands of acres and up to hundreds of tenants controlled the region from Westchester through Albany. The small scale farmer who owned his land was not the norm in this strip between the Hudson River and the New England colonies. Most of the arable land on the eastern shore was rented by the great landlords, as were most mills and stores. Mansions here were among the most opulent in all the colonies.

However, the Coldens lived in the less stratified Ulster County, north of where the Highlands bluffs narrowly squeeze the river. At the west shore precipices Forts Montgomery and Clinton were created by the Americans during the Revolution to keep the British bottled up in the lower Hudson Valley. The shoreline opens from just below New Windsor to just above Newburgh revealing a corridor to the west. From Newburgh to Kingston, for about the next thirty miles, the bank remained sparsely settled so that these neighboring south Ulster riverports dominated the area. West of the Hudson flowed the Wallkill, northward out of New Jersey. Beyond its vale stood the Shawangunk Mountains, marking the western fringe of English settlement until the mid-eighteenth century. Westward were the Indians and French. The region between the Hudson and the Wallkill was more suitable for small farm plots and cattle than for great estates. Well watered, with several rapids or low waterfalls, this area had the potential to develop small scale industries such as flour and lumber mills. Although some swamps were drained enough remained to provide hideouts for loyalist brigands and refugees during the Revolution.

The population of Ulster grew rapidly in the eighteenth century, but the county's immense size and proximity to the frontier kept its density low. The 3,000 square mile county was second in size to Albany County, but had less than 4.5 persons per square mile. Even in its eastern third, closest to the Hudson River, the county had only 14 persons per square mile. By comparison, New York County had 980 persons, rural Richmond, 50, and Ulster's eastern neighbor, Dutchess had over 22 persons per square mile.² Thus, for its entire colonial experience the county's population was huddled close to the Hudson, hardly pushing one-third of the way to its western border.

Coldengham lay in the New Windsor-Newburgh corridor to the Wallkill Valley, well located in an area which was not an outstanding agricultural region. Even though the soil was generally thin and agriculture was hard work, it paid. Because there were no wagons here until the 1750s, the Coldens and their neighbors carried their farm produce on horseback or by two-wheeled cart to market at nearby riverports.

Ulster was the home of several ethnic groups, the largest being the Dutch, who lived throughout the northern part of Ulster. Notable also were German Palatines and Huguenots, coagulated in knots throughout the county. The English, Scots, and Ulster-Scots arrived late and although some settled in Kingston, most stayed in southern Ulster. Thus the county was split ethnically. Near Coldengham was the Presbyterian Goodwill Church and the Reverend Robert Annan's Associated Reformed Presbyterian Church. Annan's sect was popularly called the Seceder Church because it rejected other Protestant meetings as too accomodating to Anglicanism and maintained its own meetinghouse in the village of Little Britain. Less numerous in southern Ulster were the Anglicans, thoroughly outnumbered by their militant Presbyterian neighbors.³ Intently and overtly Church of England, the Colden family was to lead a powerful and resented minority.

Local jurisdictions were created by the colony in reponse to the needs of the growing rural population. The precincts of New Windsor and Newburgh were probably about two-thirds as populous as Coldengham's precinct, Hanover, and the other farming settlement of Wallkill, located along the stream from Ward's Bridge to the falls. The two riverports were little more than piers and a few shops. When created from the southern part of Wallkill precinct in 1772, Hanover was populated by many British immigrants, except for its western section which contained some Dutch and Germans. Newburgh, settled as Quassaick by about fifty German Palatine Lutherans in 1719, was a British dominated village by 1732 when the original group declined and the Scottish name "Newburgh" was first used in a contract.⁴

The small riverports were important for nearby farmers even though the villages never won much traffic on the Hudson; Newburgh's only inn was insufficient to attract travelers. New Windsor was a larger commercial center for southern Ulster until after the Revolutionary War. About 1720 the founder of its leading family, John Ellison, a New York merchant, had moved to the village. By 1724, perhaps as a wedding present, he built a stone mansion on a bluff overlooking the Hudson for his son

Thomas, who ran a sloop from the riverport to his father's dock at the foot of Little Queen Street in New York City, where later he was to be an active merchant. With their ships, store, and mill, the Ellisons were a most important economic influence in the wedgeshaped area that spread out from the New Windsor point, past Coldengham, to the broad side along the Wallkill.[5]

If the Ellisons represented New Windsor's commercial present, Charles Clinton presaged its political future. His two prominent sons were the state's first governor, George Clinton, and the Revolutionary War general, James Clinton. In 1729 Charles Clinton led a group of Ulster-Scots from Dublin and in 1731 selected as their new home the inland part of New Windsor precinct, the village of Little Britain, although he lived just over the line in the Coldens' precinct. Charles' sons lived in the village which was to be the den of much hostility to Cadwallader Colden II during the Revolutionary War, even though Cadwallader, Sr. and the Clinton sire were close friends. Indeed, the surveyor-general may have been responsible for the immigrant's appointment as judge of the Ulster Court of Common Pleas as well as for young George's selection as court clerk in 1759.[6] Much anti-Colden sentiment in Little Britain was whipped up by the Reverend Annan and his leading parishioners. Four miles west of Coldengham, on the Wallkill near Ward's Bridge, was a settlement in which Arthur Park and John McGarrow operated a store and where Park hosted local political meetings at his inn.

These settlements were linked by many locally maintained roads and paths. The King's Highway ran north through Little Britain past the eastern fence of Coldengham where an important road from the Hudson crossed it traversing Coldengham as it meandered to the Wallkill. It then turned southwest to Goshen and on to the Delaware River by which Philadelphia was accessible. The conditions of these roads were sometimes less than adequate even by the standards of rural eighteenth century America. On September 19, 1762, Cadwallader Colden II protested to the county court that the overseers of highways in the precinct of Newburgh had allowed the main route from the Wallkill to deteriorate despite his former complaints. Squire of the most prominent estate in the area and son of the acting governor of the colony, Colden argued that he and his neighbors suffered by not being able to get their produce to market.[7]

These roads served Hanover in which lived about 325 families, a population of about 2,000. Property in this agricultural community was more equally distributed than in such east bank Hudson Valley settlements as the long established Livingston owned district of Claverack in Albany County in which lived many poor persons according to the assessment of 1779. In that same year the Ulster frontier precinct of Shawangunk contained about 150 families, most with little property. There surely were some impoverished colonists in the Hanover area. All precincts selected two overseers and one clerk and imposed their own rates to care for their own poor. In the 1760s and early 1770s New Windsor's poor tax reached £20, as Newburgh's went to £30 in 1769. The economic crisis immediately preceding the Revolution certainly took its toll on Newburgh's destitute, for its tax rose to £40 in 1774 and to £50 the following year.[8]

On September 11, 1767, Cadwallader Colden II was charged forty-three shillings for his share of the poor tax. Three years later at Arthur Park's house the Wallkill jury raised £33.12½ for the precinct's poor. In that year Cadwallader Colden II received £20.12.2 for expenses in caring for some of the precinct's destitute. This was almost one-third of the monies expended here for such relief. This poor rate may have been high because Wallkill was close to the frontier and had many undercapitalized enterprises and farms. In 1774 Hanover, which had just been formed from Wallkill's eastern villages, authorized £14.10 to deal with the only person on relief.[9] If this cost to support one indigent a year is typical, New Windsor, which did not raise more than £20 per year in the decade before the Revolution, supported about one and a half indigents annually. Newburgh's tax was frequently about £35, enough for about two and a half poor persons per year. Impoverished frontier Wallkill had an expense of £70 in 1772 and may have supported five persons. The figures demonstrate that little money was raised for the poor throughout southern Ulster and that there were few persons maintained by taxpayers.

Slaves of Ulster in the late colonial period appear to have been concentrated in the older northern sections of the county. Merely twenty-four lived at New Windsor in 1755—thirteen of whom were men and eleven women. That the sex ratio was almost balanced indicates slaves performed many agricultural and household tasks, for if they were used as artisans many more would have been men. Cadwallader Colden, Sr. was probably the largest slaveholder in this part of the county. Soon after obtaining possession of the land on which he was to create Coldengham, he sought the purchase of two strong male slaves about eighteen years old and a pleasant-natured female of about thirteen to work in the kitchen and be with the children. Three years later he apparently had only one slave left, but he kept looking for suitable field hands. A decade after the estate was formed the Coldens owned four men and two women.[10]

The relation between the slaves and the master's family were not unlike master-slave relations in the southern colonies. Social intercourse between young black and white children was permissible, but by puberty adult relations were created. Colden's children were expected to become young masters at an early age. When his youngest son David was ten years old the father wrote to Alice that she should remind the boy he was no longer a child, and in the father's absence he was to behave maturely. The mother was to impress upon David that he should be ashamed to play with slave children out of doors.[11] By the time the boy was ten years old and being admonished to start adult social relations with slave children, Cadwallader II was already twenty. He had been ten years old when his mother recorded that six slaves were at Coldengham, so he probably grew up in an environment similar to David's. When he was in his early twenties, Cadwallader II may have personally supervised his father's slaves who labored to clear land and create his estate farm. They would have chopped wedges into tree trunks, gathered brush, and uprooted stubs. Coldengham was not completely an agricultural factory run by slave labor, but on it lived more slaves than on neighboring farms.

Although he reveled in Coldengham, its founder was often in the colonial capital. After 1720 Surveyor-General Colden was the government official most responsible for granting land and was deeply involved in perpetuating the large estate system that he constantly criticized. His office required that he attest to the validity of an applicant's request for land, that he certify the proposed boundaries were what they were presented to be, and that the land grant be consistent with imperial and colonial law. Colden's arguments with land speculators did not keep him from enlarging grant fees paid to him, from helping his friends obtain land, and from finding loopholes in laws so he could become a landed squire. Particularly benefited was his friend Sir William Johnson of the Mohawk Valley. For one of Johnson's relatives, Surveyor-General Colden offered to draw up a petition for a patent to land in the northern frontier of New York and predate the document so the man would have a few days' priority over veterans whose land applications actually arrived earlier at the colonial Council. Colden also helped Sir William, who continued to seek land even though in 1769 he owned over one million acres in the upper Susquehanna and Mohawk valleys. To consummate a large land deal, Colden advised Johnson to create a bogus syndicate and use other people's names merely to obtain more than the royal limit of two thousand acres per person in any one grant.

Colden's own land deals were conducted on a much smaller scale. Ann Grant, a Scottish woman who lived in New York, recalled after the Revolution that his investment practices were well within the bounds of good taste. Colden worked with friendly government officials who used their influence to get land far below market value. They then sold it to Colden who was willing to hold on to it until he could sell when the market price rose. Sometimes he leased farms on his grants, but most often he profited from land sales. He participated in a syndicate to buy the "Oblong" patent, a long narrow strip of land against the border with New England and remote from river transportation. He also held some small tracts in the Mohawk and Schoharie valleys, the Green Mountains and in Orange and Ulster counties.[12] One example of his small scale operation involved his holdings in Newburgh. Had he been a Sir William Johnson he might have attempted to buy the whole town; instead he formed a syndicate with six other men and held only a few town lots. More spectacular was his purchase of Coldengham, which made him a member of the squirearchy, if not an aristocrat. On April 19, 1719, he received a grant for two thousand acres, the legal maximum per person. Contiguous were two thousand acres issued to John Johnson, Jr. on February 2, 1720, of which one thousand became Colden's on the day Johnson received it. Johnson retained the thousand acres furthest from Colden's patent in what was to become Little Britain. Colden may have acted as Johnson's agent at a fee of half the acreage granted, or he may have used Johnson as a front and paid him off with one thousand acres. Regardless, the acquisition of one-third of what was to become Coldengham demonstrates that the critic of land grabs was not above making a deal for himself as well as for political and personal friends.

Colden also used his position and status to take care of his children, and through them, perhaps to care for himself. It is improbable that Cadwallader Colden II at age sixteen controlled two-thirds of an investment with Coenrat Rightmeyer in three thousand acres near Canajoharie, south of the Mohawk River. The next year the seventeen-year-old son's name was used by the father to purchase two thousand acres in Albany with four other speculators. Also unlikely is the conclusion that two daughters of the colonial official, twenty-five-year-old Jane and twenty-four-year-old Alice Colden, obtained four thousand acres by themselves. The father was probably involved in these deals, just as he was the purchaser of New York City land for his daughter Elizabeth before she married Peter DeLancey. He likely was the buyer of land for his unmarried daughter Catherine, who at her death at age thirty-one, divided two thousand acres among two nephews and one neice and gave another two thousand acres in the Mohawk Valley to her sister Alice.[13] However, in the 1750s when his sons grew older they made their own investments; by then Cadwallader II would have been in his thirties and Alexander in his forties.

Alexander Colden's rise to prominence in New York is worth considering, for it is an example of the nepotism in British society and of what Cadwallader Colden II could have achieved in public life had he the requisite ability and the inclination. Instead, Alexander's success seems to have been a trigger for manifestations of his younger brother's jealousy. The father's purchases of village real estate were outstripped by Alexander who owned a store, wharf, ships, and mill, thereby dominating Newburgh as Thomas Ellison did New Windsor. Although he began commercial activity at Coldengham operating a store there before he was thirty, by 1743 he was fully immersed in Newburgh's development, having used his family name and his father's power. In that year he built the village's first mill on Quassaick Creek and controlled most of the waterfront lots in southern Newburgh. North of his holdings was sparse economic development, which would have added little to the Coldens' domination of the village. Nevertheless, the Coldens did own unsettled land in the area, such as Colden's Ridge a bit back from the Hudson in Marlborough, Newburgh's northern neighbor.

When Alexander obtained his mill he received from the colonial government a charter to operate a ferry to New York City and to Fishkill across the Hudson. These business enterprises constantly involved him in financial conflicts. Beginning in the May 1742 session of the county Court of Common Pleas until he left Ulster a decade later, Alexander Colden was regularly seeking payments of debts, never losing a case. As befitting such an entrepreneur Alexander Colden lived in a mansion, "Newburgh House," bought in 1749. The square, two-story frame building, with dormer windows, fronted the river on the road to his ferry at Colden's Gore, where Water and Colden streets converged.[14]

In 1753 he reduced his economic activity in Newburgh by selling the mill and several lots because two years earlier he had been appointed joint surveyor-general with his father. From then on Alexander Colden spent an increasing amount of time in New York City as heir apparent of Cadwallader, Sr. In 1761 he officially succeeded the elder Colden as surveyor-general when his father became acting governor of the colony. In that year George III ascended the throne and was welcomed by a petition from fifty-six of the most prominent men in the colony. The address included the names of such persons as Cadwallader Colden, Sr., his eldest son Alexander, and the twenty-eight-year-old youngest son David, who served as his personal secretary and as the provincial secretary. Missing was Cadwallader Colden's middle son, his namesake, who was then thirty-nine years old and still living at Coldengham. In that same year Alexander was to move his family to New York City and become a vestryman of prestigious Trinity Church. He not only held his father's old office but also was postmaster of the province. On December 12, 1774, he died at fifty-eight years. Hardly a landowner of the DeLancey, Morris or Beekman scale, at his death Alexander Colden had far outstripped his siblings. The younger brother was already in his fifties when freed of the burden of his competent older brother.

Cadwallader II now had to contend with his precocious youngest brother David, who was trained as a medical doctor, was weighmaster of the colony, and served the acting governor. He shared his father's interest in science and made his own scientific observations, wrote essays, corresponded with such luminaries as Benjamin Franklin, and owned parcels of land in Newburgh. On the death of his eldest brother, David assumed the office of surveyor-general but did not serve during the Revolutionary War. This was the last major attempt of old Cadwallader to elevate his sons. As David remained constantly at his father's side after Alexander's death, helping the old man develop Springhill after 1761, Cadwallader II lived in the hinterland remote from a prestigious life in the provincial capital.[15] David's role in New York's royal government was to be both a boon and burden to him during and after the Revolutionary War.

Nor was the welfare of his daughters overlooked by Cadwallader, Sr. In 1737 his eldest daughter, Elizabeth, married Peter, the third son of Stephen DeLancey. Another daughter, Jane, was known in Europe by Peter Collinson and Linneaus to be an accomplished botanist. At age thirty-four, after a home-centered career she married a medical doctor. The other surviving daughter, Alice, became the second wife of William Willet, a member of the prominent southern New York family. The Colden sire probably was responsible for the appointment of Alexander's eldest son, Richard Nicholls Colden, as surveyor and searcher of customs. Elizabeth Colden DeLancey's sons were well placed because of two aristocratic parents. Peter was collector under the Stamp Act until he resigned under the pressures of the Sons of Liberty. Stephen, his brother, served as clerk of the city and county of Albany as had his uncle John, the youngest brother of Cadwallader II who had prematurely died at age twenty-one. John DeLancey was sheriff of Westchester County and later served in the Assembly. James DeLancey succeeded John DeLancey as sheriff. Cadwallader II had only infrequent contact with these relatives during the Revolutionary War and they had no direct effect on his experiences. More important than his relations with siblings and their offspring, was the fact that prominent Coldens were loyalists, thereby encouraging the revolutionaries to identify the family as the enemy.

The senior Colden's manipulation of offices for nepotic purposes deeply offended many people, especially Isaac Willet of Westchester who resigned as county sheriff so that his nephew Lewis Graham could succeed him. Instead, the acting governor appointed Gilbert Colden Willet, another nephew of Isaac and grandson of the appointer. In Isaac Willet's will the former sheriff explained he had wanted to leave a large parcel of land to Gilbert Willet, but instead he passed it to Lewis Graham. Apparently piqued the elder Willet explained he did not have to consider Gilbert's future because his grandfather "is well able to make handsome provision for him."[16] The Coldens took care of their children and grandchildren.

Chapter II
The Second Son

Although Cadwallader II was born in 1722 in New York City the family moved to Coldengham in 1727. Cadwallader II was not a product of the colonial capital, for it was here on the estate that he was raised and his personality formed. By the time he was thirty-five, Cadwallader II had been a farmer, surveyor, an army officer, and above all a Colden, the son of a most important colonial official. The young man never had to fend for himself, for nepotism and patronage were normal for people of his social status.

When the Coldens moved from New York City the estate was still being developed. A bog was drained creating excellent pasture and much peat, which the family and tenants preferred for fuel because lumber was too valuable to burn. The father deepened and widened the swamp's main drainage ditch into the first canal built in New York and probably rafted on it the building stone for his Coldengham house. Cadwallader II, or Cad as he was known in the family, lived in this house only as a child. As an adult he constructed his own residence on the north side of the road connecting the Hudson and the Wallkill, across from his father's.[1]

Cadwallader, Sr.'s frequent absences from the estate thrust great responsibilities for educating the brood on his wife Alice. The father recognized he had truncated his children's development by pulling his family from the social intercourse of New York City, but rationalized the move because it isolated them from the evils of big city life. To supplement the unstimulating environment, he created educational challenges for his offspring. To his wife, and later to his married daughter, he explained that a liberal education would well expand a youngster's horizons. He criticized the specialized education that would concentrate on one subject or skill, complaining "the mere Scholar, the mere Physician, the mere Lawyer, Musician or Painter, take them out of their way, and they are often more insipid than the mere plowman." It was by this home-developed curriculum, devised by his father and carried out by his mother, that Cadwallader II was educated. However, the frail hunchbacked youngest child, David, was treated differently. The youngest son's intellectual precocity was recognized and nurtured by his father, whose scientific interests were passed on only to daughter Jane and son David. Cadwallader, Sr. encouraged David's electrical experiments and obviously favored his youngest son, a weak and sensitive child with a brilliant mind. David fondly remembered that the major part of his education was constant conversation with his father. Cad never expressed such happy memories. He never wrote fond phrases of his father.[2]

Affection appears in Colden family letters, but little humor is evident. Hardly a light touch survives in Cadwallader II's written statements. He was a sober Scottish farmer, "always more fond of working in the field than of literature." On the five hundred acres of Coldengham given him by his father he "felled the first tree, and took out the first stub with [his] own hands." To this he was trained. He served on his father's Coldengham farm learning the techniques of husbandry from his sire's instructions, passed on by his mother. When Cad was nineteen years old Cadwallader, Sr. informed Alice how he wanted his second son to perform specific farm tasks. "I would have you again assure him that I am much pleas'd with his Diligence," praised the senior Colden. Two years later the father again wrote his wife that he was still satisfied with her operation of the estate and Cad's efforts. So well did he appreciate Cad's work that he admonished his sixteen-year-old son John to continue farm work under his older brother's tutelage. The father lauded Cad's mastery of skills but the master of Coldengham trusted his wife's good sense and judgment more than the son's.[3] This reservation about Cad's abilities, in marked contrast to the father's respect for David's intellect, may well have been passed on in gestures or in casual conversation. It would be most difficult to avoid giving Cad the true impression that the father trusted his wife's acumen more than his namesake's.

Cad's attitude toward his parents is evident in a letter written when he was seventy-four years old. His comment about his mother was a loving tribute. She was "a well educated lady" who "was as capable as most women, giving the brightest example of virtue and economy." Of his wife, whom he deeply loved, he could offer no greater praise than that she was "as good a wife as if she had been brought up by my own mother." However, his father was coldly described in terms of political achievement. Cadwallader II recalled that the father's sense of duty in the prerevolutionary crisis induced many enemies to denounce him, even though "his private character was unimpeached and highly respected." Without emotion the son noted in this reminiscence that his father took his family to the colonial capital and left him in possession of Coldengham. Completely absent from this letter or from any other recollection of his father is the son's appreciation of Cadwallader, Sr.'s instructions in farming or surveying, or in any other skill. Cad offered no overt demonstration of affection for his sire.[4]

The son may have loved farming, to which he was trained, because it deeply appealed to his personality. Yet, he may also have been impelled toward this sentiment for psychological reasons. Alexander was an urban person, and David was too weak to be a successful farmer; thus, Cad eased himself into a family niche. In addition, by controlling an estate, Cad was a member of the provincial landed gentry and therefore had a high social position without having to compete with others in the family. Perhaps by wanting to be a farmer, the second son sought approbation from a father who did not lavish praise on him. However valid may be such psychological interpretations, the social effect was that Cadwallader II always considered Coldengham the reservoir which replenished his concept of self worth and provided his security. Cad's love for farming was a real and deeply felt affection.

In addition to this vocation, the father stimulated Cad to be a surveyor because land was the key to wealth in colonial America, and such skills were assumed crucial to financial success. At the age of twenty, when he was not allowed to manage Coldengham, Cad was traveling beyond Albany on surveying expeditions. When he was married and twenty-five years old, his father sent him to survey a lot on the Oblong Patent. Typical of their relationship, the father asked this of Cad through a letter to Alice, whom he also told, "you must give him [Cad] what money may be requisite." Old enough to be married, the son of one of the most powerful men in the colonly was still being addressed and controlled by his father through his mother, even as he was respected for his surveying skills. The elder Colden admonished John, who was then twenty years old, that he would learn much if he should accompany Cad on a field survey trip. Cad was not given credit for maturity or business sense, but was respected for his accomplishment in a limited sphere of activity; Deputy Surveyor-General Cadwallader Colden II issued surveys under his own name but made no policy decisions.[5]

Even though the father lacked such confidence in Cad he obtained his son's appointment as commissary for the militia at Albany during King George's War. He was characteristically as callous in this incident as he was in others. During August 1746, in conversation with the royal Gover-nor George Clinton at Albany, Colden was told that a trustworthy person could not be found for the commissary position. The father responded to his political ally and friend by recommending twenty-four year old Cad, who had just been married, because the position had a potential for advancement even though the salary was merely a captain's. The father told his wife to send Cad up "under pretence to visit me but in reality to be in readiness to receive the Commiss[n]." Colden had really wanted to recommend Alexander, whose business skills were superior to Cad's, but he thought Alexander less able to accompany the army in the field. Typically, Alice's husband concluded by throwing the matter on her capable shoulders, "I leave it to you & them to do as you shall think proper because I cannot advise any further it is attended with so many uncertainties only I would not let such an offer pass without giving my children an opportunity of using if they think fit."

Without waiting for Alice's response Colden informed the family that Cad's appointment was to be the family goal. But when the son did not receive the commission in three months he manifested enough impatience to draw a reprimand from his father by way of his mother. "I have no time to write in answer to Cad's [letter] he should learn more patience otherwise he never can be easy in this world [.] He may trust to my assisting of him in his necessities if he behave as he ought." In the meantime, the father advised that Cad knew what was required during the winter on the estate and was to get the servants and slaves to prepare for spring. In mid-November Colden informed Alice "my breast is too full when I think of him," and concluded that Alice should do what she would.

With this opinion the issue seemed dead until the end of May when the father reopened the affair by explaining that the mutiny of British troops at Albany over lack of pay had held up all administrative matters, "& Cadwallader must have patience as to his commission." The father was too busy "to think of Cadwallader's affairs." Finally on June 2, 1747, ten months after it was first raised as a family issue, the father wrote Alice he was sending out the commission, and she should tell Cad to be ready to leave for Albany in about a week.[6] Thus the second son was being cared for by his father in ways typical of the eighteenth century British gentry. The eldest son was the father's political protegee, receiving from his sire the ornaments of society. Cad, as befitting a second son, received training in surveying and farming—means of making a living, but he also obtained a commission in the army to secure his place. His younger brother John was given more civilian political opportunities than was Cad because of his frail health, and David was to become the father's secretary and after Alexander's death the senior Colden's second protegee. The father's attempts to place Cad were more normal than his remote and almost frigid personal relations to his son.

Not trusting Cad to succeed by his own effort, the father asked a friend in the Albany area to seek out his son and advise him, for "he will stand much in need of it by his being little acquainted with the world." The innocent to whom the father referred was by then a married twenty-four-year-old man. In his father's eyes Cadwallader II seemed fated never to grow up. Such an attitude could produce an insecure, dependent son. Not once did the father directly write to his son; all matters were presented through Alice who had to mollify Cad. No wonder the son recalled his mother with fonder memories than his father, for it was she who doled out the secondhand praise as well as the money to Cad when he performed estate duties or land surveys for his father.

As expected when the war ended, Cad's future would be cared for by the family head. On the son's return from the army, when this commission was no longer valuable, Colden obtained for Cad a captain's position in the local militia. According to the father's report to the governor, Captain John Bayard had been too critical of his superiors. Although the company's officers were honest men they were not fit to command; therefore, he told the governor, "I am forced to avoid greater inconveniences to propose my son Cadwallader for that Commission."[7] This ploy was typical. Later Ulster County Sheriff Egbert Dumond would be squeezed out of office so Thomas Colden, Lieutenant Governor Colden's grandson, could enter public office.

The father's use of a gentleman's power to elevate his dependents in spite of the niceties of justice was consistent with his political aggressiveness. The senior Colden was an ardent imperialist and favored a forceful policy against the French. These opinions alienated him from such politicians as James DeLancey, who feared war with Canada would destroy the Albany fur trade and might physically destroy New York's frontier. During King George's War, Colden and Robert Livingston broke over the surveyor-general's influence with the royal governor Clinton and his advice concerning an attack on Canada. Colden's desire that the governor's salary come from quit rents (a form of land tax) rather than Assembly appropriation angered popular politicians, as his suggestions to curb land speculation alienated investors. Respected and feared, the Colden family was not the darling of the people. Politically, Colden's power was the prerogative, and this alienation from other members of the gentry with power in the Assembly could be withstood by the elder Colden. Sons Alexander and David and even John were being brought up through political ranks by their father's patronage. However, Cadwallader II was not given such political aid to rise in colonial-wide positions. Feeling he lacked his father's full confidence, perhaps Cad also felt the lack of a shield to protect him from what were more politically popular aspirants.

By 1745 when he sought a wife, Cad seemed to have learned to consider people useful objects. Given by his father 525 of Coldengham's 3,000 acres, the twenty-two year old Colden first cleared the land and then started building himself a house. In that year he found Thomas Ellison's twenty-year-old daughter Elizabeth, who was a social as well as a marital prize. As a septegenarian he recalled his marriage rather prosaically.

> I thought it was proper to look for a housekeeper before my house was finished. I got one in the neighbourhood, for I could not spare time to go far, and if I had I should not have found better.

By marrying her Cad was entering a family which had its own social dreams. Thomas Ellison married his children to New York City's successful Peck family, the aristocratic Floyd's of Long Island, and the locally prominent Johnston's of Kingston. Betsy's marriage to Cad gave the Ellison's another successful alliance.

After he and Elizabeth had been married for over a decade, Cad's sister Elizabeth Colden DeLancey informed her mother that she was sorry to find Cad was not advancing economically: "I thought one great inducement for his marrying in that family was the thought that his circumstances would have been made quite easy which he tells me now are very straigh[t]." The groom soon found that he could not count on the Ellisons for financial aid and whatever successes he obtained would have to be accomplished through his own family. This helps to explain Cad's impatience with his father over the appointment as commissary the year after his wedding. He wanted money and prestige quickly.[8]

The marriage of Cadwallader and Elizabeth Ellison Colden may have begun with less ardor than the romantic splicing of two souls, but it matured. Its strength demonstrates that in this case love was more durable as a product of rather than as a raw material for a marriage. The home Elizabeth made was a comfort and refuge. Cad loved his family and his genteel squirearchy. Obviously his mundane search for a housekeeper resulted in a happy union even though no letters by him attest to his love. He did not write of his emotional experiences. This reserved Scottish colonial manifested his love as deeply as his nature permitted.

Although their economic condition seemed solid to persons outside their household, Cad and Elizabeth thought it was precarious. Of the squirearchy by birth, the five hundred acres he had in his name should have made him feel secure, but it paled by comparison to Alexander's worth. Cad had some land investments, for in 1752, at age thirty, he was one of a syndicate of four speculators who obtained a grant, and in 1760 he and his brother David were to receive a patent for a thousand acres in the Wallkill Precinct. In 1761 he was given all of Coldengham's three thousand acres when his father went to New York City to serve as lieutentant governor. He and David again were partners in 1772, buying from George Croghan fourteen thousand acres on the upper Susquehanna River. Therefore, when the Revolution broke out, Cad was part owner of almost twenty thousand acres, but much of his wealth was tied up in land, and he suffered from lack of an adequate cash flow. His inability to solve this financial problem was to produce tensions all his life.

In the 1740s with Alexander in Newburgh, Cadwallader II was the eldest son at Coldengham and one of the most prominent men in Wallkill. The voters responded accordingly and in 1745-46 he served with his father-in-law on a panel of precinct supervisors who levied the county taxes. At this time his wife and children probably remained at Coldengham, but he may have had no fixed social and economic base because several letters written to his father were sent to him at Newburgh with requests that they be forwarded to the surveyor-general.[9] This indicates Cad moved about from Coldengham to Newburgh in the late 1740s and early 1750s often enough for persons to use him as a messenger. At Coldengham he had his wedding gift of a five hundred acre farm, his new home, and his growing family. Until he was nearly forty years old his father had the estate and status as the family squire. At Newburgh he obviously was Alexander's younger brother. If he was trying to enter the commercial world there he would have to do so in a demeaning manner.

Probably for these reasons he energetically pursued a career as a surveyor, for in 1743 before he was married, he had surveyed frontier tracts as his father's deputy. Unfortunately his surveying work was to be interrupted by a respiratory illness in the spring of 1750 when he was so sick that his father noted "Cadwallader's indisposition has been inconvenient & disappointed severals as well as himself but there is no help for it [and] I am not without apprehensions of the bad consequences of it still from his lungs being affected [.] He does not recover well."[10] After his recouperation, Cad's autumn 1750 surveying trip was dutifully reported to his father, who wrote to Alice that he was too busy to answer his son and feared by the time he could write, Cad would be gone from Coldengham. This was a typical response of the father, who characteristically pushed his son when and where he thought best, but was too busy to share his son's accomplishment, and when he got around to acknowledging it, confided in his wife rather than in Cad.

The second son became a member of the Ulster bar three years later at age thirty-one, even though there is no evidence he studied with a lawyer or served as an apprentice. This achievement at an advanced age when many lawyers were already well into their practice also suggests his father's patronage helped him enter this profession. Cad's legal and surveying businesses led Alexander's wife to hope her brother-in-law was ready to make himself a success, perhaps because it would ease some resentment he bore toward others of the family. She told Cadwallader,

Sr., "I am very glad to find B^r Cad's Business is like to turn out well [.] I sencarely wish it may continue." So did his father. When Cad was thirty-two, the elder Colden was still encouraging him as he smothered his independence. The father made an arrangement with James Alexander and his son, William, to obtain with Cad a power of attorney from a land speculator. Cadwallader, Sr. thus maneuvered Cad into a business deal with the young man who was to become in twenty-five years, General William Alexander of the Continental army.[11]

In the 1760s when he was at the acme of his social status, Cad also practiced law. In one case he worked for the land speculator James Mac-Donald, trying to obtain control of part of the Minisink Angle in the southwest corner of the colony. The court decision, which went against MacDonald, was decided, according to lawyer Colden, by perjured jurors who were promised they would not be asked questions about their interests in the case and so lied by claiming they were neutral. This exculpation was to be a common tactic of the man. He did not admit to making a mistake or an error in judgment. Such a self-righteous person may well have been insecure, for such sentiment may induce aggressive as well as timid actions. His repetition that others were to blame for his failures or mediocre achievements was as symptomatic as comments by others that he was too inhibited. On another occasion James Duane implied that this trait restrained Colden's tactics when he won a land case. Duane complained that Colden was not pushing hard on the other party in order to complete the victory.

About this time Cad's eldest sister, Elizabeth Colden DeLancey, wrote anxiously to her mother of her visit with him, his inability to win Ellison financial aid, and his apparent accusation that the Coldens were to blame for his plight. Quite obviously Cadwallader's perception that he was failing in professional and commercial enterprises bore heavily on him, and he chafed at chances to succeed. He was aware that he was not building his fortune. As revealing as her report of Cad's apparent financial troubles was Elizabeth's disclosure that even though her brother was in his thirties he still, "seems to be under a very great concern that my Father prefers my Bro^r [Alexander] Colden's interest and serving of him in opposition to him which he mention'd to me in several instances." Elizabeth thought her mother should know of this anger so she might disabuse Cad of his error, but her brother was aggravated to find out that Elizabeth broke his confidence.[12]

A father's preference for an eldest son is just as normal as a second son's resentment. However, Elizabeth recognized the father seemed unable to handle the situation and avoided contact with Cad, for she asked her mother to speak to her brother about his pique. She did not approach her father nor did she suggest Alice talk to him. Alice and Cad had a close and special relation, but the personal problems had to be resolved by the men involved. This was not done.

Such an estrangement did not keep the two men from cooperating in public. The son profited from his father's influence in the colonial military. At eleven years old he served as honorary ensign under Alexander's captaincy in the Ulster militia. In the late 1740s, after he replaced Captain Bayard as commander of the Wallkill militia, Cadwallader was a defender of the Ulster frontier, responsible for the muster records of the units in the Minisink frontier and engaged in Indian diplomacy. In the spring before the French and Indian War exploded, he reported to the royal governor about his trip to the Schoharie Indians, who were disturbed that lands were taken from them and disappointed with the executive's unredeemed promises.

The French and Indian War began in 1754 in a clash over control of the Ohio Valley. In the next year military action about the northern lakes demonstrated that neither the French nor the British had developed winning strategies or tactics. In the summer of 1756 under General Louis Montcalm, French troops and Indian allies captured Oswego on Lake Ontario, opening New York to deep penetrating attacks the following year. This campaign was followed by French victories on Lake Champlain in 1758, which pushed New York's effective colonial power down to Albany. However, before the year's end a lightening raid by Colonel John Bradstreet captured Fort Frontenac, near the head of the St. Lawrence River, interrupting French communications with the Ohio and undercutting Indian support for them. In 1759 the British offensives led by generals appointed by the William Pitt regime captured Fort Niagara, sealing Canada from the Ohio. Then the British cleared Lake Champlain and conquered Quebec. Montreal fell in 1760 and so did the French empire in North America.

When this last colonial war had erupted, Ulster was so unprepared that two battallions were created to defend the southern precincts. In 1756 a new southern Ulster regiment was commanded by Colonel Thomas Ellison, assisted by Lt. Colonel Charles Clinton and Major Cadwallader Colden II.[13] The regiment's task was difficult because few fighting men were available. The weakness of the area's defense was apparent on Sunday, October 2, 1757, when Indians raided two families who lived west of the Wallkill on the eastern slope of the Shawangunk Mountains, killing a farmer, and carrying the women and children into captivity. When Lt. Col. Clinton and Major Colden received a report of the attack, they complained to the governor that while the frontier patrols were on duty there had been no attacks, but as soon as the Indians found out the troops three month tour of duty was over, trouble began. The officers wanted a permanent frontier guard supplied by the Assembly, because defending the frontier was considered so dangerous militiamen preferred the risky service on privateers rather than face the Indians. Twenty men sailed from New Windsor at the end of September for such sea duty rather than protect their homes.

The governor responded promptly, sending fifty soldiers within one week. On the day the unit arrived at Coldengham, its captain explained he was ordered to march northward across the Shawangunk Mountains to Rochester even though southern Ulster had called for the aid. From New Windsor to Rochester is forty miles, a two-day march, which in lightening-fast Indian warfare was an impossible handicap. After the militia at Rochester reported it could defend its community and the southern Ulsterites pleaded for soldiers' reassignment, the governor agreed. This was followed by a temporary respite in Indian attacks.[14]

To show provincial officials the extent of frontier damage, the elder Colden prepared a map of eastern Ulster, locating on it the principal British villages and family settlements, noting particularly that west of the Wallkill, "The Inhabitants are all fled." From the Minisink River northward along the frontier for a stretch of twenty miles, "the Houses are all either burnt or deserted." Southern Ulster had been rolled back toward the Wallkill by the Indian attacks. The provincial troops were helpful, but to create stability the people of the area wanted a string of blockhouses from the Minisink up to Rochester. This was the plea of both Coldens who reported to the governor and British military commander that local militia regimental officers recommended construction of five frontier forts, and that the Assembly send twenty-five men for each. Colonel Ellison volunteered to advance the money for the forts if the Assembly would reimburse him, and Lt. Col. Clinton offered to survey sites for the forts. Enclosed with the senior Colden's letter to the colonial capital was his son's note reporting that about ten Indians once again eluded British troops and had raided a frontier farm. "Daniell Letts went out of his house to make Watter, as soon as he was out he was Shott down." The Indians were beaten off by Letts' three sons after they scalped the dead father and destroyed the barn and corn crib. As a result the senior Colden sent Cadwallader II to New York City to lobby the Assembly for blockhouses.

The thirty-five-year-old major was for the first time delegated a significant task by his father, and although Cad's efforts may not have been crucial in the Assembly's decision, they were not counterproductive. The blockhouses were built, but it is not certain they were responsible for immediately easing the frontier crisis, for with the coming of cold weather the war season ended for 1757. Raids, however, continued into late 1758 when Major Colden went over the Wallkill toward Shawangunk to get provisions to the blockhouses and found the area greatly alarmed. The Indians had attacked a frontier residence by slipping through the woods past the family's slave who was plowing in the open field. The major concluded his letter to his father, "My wife won't hear of my leaving the house [although] I should have waited on you myself this Evening to have consulted what to do on this Occasion. I am affraid Numbers of familys will break up unless something Can be done to make them Easy." The success of the blockhouse defense may be questioned even though Ulster people thought it was beneficial. A generation later Charles Clinton's son, then revolutionary Governor George Clinton, authorized the construction of blockhouses to defend Orange and Ulster counties against Indian and loyalist raiders.[15]

Soon Cadwallader II was more concerned with the pay and bounty records of militia troops than Indians, as British military might turned the battle tide. In addition to the capture of Fort Niagara, Fort Duquesne fell to the British, easing much pressure on the frontier. The war never returned to the banks of the Wallkill, and thus ended Cad's brief military career. The colonial Assembly repaid him £36 for his limited expenditures of goods at Lake George and at the frontier of Ulster and Orange counties. Colden remained a militia major for twenty years until he was promoted to colonel on the eve of the American Revolution; however, he never served actively in that rank.[16] His brush with the Indians in 1757 and 1758 was the closest he came to fighting. He spent the entire American Revolution fleeing combat.

Chapter III
Squire Colden II

At the age of forty, Cadwallader II reached the acme of his social and political life. From 1762 until the Revolutionary War he was one of the most influential men of his community and lived more affluently than he would ever do again. Yet Squire Colden did not achieve all that he sought in these years. His will was not edict in the local Anglican churches or on the county court, although he was a force with whom his opponents had to reckon.

Cadwallader II became the master of Coldengham when his father gave him the entire estate. In March 1762 just after the old man settled in New York City Alice Christie Colden died, and he may have lost all desire to go back to Ulster. He bought Springhill, a one hundred and twenty acre farm near Flushing, Long Island for David and himself.[1] Until June 1775 the senior Colden served as acting governor five times, for a total of six years, trying to throttle the movement which was leading to a revolution. However, the crises which vexed acting Governor Colden passed by the new squire of Coldengham, who enhanced his estate by changing the function of his father's home into a militia training center and drill site, and probably an armory. Edward Rigs, who served for a time as schoolmaster at the estate, may have taught Cadwallader II's and perhaps neighbors' children in this "Academy" building when it was not being used by the militia.[2] Less elaborate than the Colden houses were the homes of about a dozen tenants scattered across Coldengham and the grist and saw mills on Tinn Brock. By 1770 the ornament of the estate was the new home of its second squire, built to be worthy of Cadwallader II's dreams.

The Georgian mansion, with a datestone marked 1767, was a hipped roofed two story rectangle. It had centrally located front and rear doors with a connecting hall and a staircase of black walnut that swept from the entrance around the foyer to the second floor. Later Colden would add a wing to make the building "L" shaped, and still later he would restore its rectangular form with another wing. The rooms were spacious, with ten feet high ceilings, rich interior wood paneling, and fluted base relief columns balancing the doors and fireplaces, typical of its genre. Neatly sculptured cornices topped the clear vertical lines of wood paneled walls. The features of the mansion were British, not northern European, Dutch, or Germannic as were popular in Ulster. Colden built to emulate the estates of the southern and eastern Hudson Valley gentry.[3] For years after his death his house would remain a symbol of Georgian aristocracy on the west side of the river. As sole Colden of the Hudson Valley, the proprietor of an estate, and the eldest son of the acting governor, he deserved such a home.

By the time the Coldens moved into their stone mansion almost all their offspring had been born. Elizabeth was to bear twelve children, of whom eight survived childhood. Cadwallader III (who was to demonstrate flashes of independence from family influence and was to be unhappy in economic pursuits) was born in 1745, the year of his parents' wedding. Alice was born the next year, but was to die at age thirty leaving her parents to raise two granddaughters. In 1748 came Jane who remained a spinster at home until after her father's death. Thomas was born in 1754, and with John whose birthday is unknown, fought with the British in the Revolutionary War. John died in the war and soon after the peace Thomas returned to the estate, where he lived the rest of his life. Alexander, born in 1757, remained a civilian on the estate as did David, born in 1762, who was too young to fight. The birthdate of the Colden's youngest child, Margaret, is unknown. According to the published inscriptions on Coldengham cemetery tombstones, she died in 1855 at age seventy-five, and so was born in 1780, when her father was fifty-eight and her mother was fifty years old, an unlikely age for childbearing. Margaret must have been born before 1780, for in 1787 she was married!

Thus, by 1770 Coldengham was again alive with children. Cadwallader, Sr. had eight offspring and the second squire's family had about the same number. Unlike his father, Cadwallader II wrote no letters instructing his wife on how to raise their children. He remained at home most of the time after the French and Indian War, but even more importantly he demonstrated little interest in scholarly activities and seems not to have been concerned with educational matters. At this time, life at Coldengham was happy and probably was genteel, but it was not intellectually stimulating.

The squire's wealth is almost impossible to determine. During the Revolution he estimated Coldengham alone was worth more than £20,000. In 1779 thirteen tenants on the estate paid taxes to New York State for their 705 acres of leased land; the assessments of the remaining Coldengham property was £2,072, the largest in Hanover. If to this is added Colden property held elsewhere, the family was the wealthiest in town.[4] Colden's estate and his ownership of speculative lands were part of his real estate assets. In Ulster and Orange counties he held mortgages worth almost £1,000 on six lots of about one hundred acres each. In addition, land records suggest the existence of other unrecorded land deals. Colden obviously was not a large scale land dealer, and since he was paying on only one mortgage he seems to have bought much less real estate than he sold.[5] He added less than he took from the family fortune, and so his complaints about his economic condition were based on realistic long range views of his situation. He lived as did Chesapeake planters who drifted into debt in the same prerevolutionary period. Wartime chaos and punitive revolutionary measures accelerated a degenerating economic process underway in the early 1770s when Colden was already over fifty years old. To keep alive Colden family pretensions his descendents would have to become sharp businessmen.

Colden was called "Merchant" in addition to "Esquire," for he was the proprietor of the store on the estate, a small scale source of income, which his brother Alexander had run. Cadwallader's tenure ran from at least the early 1760s, although only the 1767 and '68 daybook has survived to record business. From these pages it is obvious that Colden had little knowledge of accounting, for he entered all his financial transactions in one long list, such as: credit extended to customers, cash income, and personal expenses, including £5.17.6 paid for twenty-one days of plastering on the estate mansion and mill. Therefore, one cannot tell from the daybook what were Colden's private or business expenses or profits.

Most of the store's customers were from his immediate neighborhood; only occasionally did one come in from an outlying region, such as Shawangunk. Friendship may have regularly brought Peter DuBois from the Wallkill, but very few customers came from Newburgh and none were from New Windsor where his in-laws controlled trade. Colden's mercantile activities may have dominated little more than his neighborhood, and most of his retail sales were for small amounts of money. For example on August 11, 1767, he conducted ten transactions, the largest of which was for £2.8.7, with the total for the day being £7.17.5. His business was better in the following year: on August 15, 1768, he had twenty-four customers who spent £20.1.7. One of the biggest sales that autumn was for £10.12.9. Regardless of the increase he was still not bringing in much money through his store. Such small transactions could not sustain a genteel style of life, even though he supplemented these sales by shipping lumber down river to the port.

Daily Colden vended to his neighbors such luxuries as rum, tea, sugar, textiles (such as mohair, linen, silk, chambray, and buckram), nails, and writing paper. The area about Coldengham contained people wealthy enough to buy silk and mohair and to use writing paper, so it was not an impoverished frontier. Yet few of Colden's sales were noted in his record as "Cash." He generally sold on credit and bartered goods: on October 7, 1767, he was paid £14 in the form of a £10 note and a cow worth £4; on October 19, a debt of £4.10.1 was paid with £3 worth of butter plus a credit of £1.10.1; on October 31, Colden bought £29.12.1 of wheat and paid £25 in cash and extended the seller £4.12.1 in credit against future purchases. One year later on October 12, 1768, the merchant bought thirteen bushels of flaxseed and nearly twenty-three pounds of butter from a customer whose credit was raised at the estate store to £10.7.2.

Colden may have maintained the store as an obligation of a major landowner who provided a service for his tenants and neighbors. His sense of noblesse oblige may have been as strong as his profit motive, for he carried debts for many weeks. Most of his sales were for less than £1, and few customers came in more often than twice a week, so when Colden received a payment of £10 he was probably being paid for over a month's debts. Such may have been the payment of Hans Yurry Rand's wife, who on August 12, paid £10.13.21/2, which Colden recorded as, "This is supposed to be in full of his and the books not being Posted Some may be overlooked." This note on the Rand payment indicates he knew that his books were incomplete. That he accepted Mrs. Rand's version of the debt also indicates Colden's mercantile operation was typical of many village storekeepers whose profits were dependent on customers' welfare. Rather than bleed his neighbors he maintained their credit and gave them some benefit of the fiscal doubt. Fifty years after Colden's death a neighbor recorded that:

> The first descendants of the Lieutenant Governor had large landed estates in the town, which they sold out from time to time; and we never heard aught of hard feeling or oppression on their part, but on the contrary much of that which was of fair, honest and liberal character.

Colden was generous to his debtors, but not so lenient that they could easily take advantage of him.[6]

He sued recalcitrant customers for nonpayment of debts in the Ulster County Court of Common Pleas, the records of which are mere minutes not transcripts, so only the results of litigation are known. The squire won many cases by default when the defendants did not show up in court, and rarely did he appear before the bar as a defendant. In the 1760s and early '70s he brought into the county court more than thirty cases. Colden's many suits for debts due him suggest he acted as a money lender to people throughout much of southern Ulster, including Newburgh where he kept Colden family influence alive.[7] That not one defendant came from New Windsor again demonstrates he could not crack the commercial power of the Ellisons. Unusually large was the judgment he won against Jonathan Belknap, a yeoman of Newburgh, later to be an active revolutionary. The court ordered the defendant to pay £412.5.4. So eager was the squire for payment that if Belknap paid him half within six months he agreed the debtor would be released from the remainder.

This case demonstrates that Colden was vexed with cash flow problems, for he accepted Belknap's £206 in May and forgave the rest. In most of his cases Colden won small amounts of monies: as little as £6.7.2 from a store customer.[8] Because the average of these civil suits' decisions was about £15, Colden seemed to carry a customer for about three months before he pressed payments in court. He had too little cash to be a moneylender or proto-banker of large proportions. Although he was generous his capital was too scarce for him to be philanthropic.

As a suitor in court for almost fifteen years, the squire worked twice a year with the elite of Ulster County in Kingston. Here the county seat bustled with energy and taverns filled with people who enjoyed the various social activities which accompanied the local governmental processes in British colonies. By 1770 Colden met prominent mid-Hudson Valley people who would later be important in his life. Except for the years 1769-73 his constant lawyer was the revolutionary governor-to-be, George Clinton. In the interlude when Clinton did not represent him, Robert R. Livingston, of the important manorial whig family, was his spokesman. Here he also encountered Roeliff Eltinge, the New Paltz merchant with whom he was later to share a cell and exile.

While the squire was moving in this echelon of society, the colony's capital witnessed increasingly strident arguments, even though no one anticipated a revolution. The Grenville program of imperial administrative and tax reform was passed by Parliament to tighten enforcement of customs law and to raise revenues. Merchant-led popular resistance to these new administrative rules and the Sugar Act of 1765 was not as violent as the actions opposing the Stamp Act of that year, against which the militant Sons of Liberty coordinated public demonstrations, civic violence, and with moderate protestors, enforced a boycott of British goods. In New York City the Stamp Act Congress met to produce petitions seeking repeal of the hated act. Exasperated at Lt. Governor Colden's adamant promises to enforce the Stamp Act, the Sons of Liberty in November 1765 led a riot, burning the official in effigy and destroying his coach, sedan chair, and two sleighs. Because it was impossible to enforce, the loathsome tax was repealed. But further colonial protests were generated by suspension of the provincial Assembly when it refused monetary support for the British troops stationed in New York, the headquarters city for the army in North America. Further boycotts and riots from 1767-70 were induced by increases in Parliamentary levied import taxes imposed under the program of Charles Townshend.

During these prerevolutionary crises, the acting governor and other loyalists witnessed the hubbub of port agitation but denied that the rural populace was involved in the arguments. Throughout the 1760s the senior Colden told the secretary of the Board of Trade in London that the majority of the colonial Assembly were loyal rural parochials who were being wooed by port lawyers.[9] However, absence of demonstrations in the agrarian Hudson Valley was caused by lack of provocation there. If stamps had been distributed in Ulster it too may have experienced riots similar to the ones enacted in the capital.

Yet, the loyalists' analyses were partially correct. Political life in the rural Hudson Valley communities was concerned with local problems and had little if anything to do with imperial issues, unlike their counterpart towns in agrarian New England. For example, the town meeting records of Cornwall, New Windsor's southern neighbor, do not indicate the transition from imperial through confederation to federal regimes. In this valley elections were dominated by freeholders who owned or rented land for life or at least twenty-one years. Such officials as judges and justices of the peace were appointed by the governor, but each year the freeholders and inhabitants elected officials who levied and collected taxes, without major consideration of imperial imposts. The precinct supervisors met in the county seat to determine the county budget and each community's contribution in taxes. These figures were then turned over to elected assessors who valued properties in their local jurisdictions and established the tax rate. This information was passed on to the elected collector who delivered to the county treasurer the monies raised. The 1768 and '69 supervisor's elections of the Wallkill precinct were won by the squire of Coldengham, but in New Windsor none of large landowning proprietors consistently held any office or bothered to administer the community's ordinances or colonial laws.

Rural isolation and freeholder control of many aspects of local government determined the issues over which Ulsterites argued during the 1768 election in which Cadwallader Colden II sought a seat in the Assembly, but had to settle for a supervisor's position. Politicians in New York City threw epithets at each other over imperial and provincial matters. Public opinion in the capital should have been at a peak, for the eighteenth century version of the news media certainly was. However, this impressionistic evidence is misleading. In the Assembly election of 1768 almost 54 percent of the adult white males of the city participated. Yet the election of 1735, which followed the Zenger trial, had drawn almost 56 percent of New York City's eligible voters. The election of 1761, which occurred during the French and Indian War, had attracted votes from over 56 percent of the enfranchised. Even more surprising was the city's poor turnout of less than 41 percent in the election of 1769, conducted after a full year of political wrangling. Westchester and Dutchess counties apparently experienced active campaigns, but there is no way of knowing if the issues were directly related to local or imperial matters.[10] No election statistics are available for the Hudson Valley's west bank, but one may question whether imperial political arguments permeated society in Ulster when Colden ran. His perception of the issues of the 1768 campaign had little relation to the crises his father faced, for he did not run on a platform which mentioned the mother country. Although this may have been a way for him to avoid psychological dependence on his father, it also reflected what he perceived were the issues that upset Ulsterites.

As part of his campaign Colden circulated his "Confession of Faith," a manifesto of principles on the issues of the election.[11] He began his "Confession" typically explaining that neighboring worthies were nominating him and that he was not seeking the Assembly seat. This statement was his answer to prejudiced critics. First, he addressed the issue most "destructive of the peace and well being of the County." It was not stamps or tariffs which caused the greatest public disorder in Ulster but the fight between Dutch Reform Church factions: the Conferentie, which wanted to retain ties with the Classis in the Netherlands, and the Coetus, which tried to sever most connections. This religious dispute, which was not to be settled for three more years, caused physical violence in the small Dutch settlements and threatened the stability of even non-Dutch towns. Southern Ulster had few Dutch families, but northern Ulster had many. Colden declared his neutrality in the most important problem of the most heavily settled part of the county, obviously hoping he could avoid offending either side.

Second, the candidate declared he would not vote for any law which infringed upon "the Religious principles of any Church Sect or Society of protestants whatsoever." In rural eighteenth century New York such a statement had significant political connotation. In 1768 New York Church of England leaders defeated the fourth attempt of the Presbyterians to incorporate their church. It is no wonder Presbyterian leaders militantly opposed appointment of an Anglican bishop in America and a revitalized Society for the Propagation of the Gospel in Foreign Parts which threatened to embark on a crusade that would seek, under political power, the creation of an Anglican religious orthodoxy. In general the religious-political arrangement of New York before the 1770s found the Anglicans allied with the Huguenots and with many of the Dutch whose appreciation of New York's cultural freedom allowed them to slide from traditional Dutch ways.[12] In opposition were many Protestant Dissenters led by Presbyterians, who feared for their religious institutions. In the 1768 Ulster campaign, these problems were critical to such religiously motivated persons as Cadwallader Colden II, who declared himself to be a liberal Anglican. He would not force such groups as Presbyterians to change principles or to debate their virtue with Anglican leaders, but he did not rule out attempts to convert them to his church by S.P.G. missionaries. He merely stated that he would not proscribe any sect by law. No wonder he was to have difficulties with militant Presbyterians in communities surrounding Coldengham, especially in Little Britain.

Candidate Colden's third plank addressed the cultural differences and distances within Ulster, which would lead to the county's eventual reorganization in 1798, when settlements from Newburgh south to the county line were reassigned to Orange County. The distance from Kingston to the Newburgh-Wallkill-New Windsor triangle, in which Coldengham was centrally located, was so great that court days were just about the only institution that held Ulster County together. Colden declared himself neutral on the issue of whether to put another Ulster courthouse at New Windsor or create a new county in this British settled area. He would do what the people wanted, he averred.

As a campaign document, the style of Colden's "Confession" is heavyhanded, complicated, and in part almost incomprehensible. Here may be seen an important reason for his failure as a public person and, perhaps, as an entrepreneur. His words did not flow well. Where simple forthright statements would do well, he composed complicated ones. His choice of words and phrasing weakened his chance for elected public office. Such platitudes about following the will of the voters and his refusal to take a stand on each of the three major problems of the county demonstrate he had a keen desire to hold office, but little political sense. Unfortunately for him, as the revolutionary ferment oozed into rural New York, such sense was needed to be elected. His "Confession" was as clumsy as a hippopotamus dancing a ballet.

In the election of 1768 the two winners in Ulster were the pro-Livingston faction candidates: forty-year-old Charles DeWitt of Kingston and twenty-eight-year-old George Clinton. The loss by the forty-six-year-old Colden was part of a pattern. The Anglican-DeLancey led politicians won the port area counties and Dutchess, but the Livingstons won most of the rest of the colony. The Colden family salvaged one victory in the Assembly election; Elizabeth Colden DeLancey's son won a Westchester seat. However, control of the legislature was so balanced that the DeLancey majority was too small to dominate the body, and in the following year the fight was rejoined when Governor Moore dissolved the Assembly for supporting Massachusetts' circular letter protesting British colonial policy. Politicians who were deeply involved in the empire's crisis noted the intensity of the contest. Peter DeWitt of Dutchess County, informed his cousin Charles DeWitt across the river that "as our election is near at hand, which I expect will be the hottest that ever was in this county, makes upon that account time very scarce with me."[13] If this was indeed the most hotly contested election ever held in Dutchess, it was not a colony-wide characteristic. In New York City fewer votes were cast than in the previous year. Perhaps for politicians who felt that vital interests were involved, the campaign was all consuming. No election results for Ulster survive.

At one time campaigns may have been fought in New York City on issues closely related to the Presbyterian-Anglican hostility. However, in the late 1760s the lower counties' electorate seemed to lose interest in the religious issue. There the Anglican-DeLancey alliance with some leaders of the Sons of Liberty carried the day. Temporarily, this coalition seemed to lead the protest movement, although by the Revolution the Livingston and DeLancey factions were to reverse their attitudes toward militant anti-British protest. The old Lieutenant Governor, who was having problems with both factions, seems to have accurately described the political conflict of 1769 in southern New York: "Church & the Dissenting Interests were made the Pretences the true motive was whether the DeLancey or Livingston Interests should have the Lead in the Assembly for the future."

Although not the major issue in the capital, religion seemed to be still important in Ulster. The Reverend John Sayre, who was to assume the pulpit of Newburgh as an S.P.G. missionary in January, 1769, did not take up his duties until after the election because Dr. Samuel Auchmuty of Trinity Church and several gentlemen in the port advised him there was likely to be "a great heat of contention" in Ulster during the campaign. A couple of years after he arrived, Sayre unsuccessfully tried to move the seat of the mission and glebe to the wealthier and more populous New Windsor, but the members of the Newburgh church refused. They "urged their fear of the people of Newburgh if they should consent to such a step, and it would be unsafe for them to ride roads for fear of assassination." Not only did the Anglicans of Newburgh resent the attempt to move their church out of their village, they also feared for their safety if they had to ride through Dissenter settlements to receive sacraments. In 1775 Cadwallader II explicitly linked the Ulster protest movement to religious sentiments, confiding to Miles Cooper, the exiled loyalist faculty member of King's College, "All Church men in this part of the county [who] have appeared averse to public measures are consequently called Tories." Obviously historians are correct to state that religion did not split the port's population as the revolutionary issues became critical. Yet, some communities, such as those in Ulster, still responded to the old appeals and lagged behind the new political opinions of the more sophisticated lower counties.[14]

During the 1769 campaign Colden tried to make peace with the Clinton family by relying on his friendship with Charles Clinton, hoping he would apply pressure to his son. To his militia comrade and friend of his father, the squire lamented that the families had became estranged because of political enthusiasms. He also hoped the Clintons would help "to unite this end of the county again." Colden could see only one way to bring these about—a neutral person should hold Ulster's Assembly seat. To accomplish this he offered to step out of the campaign if his friend would get his son to do likewise. Colden claimed that holding an Assembly seat was but an empty honor, and if Charles Clinton could not get George to resign from the race, he would know that it was because of animosity toward the Coldens and that the Clintons could not be relied on as friends.[15]

Colden's letter demonstrates his myopic view of the Clinton family's interests. Assembly membership may have meant little to him, but to George Clinton it was a path upward. The second generation of Clintons could not continue to ride the Coldens' coattails; George needed his own vehicle for advancement. If he wanted to succeed through nepotism, he could not rise above the county level. Beyond that he had to forge his own advances. Yet, one may wonder whether Colden was being honest, even to himself. Certainly an Assembly seat would have been psychologically gratifying to him. His plan was not accepted by the Clintons, and the incumbents were reelected. George Clinton and DeWitt joined the minority of Livingstons in the new Assembly and became backbench critics of the administration.[16]

The elections of 1768 and '69 did not shut Cadwallader Colden II out of public office. In addition to retaining his supervisorship he benefited from nepotism. On November 17, 1769, acting Governor Colden appointed judges to the Ulster County Court of Common Pleas, reassigning Charles Clinton, Levi Pawling—later to be a revolutionary—and selecting his son. The thirteen assistant judges included Kingston's Henry Sleght, a revolutionary who remained Colden's friend, and Wallkill's Peter DuBois, fellow Anglican parishioner and later ardent loyalist.[17]

The court sat in a spring and fall session each year, but not all of the judges sat together. Often only two judges presided with about six of the assistants, and they heard the cases as a panel, often reaching decisions without a jury. The court met mornings and afternoons for about five days in each session and considered about one hundred cases. At an

average of twenty cases per day justice was swift in this court. Problems
were dispatched quickly when one party declined to fight the issue or
when only one party appeared in court. Many cases which threatened to
take long to settle were turned over to a mediator or panel to recommend
a decision to the judges at the next session. Judge Colden first sat on the
bench in the spring 1770 session and presided over his first trial by jury
two years later.[18]

From his powerful position as a judge of the court, Colden worked
with many future leaders of the Revolution in Ulster. George Clinton,
clerk of the court in the 1770s, signed the writs which Judge Colden
issued until the May 1775 session, more than a month after the Battle of
Lexington. Colden's 1773 return to Clinton as his attorney marked the
end of hard feelings left over from the Assembly election campaigns.
Clinton was one of the most popular lawyers in the court, perhaps
because he had influence, serving as clerk while his father was a judge. In
addition Colden also worked with other Ulster revolutionaries: Thomas
Palmer, who acted as a court surveyor and later was to arrest and villify
him, and Robert Boyd, Jr., who served on a committee to determine the
merits of a case and later chaired the committees which imprisoned him.

Colden was the only county judge to be a litigant before his own court.
He certainly was not the most prominent businessman in Ulster, yet his
appearances before the bench as both plaintiff and defendant while serving as judge suggest he either suffered more legal affronts than did other
jurists or he was extremely sensitive to offenses. Perhaps Colden perceived hostilities more readily than did the Ellisons, who were more prominent merchants but who appeared less often in court, or perhaps he
was less astute in making business decisions than were they. The judge
went through the formalities of absolving himself from conflicts of interest in these cases by stepping down from the bench for the duration of
the trials in which he was a litigant. Yet Colden did not win all of these
cases. In fact he lost more suits after he became a judge than before. For
example, twice in the September 1773 session he was the defendant. In
one case, "To save the expense of executing a Writ of Inquiry [Colden]
confesses Judgment to the Plaintiff for Ten Pounds one Shilling and
seven pences Damages with Costs of the Suit to be taxed—on Motion of
Mr. Clinton Attorney for the Plaintiff—Ordered Judgment
accordingly."[19] Occasional losses in court may have been a small price
for Colden to pay for flaunting his social and political positions in the
early 1770s.

Colden also served as one of the socially prominent justices of the
peace. An example of the quality of persons who served in this position is
evident in Kingston where only one-third of the justices could be con-

sidered members of the local aristocracy. The selection of such middle-class tradesmen as carpenters demonstrates that either many upper-class persons rejected such low-level offices or there were not many of the elite available for these positions in Ulster.[20] The status of most of these officials is further evidence of the democratic tone of local government in Ulster, which had less aristocratic local officials than did Dutchess and many southern provincial counties. Colden's appointment as justice of the peace suggests more his desire to hold office than the gentry's control of local government.

Keeping the peace in Ulster County was not nearly as historically significant as such activity in the colony's capital. In Ulster neither imperial issues nor renters' or tenants' rebellions disturbed the social calm. Here more universal problems were omnipresent: tavern brawls, petty thefts, and family feuds were the common violations of the law. The justices of the peace who met as the panel of judges of the Ulster County Court of General Sessions heard "Assaults, Batteries and other Misdemeanors" as simple as that of a slave and two white persons who broke into a garden to steal two watermelons, and of a Kingston wheelwright who stole about twenty household articles and broke out of the town jail in which he was confined. Colden sat on the bench hearing such petty cases as late as September 1775, five months after the Battle of Lexington.

As a member of the court, Colden issued orders and took depositions in locally caused disturbances of the peace, such as the series of brawls which lasted for ten months and involved twenty-six residents of New Windsor and Hanover. The dispute began September 1772, when George Denniston of Little Britain married Mary, daughter of Patrick McClaughrey. Later that month a group of men led by Samuel Falls from Little Britain broke the peace at Patrick McClaughrey's house when Denniston was there with two Hanoverians: Alexander Trimble and James McCobb. From that incident until May 1773 Falls seems to have been involved with several groups that attacked McClaughrey, Trimble, and Denniston, most often at McClaughrey's home. Although the public record does not explain the cause of these disturbances, these acts seem related to the arrest of Mary McClaughrey Denniston on May 1, 1773, on a complaint that she gave birth to an infant "and has either murdered it or secreted it away" about seven months since her marriage. Later in May Mary Denniston's accuser was indicted for falsely swearing before Justice of the Peace Colden that she had murdered the infant. During the year twenty-five men of the two precincts were indicted for fighting, and Samuel Falls was twice indicted for his assaults. Finally Alexander Falls, Jr. was indicted for attacking Mary Denniston. The British were not needed to keep life in southern Ulster from becoming a bore.[21]

In 1774 Judge Colden was also appointed colonel in the Ulster Second Regiment, but never served a day on active duty. Soon after his promotion, New York City had its version of a tea party and the Coercive Acts passed Parliament to punish the colonists for destroying British East India Company property. By the end of the year the First Continental Congress met, and Ulster's militia was being transformed into a revolutionary force with Colonel James McClaughrey of New Windsor in command. During the following fall as the Revolutionary War was being fought in New England and at Fort Ticonderoga, as General Richard Montgomery led the ill-fated American invasion into Canada, and after Mecklenburgh County, North Carolina voted to support independence, Ulster County judges continued to meet with Colden, already a suspected loyalist, sitting beside such men as Levi Pawling who was a member of New York's Provincial Congress.

In addition to these secular posts, Colden was integrally involved with the Anglican Church. He served as vestryman at St. George's in Newburgh and warden at St. Andrew's in Wallkill. The first step toward creating an Anglican parish in southern Ulster was begun in 1729 when the Society for the Propagation of the Gospel in Foreign Parts (S.P.G.) created a mission. In 1731 a minister was sent and a dozen years later three stations were established: St. Andrew's, St. George's, and St. David's, west of Little Britain. In the 1740s the squire's older brother Alexander and Richard Albertson led the Anglican majority in Newburgh to vote themselves control of the German Lutheran parish and patent of the village. Elected as the two trustees by the British inhabitants in 1751, Colden and Albertson obtained a new patent for the Church of England parish there. In a decade this Anglican majority was to lose control of the glebe and congregation to a new majority of Dissenters. The Church remained anemic in Ulster, for the Dutch and Huguenots did not convert and the Presbyterian-led Dissenters were intrepid foes. During the career of the Reverend Hezekiah Watkins, the missionary sent to this mission by the S.P.G., nonconforming Protestants poured into southern Ulster and northern Orange. Until his death in 1765, Watkins tried to stem the tide, traveling as far as seventy-five miles from home, regularly calling on congregants at the Wallkill where he ministered to about "30 Families chiefly from Europe" who appeared "Zealous." Yet the baptisms and sacraments he performed could not keep Anglicans a majority in the area.[22]

In 1764 the Reverend Samuel Auchmuty, rector of Trinity Church, passed on to the S.P.G. Colden family lamentations over the fatally-ill Watkins' work and the religious situation in Ulster. After Alexander Colden left for New York City, Cadwallader II assumed patronage of the Newburgh mission and offered to aid the S.P.G. On behalf of his Anglican neighbors Colden proposed that he would give fifty acres for a parsonage near Coldengham and "stir up the people to build a Church." The society responded by agreeing to reestablish an active mission after proof that Colden's Anglican neighbors committed themselves to support adequately a minister. Watkins' death made this discussion even more timely.[23]

The new missionary was not yet appointed by 1768, as the Assembly election was being fought. Colden's participation in the search for a minister may have antagonized the Dissenters in time for their resentment to be manifested politically. Later that year the Reverend John Sayre was appointed by the S.P.G. to begin in the summer of 1769. Eager to get on the job, Sayre arrived in New York City as the political campaign of January 1769 reached its climax, but there he remained until anti-Anglican sentiment in Ulster cooled. When the minister did arrive in Newburgh in March, he immediately noted that the glebe was under the absolute power of the trustees, "who are now Dissenters, & are always likely to be so." To fight the trend Sayre embarked on a circuit of the area delivering sacraments to Anglicans throughout southern Ulster. Vestryman Colden supported Sayre's plea to the S.P.G. for a raise in salary by extolling his efforts among the widely scattered clusters of poor Anglicans who could not give their minister "any more than a Bare and Scanty Support for him & his Family." The paucity of Anglicans and their poverty had political implications in the crises leading to the Revolutionary War.

Colden personally supported Sayre by letting him live at the Coldengham mansion for two years and by aiding in the attack on Dissenters. To the squire the nonconforming Protestants were ignorant boors who argued vehemently among themselves, had "no Regular Plan of Church Government and [were] Generally in Great Confusion and Anarchy." They agreed only in their "Blind Bigotted prejudice, and opposition to the Church of England." This opinion of Dissenters was penned in June 1769, less than six months after the Assembly election. An ardent member of the Anglican minority among a majority of militant Protestant Dissenters, Colden was becoming increasingly alienated from his neighbors.

Having estimated that he rode three thousand miles since he arrived, Sayre went in 1769 to New York City where he raised £250 for the brick church slowly being built on the Wallkill.[24] His presence in the capital to raise money was the excuse he gave to the S.P.G., but he had another reason for being there. He lobbied the colonial Council on behalf of a petition drawn up at Colden's home by St. George vestrymen and wardens, plus interested laymen such as William and John Ellison. On December 12 the Council, chaired by acting Governor Cadwallader Colden, approved and passed on to London the request that the Newburgh mission be given a royal charter. It was granted on July 30, 1770. Two years later Sayre sought to move the parish site of St. George's to New Windsor, arguing that in the infancy of the mission Anglicans from Otterkill, Wallkill, and Newburgh had agreed to make New Windsor the seat. The minister now wanted the mission out of the village that had caused so much trouble for his predecessor. Sayre's unstated reason was probably that in New Windsor lived some Anglicans, especially the wealthy Ellisons, who might become patrons of the parish. This proposal was refused by the Newburgh Anglicans, who feared commuting several miles to their closest church, for they would be traveling among militant Presbyterians.

Under Sayre's leadership, with Squire Colden's active support, two new missions were created and one mission became a parish. On the Wallkill was a new brick church, St. Andrew's, which was usually filled by its twenty-three congregational families. At Otterkill thirty-two communicants worshipped at St. David's. According to Sayre there were more Anglicans on the frontier of southern Ulster than in the Hudson River settlements. Therefore in disgust he resigned in 1774 to go to Fairfield, Connecticut, vexed because he was unable to obtain a new prominence for New Windsor or serve the frontier settlements without physically weakening his health. Anglican churches in southern Ulster remained without a minister until after the Revolution.

Cadwallader Colden II's efforts were not limited to St. George's mission. He was one of St. Andrew's wardens and both donated land and loaned money to the congregation when it strove to erect an edifice. When Sayre left, his efforts in the short run were aborted. Nevertheless frontier Anglicans would be a problem for revolutionaries as the war broke out. In addition to these local actions Colden corresponded with many church leaders and was related by marriage to one of the important clerics of New York, the Reverend Charles Inglis—curate and later rector of Trinity Church, and after the Revolution, Bishop of Nova Scotia. In several ways Colden was tied intimately to the Anglican Church.[25]

As the crises which led to the Revolutionary War moved toward violence, southern Ulster seemed to be left behind. Its population was still splintered over religious issues that were not arousing passions in other parts of the colony. In the early 1770s Cadwallader Colden II was slipping into a comfortable social position. Although not the idol of the many anti-Anglican small farmers or townsfolk, he was elected a supervisor by his immediate neighbors, was appointed a county official, and was a supporter of the prestigious and disliked Church of England. He was solidly a squire, perhaps respected, perhaps feared.

Chapter IV
The End of a Dream

Few rural Americans of the northern colonies were deeply concerned about the British government's imperial policies after the Seven Years' War because most of them did not feel the direct impact of the new taxes and administrative procedures. The American Revolution began with riots and demonstrations in northern cities where the people's well-being was hit hard. Several New York City committees led the attack on the British policies: the Sons of Liberty and the committees of Fifty-one, Sixty, and One Hundred rallied protestors at various times. Finally in 1774 the port's Committee of Fifty-one, by linking the oppressive Intolerable Acts to the question of New York's representation at the coming Continental Congress, induced a few provincial settlements to create local committees. Such community groups served as extensions of the revolutionary legislature, the New York Provincial Congress and also acted as courts and enforcement agencies for provincial revolutionaries, obtaining obedience by coersion. Common was the threat of tar and feathers and of social isolation, a form of ostracism. Some loyalists were either jailed by committees where the protestors controlled appropriate facilities or placed under house arrest. Others were banished if local control seemed inadequate or impractical. The lucky ones were investigated, warned about pro-British actions, and let free on a form of parole. Often suspected loyalists, against whom town or precinct committees had little evidence, were sent up to the county committees for hearings. Occasionally a county committee kicked the case of a local aristocrat up to the Provincial Congress. At times a higher board refused to get involved and remanded the case back to the local body. In such an instance a suspected loyalist might be imprisoned for months awaiting a jurisdictional decision.[1] Cadwallader Colden II was to be threatened by all of these procedures.

Even though many local revolutionary positions were filled by persons of respected status not all could be occupied by the old aristocracy. Some people remained loyal to the crown, and some revolutionaries preferred military service. The needs of the revolution gave persons of moderate local prominence a chance to widen and enhance their activities and so move up the social scale. In Hanover the political and military leaders of the protest movement came from the respectable upper middle class of the precinct. Five revolutionary militia companies were formed in Hanover, each with four officers. The precinct committee had seven persons. Of these twenty-seven men, twenty-two appeared on Hanover's tax assessment roll of 1779. None was impoverished or affluent. Almost half of them had property assessed between £251 and £500.[2] Colden's local enemies were solidly members of the precinct's society; none was rabble or mob.

In addition to Hanoverians, protestors who operated on the provincial level threatened Colden's life during the war. They easily identified and controlled blatant enemies of the Revolution. More onerous were those who claimed to be neutral, who were secretly loyalist, who clandestinely created arms cachés, who recruited soldiers for loyalist brigades, and who circulated propaganda to weaken American morale. To control them the New York Provincial Congress created a small body called the Committee for Detecting and Defeating Conspiracies, and then gave it more authority by changing it to a commission. When a British raiding party ascended the Hudson River in October 1777 and destroyed the temporary state capital in Kingston, a revitalized ten-man commission was created for the year. The job became so difficult that a large thirty-man commission was soon organized with a quorum of merely three members, making it possible for ten simultaneous investigations to be conducted.

In spite of authorization from the new state government, the persons who sat on these committees and commissions were uncertain of themselves, seemingly torn between two policies: trying to win support for the revolution by demonstrating leniency and trying to win the revolution by harshly treating suspected loyalists. The ambivalence and uncertainty of these antiloyalist bodies allowed enemies to escape by slipping down the Hudson to New York City or northward to British controlled Canada. Not until the law of June 30, 1778, did the Commission for Detecting Conspiracies virtually outlaw neutrality by requiring an oath of allegiance (or affirmation from Quakers). Those who refused were to be shipped behind enemy lines. From then to the end of the war this policy was modified but remained basically intact.[3]

As the most prominent Ulster Colden, the squire would have been suspect merely because of his name, even if he had done nothing suspicious. He may have attracted animosity because during the prewar crises his father and brother had been critical of the protestors. At Springhill David Colden actively supported royal government and, as a leader of the loyalists who so outnumbered whigs in Flushing, prevented the creation of local protest committees in 1774 and '75. Queens County had so many loyalists the Continental Congress outlawed the county, ordered it disarmed, and foolhardily ordered the arrest of royal adherents there. "But unawed by these threats," reported the last royal governor, William Tryon, "Lieut Governor Colden and his Family have much merit in promoting this laudable Spirit of opposition to the Measures of Committees and Congresses in Queen's County." The Americans also recognized the family's allegiance on June 5, 1776, when they included on a list of one hundred suspected loyalists both David and Alexander's son Richard Nicholls Colden.[4] Omitted from the roll was the eldest Colden, who was by then terminally ill and was soon to die.

Shortly after the capture of New York City by British troops, David Colden petitioned Governor William Tryon in the name of 1,293 freeholders and inhabitants of Queens, seeking reinstatement of the king's peace in the county. Such a grant would have restored civil government and probably would have raised David Colden to a significant official position. However, civil government in royally controlled New York was never restored and this generation of Coldens was now out of power.[5] Thus, as the squire of Coldengham remained in Ulster, his father and brother were active in the king's cause. Little wonder that he was studied suspiciously by members of local committees.

The senior Colden died on September 20, 1776, leaving as executors Cadwallader, David, and Elizabeth Colden DeLancey. To the deceased Alexander's eldest son, Colden left mineral rights to several tracts of frontier land, and to David went Springhill. The rest of his property went to the three executors.[6] Thus, in October 1776 Cadwallader Colden II was an executor of a will while living on the other side of a military boundary. When his father died he was on parole at his home awaiting what he thought would be a final desposition of the charges against him. At age fifty-six he was the head of the Coldens, yet he lacked the political power to maintain the family's social position.

When the protestors' committees had begun to meet in Kingston, New Windsor, and other Ulster villages he may not have realized how precarious had been his status. The first gatherings in early 1774, a start of revolution by committee, were followed in Hurley on January 6, 1775, by a meeting of delegates from five northern county towns. Dominated by Dutch and German families, this body organized a committee for the entire county without representation from the predominantly British southern Ulster villages. The gathering adopted five resolutions that were to be promulgated by other local Ulster committees during the next few months. The measures of the Continental Congress and its Association were to be enforced; the recently published loyalist pamphlet, "Free Thoughts on the Resolves of the Congress," written by Samuel Seabury over the pseudonym of "A Westchester Farmer" was condemned as destructive of American Liberty and was publicly burned.[7]

Twenty days after the Hurley meeting had called on each settlement to form its own committee, Shawangunk acted when "a number of the most respectable Freeholders and Inhabitants" met to obtain a broad base for protest and passed resolutions similar to those adopted at the delegates' meeting. Thus here on the frontier, where few persons owned the land they worked, the protestors tried to unite all adult residents. On the next day two precincts held meetings. At Martin Wygant's tavern in Newburgh an eleven-man committee was elected by a gathering of protestors. In Colden's home precinct, at Arthur Park's house on the east bank of the Wallkill, some freeholders conferred. Park was to serve on the committee elected by this group and thereby embark on a career of revolutionary politics that carried him to the state Senate for eleven years. With him on the precinct committee were five freeholders who held no important local offices. Only Charles Clinton, the first chairman of Hanover's committee, was a precinct leader capable of mingling with the county aristocracy. Clinton informed the Provincial Congress that the Hanover meeting of freeholders unanimously approved the Association and other measures of the Continental Congress. The Hanoverians also resolved to employ "the utmost of [their] power, [and to] use every prudent measure to render them effectual," as well as publicly burning Seabury's pamphlet. Three days later "a great number of the most respected freeholders of the Precinct of Wallkill" met, elected a six-man committee and did "heartily approve" by unanimous vote the Association, the Continental Congress, measures to enforce the movement's policies and burning "Free Thoughts."[8]

Such protests were opposed by loyalists of Ulster County. On February 11, 1775, an anonymous loyalist denounced these committees of inspection, the mechanisms by which "the leaders of the Republican faction in this Province" excited "their despicable tools . . . [to] licentiousness and Violence." Lies, this loyalist averred, have led the ignorant and credulous to erect liberty poles and tar and feather loyal "Lovers of peace, order, and Government" merely for reading or disseminating anti-Congress literature. As evidence of the desperation of the "Republican faction," the writer described one of their outrageous lies. When the Quebec Act established Catholicism in America, George III broke his coronation oath to support Protestantism. Therefore, supposedly "the people were discharged from their allegiance, and were justifiably in association to make proper provision for their common safety." The anonymous loyalist argued that a religious issue was a prime cause of anti-British protests. The American Revolution was not a religious crusade, but in Ulster it seems to have been partly based on militant Protestant distrust of Anglicanism and hatred of Catholicism.

This loyalist also noted that on February 10 "a very respectable number of his Majesty's loyal subjects met at the house of Mr. John Graham, at Shawangunk," merely one week after the committee of inspection in that precinct was formed. At Graham's house the loyalists raised a seventy-five foot mast, capped by a "Royal Standard," and bearing an inscription which attested to their "unshaken loyalty and incorruptible fidelity to the best of Kings," their affection for Great Britian and its constitution, their abhorrence of republican government, of treasonable associations, committees and execrable mobs, and of all measures calculated to lessen the people's affection for what the king's friends favored.[9] Except for John Graham, the host of the meeting, no Ulsterite's name was attached to the event, and no petition was signed. Although this meeting is purported to have been attended by Ulster men from beyond Shawangunk, it seems to have been held where a large number of loyalists were available. Probably few traveled to this frontier precinct; most of those present were Anglicans to whom the S.P.G. missionaries had ministered. The Anglican conversions here may have had important political repercussions, connecting loyal affiliation to Anglicanism. Also, this gathering did not create a committee to execute its sentiments as did the protestors' meetings. The loyalists apparently reasoned they need not act in an extralegal manner when the lawful government existed. By relying on lawful authorities, Ulster loyalists depended on existing civilian power, which was rapidly diminishing. Regardless of their numbers, loyalists rarely were active. They did not organize public opinion or the enthusiasms of mass meetings. Instead they assumed legal officeholders would restore law and order, as they had previously done whenever the provincials had rioted or broken the peace. Later, when the extralegal committees operated as governments and royal officials could not command obedience or compliance, it was too late for loyalists to control their communities. They lost their part in revolutionary society by 1776, and thereafter they were often refugees behind British lines, cowed into cooperating with Americans, or neutrals behind American lines.

On March 4, one month after the loyalist meeting in Shawangunk, the protestors resumed the pace of their movement. At New Windsor a mass meeting was called to create a committee comprised of not only the freeholders, but of all the community's adults. George Denniston, the object of Fall's attacks, was chosen chairman, and the rest of the committee was composed of moderately propertied men from Little Britain. The Ellisons, who were not included, were to keep out of active participation in the war, except for John who was to serve as a military officer.[10] In the next month committees throughout Ulster sent delegates to New Paltz where county revolutionary leaders met to reinforce local vigilance and to elect county delegates to the Provincial Congress, which was in turn to elect delegates to the Second Continental Congress.

To this the squire of Coldengham objected. On April 14, one week after the New Paltz meeting and five days before the Battle of Lexington, he and Walter and Peter DuBois published a protest against the election of George Clinton, Levi Pawling, and Charles DeWitt as the Ulster Committee's three man delegation to the Provincial Congress. Colden and his two comrades denounced as "pretended" the New Paltz gathering's claim to have been elected by the "Freeholders and Inhabitants." The anticongress men contended the New Paltz attendees were not elected, but either were privately appointed by cliques of less than one percent of their constituents or were chosen in rigged local elections, which violated rights under the constitution. The three authors also claimed the Assembly was the only legitimate representative body in the colony, and that intra- and intercolonial congresses were illegal. Therefore, the signers formally and publicly protested any action taken at the New Paltz meeting or at any so-called Provincial Congress and stood "against all and all Manner of Proceedings Acts and Deeds of any illegal Congress whatsoever," vowing to remain loyal "to our Parent State and the British Constitution." The only support these anticongress men achieved in southern Ulster was in Newburgh where the proloyalist protest was signed by about sixty men. By 1777 probably about fifty of them were either fighting for the British or in prison because the Americans thought they were too dangerous to leave free.[11] Here in Newburgh, as on the frontier, active Anglicanism and loyalism were geographically linked.

As the Ulster protestors belatedly mobilized supporters they had nothing to offer Cadwallader Colden II. He could raise his social status only by becoming active on a provincial level. This was impossible for he had no base of power. The Clintons were the most prestigious spokesmen of southern Ulster, and they controlled the local Assembly and Provincial Congress seats. It is no wonder that Colden remained true to this conservative social outlook and values. Yet compared to his father and brother, he flirted dangerously with the rebels and vacillated. The squire had publicly denounced the county committee and the Provincial Congress, yet under pressure from the Hanover committee he signed the Association later in the Spring of 1775. According to his father some of New York's political elite worked with the committees because, "if they did not the most dangerous Men Among us would take the Lead."[12]

But Cadwallader II justified his actions with more personal reasons than this. He complained that his "life and property" were "threatened," and that he was "compelled to sign the Association Papers," because "some who refused to do so [were] tied hand and foot and sent down to the Provincial Congress." He signed because, "the threatenings & insults I have receiv'd from our Tarring & feathering Gentry" weighed more than did political reasons. In 1775 such protestors' punishments were imposed because the committeemen lacked control of law enforcement machinery, but when the state was established these sanctions were replaced by more normal criminal procedures.

Colden probably succumbed to committee pressure similar to that applied by the Newburgh Committee. The Newburgh protestors persuaded people to sign the Association "in a most friendly manner," but warned that by the end of May all abstainers were to be "deemed enemies of their country" and subjected to a boycott. The committee also threatened a secondary boycott against persons who had "connection or dealings" with those who withheld support.[13] Colden's regard for his property was too great for him to entertain seriously any thought that would subject him to economic ruin. These threats were made in most communities, and Hanover committeemen probably acted as did their Newburgh neighbors. Little wonder that Colden signed the Association against his conscience.

As political pressure was developing in southern Ulster, another county committee meeting was held in New Paltz on May 11, with Charles Clinton, Arthur Park, and Alexander Trimble from Hanover. The New Windsor delegation included Colonel James Clinton, brother of George and in-law of the revolutionary DeWitt family. Again no Ellison served this precinct's protest movement. Among those selected from the northern part of the county was a delegate who had personal reasons to dislike Cadwallader Colden II—Egbert Dumond. Dumond was born in Kingston in 1732, a decade after Cadwallader II, and starting as a sailor, rose in 1771 to become sheriff of the county. In that office he worked with the county court on which Colden sat as judge, but whatever friendly personal relations existed were probably scuttled in 1774, for while Dumond was in England on a visit Thomas Colden, the twenty-year-old son of Cadwallader II, was appointed sheriff. Dumond was reappointed by the newly formed state government and became an active tory-baiter.[14]

Later in 1775 the Hanover Committee mobilized its precinct militia defenders, per the requests of the Continental Congress and Provincial Congress. In October at Arthur Park's house, Alexander Trimble replaced Charles Clinton as chairman, and five companies were organized in the community. One of them was commanded by Captain Cadwallader Colden III. During the previous year, Colden's thirty-year-old son had married Elizabeth Fell, daughter of the militant revolutionary of northern New Jersey, Judge John Fell. However, this Colden son, who came closest to being a revolutionary, could not sustain participation and resigned his command.[15] This Cadwallader's resignation was probably related to the discomfort he endured during brother Thomas' showdown with the local committee earlier that month. Sheriff Thomas Colden tried to read from the steps of St. Andrew's Church in Wallkill on Saturday, December 2, 1775, a royal proclamation and a statement by the governor concerning the colonial fighting. As sheriff of the entire county he could have read the proclamation at the courthouse in Kingston, but St. Andrew's was nearer his home, and presumably he would have a friendly audience. However, when the Hanover Committee heard of the sheriff's plan, it claimed jurisdiction and asked Colonel James Clinton, commander of the "Second or South End Regiment" of the county militia, to stop the meeting. He ordered seven militia companies to the church. Present were "all the officers (Capt. Cadwallader and C. Colden Jun. [who was still officially an officer], excepted) and most of their men attended." The regiment "under arms" obviously was too strong for Sheriff Colden to overcome. He succumbed. In front of the militia and a "great number of spectators" he put away the statements he brought and instead read and signed the committee's declaration in which he admitted to having acted contrary "to the true interests of the United Colonies" and the Continental Congress. He was "sorry for it" and promised to work with the committee to carry out the resolutions of the Continental and Provincial congresses.

The absence of Thomas' father from this incident was typical of his behavior, for he constantly tried to avoid such clashes. On the other side, Cadwallader III stifled his whig inclinations by his absence. He had been one of several persons whose signatures validated the election of Clinton, Pawling, and DeWitt to the Provincial Congress, and later, during the war, he openly expressed irritation with his father's politics. This public posture, friendly to the revolutionaries, but active only as a civilian on the family farm, allowed Cadwallader III to live through the war with a minimum of martial activity. He never fought with the Americans nor held public office. As the two sides in the imperial crisis became increasingly militant, the most provocative act Cadwallader III took was to marry the daughter of John Fell.[16]

Such family cleavage was common. The revolutionaries believed that families split, with some members becoming protestors and other loyalists, merely to save family wealth and guarantee that whichever side won nothing would be lost. This may have happened in some families, but such crass calculating must also have involved some personal political commitment. To declare an open allegiance meant one must risk capture or punishment by the enemy. An outstanding example of a family split by the American Revolution was Colden's in-laws, for while Elizabeth

Ellison Colden's brother Thomas, Jr. remained in New York City and served as vestryman of Trinity Church during the British occupation, her other brother, John, served in New York's fifth Continental Regiment and was taken prisoner in 1777 at the Battle of the Highlands. Another example of brothers who took different sides was Donald and George Campbell, the sons of Lachlan Campbell, who kept "Campbell Hall" a few miles southwest of Coldengham. The eldest son, Donald, a half-pay, pensioned veteran of the French and Indian War, sought in London compensation for what he claimed were reneged promises of land grants to his father. He came back without success and in 1775 obtained a commission as deputy quartermaster in General Richard Montogermy's ill-fated Canadian army. He then retired to his home and sat out the rest of the war as a prorevolutionary civilian. His younger brother, George, also served in the French and Indian War and later in India, but when the Revolution broke out he fought as a loyalist soldier. The prominent New York family of Crugers was also split. John Harris Cruger married a daughter of Oliver DeLancey and served as an officer in his father-in-law's loyalist brigade. His brother, Henry Cruger, Jr., was mayor of Bristol and was twice elected to Parliament where he espoused the American cause.

A most bizarre instance of family members who were of different temperaments and who worked at cross purposes, was that of the Jay brothers, John and Sir James (who received his title in 1763 in recognition of his fundraising for King's College). The Jay family included seven children, of whom four were either physically or mentally handicapped. Of the other children, James was the eldest and John was thirteen years younger. Sir James was headstrong, aggressive, rampantly vain, and flamboyant. Not surprisingly, John was sober, conservative in manner and thought, and obsessed with what he perceived his responsibilities. He and Sir James were both revolutionaries, but were in hostile Continental Congress factions. In the New York Senate Sir James ardently supported an attainder law for loyalists and confiscation of their property, whereas John opposed such proposals. In 1782 Sir James was captured by the British—perhaps by design. While John was in France as part of the congressional delegation to the Paris peace negotiations, his brother was in Great Britain pursuing his own financial projects and indulging in unauthorized personal diplomacy to end the war on his terms. When he heard that Sir James was in England, John Jay was reported to have said, "I shall endeavour to forget that my father had such a son."[17]

Not always is a family's most productive achiever the eldest child. Not always is the next on an underachiever. More likely, when one child demonstrates one set of qualities, the next sibling manifests another, and sometimes contradictory, set. The Colden clan was no different. In the second generation of American Coldens, Alexander and Cadwallader II had different personalities. In the third generation Cadwallader III's political sympathies varied from those of his father and brothers Thomas and John. Cadwallader III, his much younger brothers, Alexander and David, and his sisters, Alice, Jane, and Margaret, remained at Coldengham through the war.

On the estate they lived among emphatically revolutionary neighbors. When Boston port was closed Ulster farmers donated about 450 barrels of flour, which George Clinton offered to grind, bolt, and pack without charge. More flamboyant was the Reverend Robert Annan, minister of the Associated Reformed Presbyterian Church of Little Britain. To relieve New Englanders during a scarcity of food he argued heartily at a meeting for the American revolutionaries to stand together and ship the grain. Annan capped the discussion with an impassioned plea, and then asked that whoever favored assisting his political bretheren "and the cause of liberty, follow me" out the door. The hall nearly emptied behind him.

Such militancy also produced soldiers for Ulster's second regiment, composed of the southern precincts. Because half of the twelve regimental companies were drawn from west of Hanover, the militia organizers obviously anticipated equal support from eastern and western parts of the regiment's region. Yet less than 420 men served in the six western companies, and 544 were in the six eastern units from New Windsor and Hanover. Of the regiment's twelve companies, seven had over 80 men in March 1777. Five of these large companies were from east of the Wallkill. The distribution of men in the second regiment indicates far less revolutionary sentiment on the frontier of southern Ulster, where loyalists rallied at Graham's house, where Indian and loyalist raiders threatened devastation, and where Anglicans were numerous.[18]

This militia regiment and the local committees were the political arms which carried out the enthusiasms rampant with the mobilization of the American cause. Provincial antiloyalist sentiment was repeatedly buttressed by such statements as that of John Alsop, who on May 24 claimed in the New York Congress that loyalists were organizing into their own committees of correspondence to disseminate propaganda. Less than two weeks later the Provincial Congress attempted to define its enemies by ordering the arrest and questioning of one hundred suspects who held royal office, who did not sign the Association, and who had "maintained an equivocal neutrality," which put them in "a suspicious light." In two weeks New York City was shocked by an antitory riot that swept the streets and the disclosure of a plot to capture General George

Washington. The villains included Thomas Hickey, one of the general's guard, and the royal governor, William Tryon.

Throughout June 1776 the Hudson Valley loyalists drew the attention of revolutionary leaders. One hundred and fifty militia men were needed to put down the king's men in Dutchess, and the militia of Orange was so permeated with loyalists that the Provincial Congress feared to trust it. However, merely a squad of twenty-five men was sent to Ulster "to get the rascals apprehended." Loyalism in this county was certainly less of a concern than in Queens County, where five hundred men tried to control the disaffected. In spite of the paucity of organized Ulster loyal activities, revolutionaries there perceived that they lived among many enemies, an impression that may have been induced by contact with the fears of other counties' leaders. In early 1777 two Ulster commissioners asked the state Convention to authorize county precinct committees to take inventories of property removed with loyalists who fled to the British. Whether these sentiments were justified is immaterial. That Ulster never faced the problems of Dutchess or lower Hudson Valley counties did not prevent its leaders from thinking they were faced with severe threats and imminent loyalist uprisings. In southern Ulster, the most prominent family was the Coldens, who had intimate ties with the enemy. The revolutionaries were bound to demand that the squire commit himself by overt act. His status demanded such.[19]

Chapter V
Prisoner of the Revolution

Because New York had more loyalists than any other province (about one-third of its population), its revolutionaries had particularly difficult problems. However, here as in every colony, the number of loyalists varied depending on transitory conditions, such as when the British army entered an area and encouraged open loyalist actions from moderate and timid persons who until then had been neutral or had cooperated with the revolutionaries. Also, the intensity of allegiance varied across the war years, as did its definition. To the British, who relied on the army and government officials, a neutral who did not impede the royal cause was not an enemy. To Americans, neutrals were often disguised loyalists, especially during military crises.

By using only the restrictive standard of who fought in loyalist regiments or applied for compensation from the British government after the war, New York ranked as a tory stronghold. This colony produced a plurality of the war's loyalist soldiers and of the postwar claimants for compensation. Yet the many New Yorkers who remained loyal were suppressed by the revolutionaries with surprising ease. The vast majority of loyalists were not militant, relying on government to maintain law and order. Some were hostages of their wealth who feared that drastic action might bring down on them and their property the wrath of the revolutionaries. By fleeing, other tories strengthened their enemies, for flight siphoned off active persons and made more property available to the new state. Moreover, if they left families behind, these hostages could be punished for their relatives' militancy.

Scattered throughout New York were several enclaves of loyalists. One center was the port area, the headquarters of the British army, surrounded by farmers in nearby counties who sold produce for specie to the urban market. In addition, the British navy probably influenced allegiance on Manhattan, Staten, and Long Islands, an influence that also seems to have been felt in such coastal regions as Cape Cod, the Delmarva Peninsula (between the Delaware and Chesapeake Bays), the coast islands of South Carolina and Georgia, and in the ports that served these areas.[1] The British presence in Canada strengthened the loyalists along the northern and western frontiers of New York. A different situation developed in the area from the upper Hudson to the upper Connecticut rivers, where settlers under competing New York and New Hampshire grants waged a civil war from the early 1760s to the 1790s. Here during the Revolution the Yankees were overwhelmingly rebel and the Yorkers tended to be neutral or loyalist; prewar enemies seemed to remain wartime enemies.

The Hudson Valley also contained loyalists, but they were not a threat to revolutionaries except in parts of Dutchess and Albany counties. The people in this valley of small farms entered the protest movement late, but became its strength. Yet, the new state leaders feared prominent loyalist aristocratic leaders, such as Colonel and Judge Cadwallader Colden II. Colden's first argument with a revolutionary involved a frequent customer of the Coldengham store, Dr. John Hill, from whom he held a £200 mortgage. In 1775 to avoid default the debtor had to sell property, but was paid in revolutionary paper money. Colden refused to accept payment in this form. Unable to find someone to change the £200 into acceptable currency, Hill took his case to the Hanover Committee, and on February 28, 1776, sought advice of the Provincial Congress.[2] At this early state in the war refusal to accept revolutionary currency was not damning, but in conjunction with Colden's other actions, this may have been additional cause for suspecting him of being loyalist.

Actually the anti-Colden crusade was led by Robert Boyd, Jr., chairman of both the Ulster County Committee and the joint committee of Newburgh-New Windsor. He was a gunsmith who contracted to supply the New York revolutionaries with fully equipped muskets (for £3.15 each). Although the joint committee lacked jurisdiction it acted because Coldengham was on the eastern boundary of Hanover, close to the other precincts, and in a revolution lines of jurisdiction were superfluous. However, Boyd justified Colden's arrest because the Newburgh-New Windsor militants had received orders from the county committee "for disarming all suspected persons, of whom they freely thought Mr. Colden one." Nevertheless Boyd's committeemen held off action until they "were induced to believe the common report to be true, i.e. that the committee of the precinct of Hanover were afraid to treat Mr. Colden as he deserved."

Boyd had earlier confided to George Clinton he was flabbergasted when the Hanover Committee voted no on the question of whether there were "suspected Persons in our Precinct who ought to be disarmed." "Your old Friend, the Coll [Colden]," he informed Clinton, "had an active hand in this," for the committee "seems to be under such a kind of Influence relative to the Ellisons & Coldens, that I cannot fully understand."[3] Perhaps old Charles Clinton as chairman of the Hanover Committee was a moderating influence on the Hanover Committee. Apparently the middling people who made up the precinct's committee were not social revolutionaries bent on overthrowing a landed aristocracy.

The disarming of Colden was caused by the squire's behavior from early 1775 to mid-1776, according to Boyd. After he signed the Continental Association which was pledged to boycott British goods Colden violated his oath by distributing loyalist, antiprotest material. The Hanover Committee disregarded this, argued Boyd, and also overlooked the obvious reason why Colden signed the Association: "He only meant it as a sanctuary for his person and property, never having acted in the smallest degree agreeable to the spirit of it, or in his heart bid it God speed." When Colden admitted he wanted "to ward off those calamities" that would result from ardent protest, Boyd seemed to reason that by calling the effects of militant action "calamities," the squire was an enemy. In mid-1776 Boyd argued that in spite of Colden's claims of neutrality he actually maintained his antipathy toward the Revolution. The chairman considered the squire's printed opposition to the congresses "as the evil seed sown in this county, from which the whole of the fruits of toryism sprung." Boyd claimed that about sixty poor persons in Newburgh subscribed to his petition. Loyalists in southern Ulster could be found among the poor of that village and on the country's southwestern frontier.

In addition, the artisan argued, these Newburgh loyalists, who had the integrity to stand by their loyalist beliefs and would not assent to the Association, were abandoned by Colden when he signed. These aboveboard loyalists understood their signatures on the document would have committed them to obey the congresses. However, instead of arming his household, as Associators throughout the colonies were doing, Colden kept only a broken gun. If he had true moral fiber he would have been armed to defend what he swore to support when he signed the Association. Therefore, in the crisis of June 1776, his arrest was justified, argued Boyd, who concluded that "Mr. Colden appeared, all things considered, to be a person dangerous to the welfare of the United States of America."

Colden's version of his prewar political stance was unlike Boyd's. The squire claimed he was arrested because he was suspected of "being inimical to the American Cause." This, he admitted, had been his sentiment when he thought he could still prevent calamities, but when he saw rapprochement was impossible he "entirely avoided interfering in any shape in public affairs."[4] For his criticism during the months before the fighting, he was called an enemy of the people, insulted and threatened. As did many other loyalists, he insisted on "the freedom of disquisition and debate," even though he discreetly decided to keep quiet on public issues. He claimed his one nonneutral act was to sign the Association, even though he continued to remain silent and never "perswaded or disswaded any man from pursuing the propensity of his own inclinations."[5] He never publicly admitted to disseminating any loyalist published material, nor did he openly respond to Boyd's accusations about his attempt to sway Newburgh opinion. Quite obviously there were differences between Colden's and Boyd's claims. To Colden signing the protestors' document meant he would not oppose those pursuing its goals. According to Boyd, by signing the Association the squire pledged to help achieve its ends.[6]

Much of this argument was articulated after Colden was arrested on June 24, 1776, when the joint committee of Newburgh-New Windsor, under Boyd's chairmanship, disregarded the Hanover Committee's jurisdiction and took the matter of Cadwallader Colden II into its own hands. It sent a detachment commanded by Colonel Thomas Palmer and Major Samuel Logan to rouse Colden from his bed just before midnight and search his house for incriminating evidence. All that they found were an old left-handed gun with a broken stock and a fowling piece owned by his son-in-law. The missing arsenal seemed to pose a problem for the arresting party. Because Palmer so emphasized the limited amount of weapons found, he must have expected to find a cache. Some operating guns were openly kept available for the militia in the "common room," probably in the "Academy," where the local militia had drilled. That the reputed leader of local loyalists was not maintaining an arsenal was perfectly consistent with his personality and character, for such scheming would be too risky for him.

In the morning the prisoner was taken to New Windsor where he was confined at the home of a patriot after the committee refused to let his father-in-law, Thomas Ellison, pay bail. Held for five days, he was given up to the Ulster County Committee, which paroled him to his home pending its hearing. While he was on the estate, Palmer and his friends tried to destroy Colden's reputation by circulating a story that they were scouring the neighborhood for a sailor who had escaped from a British man-of-war in the Hudson River. Actually one of their party was acting the role and when seized, publicly confessed he had slipped away from Colden's house while Palmer was busy arresting the squire.[7] By such ruses was Colden made the butt of lies that could have led to mob violence. Threats and other forms of psychological warfare kept loyalists and neutrals in line.

On July 4, 1776, a guard of militia brought Colden to the county committee for his hearing. At his trial by committee the issue of the captured sailor was settled by Palmer's admission that the ploy was "only a piece of fun." Next, when the prisoner affirmed that since fighting began he had kept silent about his principles, the county board asked him to identify those ideas. According to Boyd, Colden responded that he had opposed the measures taken by protestors that were aimed at "independency, which he should ever oppose with all his might, and wished to Lord that his name might be entered as opposed to that matter, and be handed down to the latest posterity, to show them his disapprobation of it."[8] Colden's version of the hearing explained that as a neutral he kept no arms at Coldengham. He omitted any mention of his outburst against independence, which at this time was being voted in Philadelphia. The squire emphasized the foolishness of his arrest and his willingness to abide by the Provincial Congress's Association and orders, but he wanted some days to consider whether to sign an oath swearing to do this. Denied this delay by the county committee, he agreed rather than go to jail, "which I found was like to be the case." When the county committee added a codicil, the prisoner changed his mind and was jailed as a loyalist.[9]

Boyd justified the amendment because the squire had tried to stir up loyalist feeling. The provision required that Colden pledge to arm himself for battle and, in case of invasion, to fight against the British. This special oath would have required Colden at age fifty-five to perform military service from which fifty-year-old men were exempt by militia law. Actually the committee merely sought his moral commitment to the American cause, reasoning that "Mr. Colden being upwards of fifty years old, of course an exempt by the militia laws, and found destitute of arms, the committee was of opinion Mr. Colden should be somewhat explicit on that particular." By using this pledge the committee seemed to be baiting Colden. One can almost visualize the sarcastic smiles on the committeemen as they told Colden they "would use no compulsive means" to obtain his signature; he must sign freely. Especially manipulative was the committee's reply to Colden's suggestion that on refusing to sign the oath he might be jailed. The committee answered that it had not yet decided what would be its reponse but observed, "It was inconsistent with the character of a gentleman to sign anything contrary to his sentiments for fear of a little punishment." To a person such as Colden this offer was an invitation.

He would be worthy and would take his punishment as a martyr for the obligation of his rank. He told the committee to do with him as it pleased, but he would not sign. The county committee then meted out a penalty that may have been psychologically gratifying to him; on July 4, 1776, he was sentenced to the county jail until the committee or the Provincial Congress discharged him.[10]

The jail where Colden was confined was in the basement under the Kingston courthouse. In the early months of the Revolution so many prisoners were crammed in there that the stench in the courtroom upstairs, where the State Convention met, was obnoxious. On March 18, 1776, the odor was so overpowering that Gouverneur Morris, who did not smoke, moved to mask the putrid smell that rose from the basement.

> From the past want of care for the prisoners now confined in the jail, immediately underneath the Convention Chamber, the same is supposed to have become unwholesome, and very nauseous and disagreeable effluvia arises, which may endanger the health of the members of the convention; therefore *Resolved,* That for the preservation of their health, the members of the Convention be at liberty at their pleasure to smoke in the Convention Chamber, while the House is sitting and proceeding to business.

Dissatisfied, John Jay tried to lessen the crowding by inducing prisoners to take the oath of allegiance to the state. Fourteen inmates did and were released in four days. A loyalist prisoner with whom Colden was later confined survived to tell the British authorities that the Convention ordered prisoners moved out of the courthouse jail, "lest a mortality should enter, in which they themselves might suffer."[11]

For Colden to be assigned to this dungeon, into which he had condemned men several months before, was degrading. The former judge was locked up for five weeks with a convicted murderer in a cell so foul he paid someone to clean it rather than wait for the town fathers of Kingston to get around to the job. Colden's appeal to the state for release was kicked back to the county committee, which refused to reverse itself. Boyd argued that Colden had never changed, was still hostile to the Revolution, had always been duplicitous, and remained "all things considered to be a person dangerous to the welfare of the United States of America, at this alarming crisis." Yet in spite of such vehement criticism of Colden, on August 6 the committee did modify his punishment by paroling him to his farm. "The Committee, out of compassion to his son, Cadwallader, who appears to be a decent young man," agreed to the parole and a £2,000 bond. Colden did not admit his son's role in this matter. He claimed that "with much difficulty my friends prevail'd" convincing the committee to accept his security to stay at Coldengham. The revolutionaries asserted Colden's release resulted from the influence of the only mature rebel in the family, implying that he had no friends who could sway the committee. For Colden it was just as crucial to have his release appear to be based on popular outcry against the injustice of his imprisonment. His appeal to the state legislature, his prestige, and his psyche required that he demonstrate he had many friends. If he accepted Cadwallader III's responsibility for his liberty, he would be manifesting his weakness and social isolation.

Later that month he sought complete freedom rather than parole so he could visit his dying father. Colden was so certain of his rectitude and his family status he did not realize that his father was hated as the acting governor who had tried to stop the protest movement. Certainly the Americans were not going to let the squire shuttle across military lines on such a pretense. Probably at the same time as Colden unsuccessfully sought travel permission from the state, two of his daughters requested a pass from the Continental Congress to visit their dying grandfather. On October 22 Congress allowed them to pass but the resolution arrived at Coldengham too late. Cadwallader Colden, the elder, had expired on September 20. Also at this time the squire's daughter Alice and her husband, Dr. Lewis Antill, died, and their children went to various relatives, with one young girl and her infant sister coming to live at Coldengham where they were raised as Cadwallader and Elizabeth's children.[12]

On August 22 Colden's case was given to the newly created state Committee for Detecting and Defeating Conspiracies, yet for three more months he continued to live at home. This committee, chaired by the aristocratic protegé of the Schuyler family, William Duer, eventually ordered that Colden and his papers relevant to the imperial crisis, be called in because the squire

> hath been represented to this committee as a person who hath long been notoriously disaffected to the American cause and who from his disposition and influence as well from his vicinity to the enemy may justly be considered as too dangerous to be permitted longer to remain at his present abode and the more so as this committee have reason to believe that he hath Countenanced and abetted measures prejudicial to the rights of America.

The day after the resolution was adopted Colden was taken into custody with his papers and brought before the body at Fishkill. At that time the arresting officer laid before the committee twelve suspicious documents seized at Coldengham.[13] The accused was permitted to lodge in town on parole for an additional day while the evidence was studied, a distinct contrast to the charge that he was a menace to the revolutionary effort. Apparently official condemnation of Colden in minutes and documents were pro forma and did not accurately portray the personal attitude of committeemen toward him. They feared his status and his family name, but seemed to realize he posed no danger.

Revolutionary committees like those investigating Colden were common and so were loyalist condemnations of their illegality. Colden's censure was typical.

> By an order of a Committee of the Convention appoint'd for inquiring into and Detecting Plotts and Conspiracies (but more Generally known by the Name of the Torie Commite) who's Busyness it is to take up all Persons Suspect'd of Loyalty who they Call Tories, to Punish them according to their discretion which god knows they

have but Litle of, for they have Sent hundreds of Poor inocent People after keeping them Weeks under guard in Nasty Dirty Vaults of Baracks.[14]

On this committee sat such worthies as John Jay, William Duer, Gouverneur Morris, Leonard Gansevoort, and members of the Livingston clan—Robert R., Peter, and Philip—along with such aspiring and emergent revolutionaries as Melancton Smith. Together these men used their positions as prosecutors and persecutors to preserve, in the civil phase, the Revolution to be won by the military. Whereas the American continental and state armies fought the British forces, the committeemen pursued the civilian fight against British sympathizers who would destroy the new state. Firm but not bloodthirsty, these men were running the state to protect their position and goals. Their legal training and aristocratic background and pretensions prevented purges. They could severely punish poor loyalists but had greater difficulty in dealing with the genteel enemy. In meting out punishments to squires they seem to have had in mind the cliché, "There but for the grace of God go I."[15]

When Colden appeared before this "Torie Committee" he was not afforded rules of evidence to challenge consideration of letters taken from his home without a warrant and was never accused in court of having acted against the new state. The committee noted that "he conceived the former oath of allegiance which he had taken to the King of Great Britain to be binding upon him & professed a desire of being permitted to observe a state of Neutrality." Neither Colden nor the committee at this time fully discussed the seized papers. The body then speedily decided that he should be removed from the Hudson Valley to Boston, Massachusetts, where he would be paroled at his own expense under control of the selectmen of that town. He was then allowed home on parole for ten days after which he was to report back for banishment. He was given this favor probably because officials as yet had no system to banish loyalists and recognized he was not a violent man but would go to Boston quietly rather than create a disturbance that would threaten the new regime, his family, or his property. Colden never considered escape.

The only clues to what the committee thought important in this short meeting are two sentences in its minutes. The first referred to the committee's question of "whether the paper containing reflections on a Sermon preached by the Rev. Mr. Anan was his own hand writing—confessed it was." Two months later, when defending his supposed neutrality before the state legislature (then called the Convention), Colden specifically considered his notes on the Reverend Annan's sermon and probably reasoned similarly then. Accordingly, Annan was "a very war firey Man who Makes Politics more the Subject of his Sermons then Either Morrality or Religion, Yet he is Continuously luging in Religion head and Shoulders as the Primary Cause of the War with Great Britain, by which I think he Dose more hurt to the Cause he ought to Mean to maintain then good." In addition Colden was told that he was the object of Annan's snide comments about the Anglican Church: "And it is to some of the Members of his Church that I owe all the abuse & ill treatment I have met with in the Country. Even that of being sent to jail in the Scandleous Manner I was." Therefore Colden felt obliged to send to Annan a response to the sermon that claimed that when the British suppressed the rebellion "a Religious Persecution would Emediately insue." The contrary was true, claimed the squire. The civil persecutions carried out by the revolutionaries are "Evidently a forerunner of what may be Expected with Respect to Religious Matters" should they win.

The other matter considered by the committee was the affidavit of David Pembrooks, in which he swore James Robinson frequently talked "of going to see Major Colden." This hearsay evidence that Robinson, an active recruiter of men for the King's service, often went to Coldengham was by itself certainly inadmissible in a court proceeding but carried much force in a committee hearing. Colden denied knowing Robinson and the committee did not question his denial, but "was then Pleased to Say, that my Character as to veracity was so Well Establish'd that they Wanted no other Proof of what I asserted" about this accusation.[16] He thought he was believed by interrogators for he was never contradicted. He seems to have been the victim of that genteel tradition that discourages casting a direct refutation in the face of the aristocratic witness. In private the committee evaluated his pretensions and arguments. The result was obvious in the order of November 27, which banished him to Boston.

Soon thereafter he composed to his neighbors a farewell letter filled with his deep religiosity and love for the life he had led as squire of Coldengham. Written by "a fellow Sufferer both in Body and Spiritt on account of the Heavy Judgements from Allmighty God," Colden lamented having to leave "a Fond and tender Wife with a Large family of Dear Children Some of them yet Babes, and Whether I Shall ever See any of You or them again God only knows." He told his neighbors it was the action of "those you Call your Representatives" who implemented this tragedy. This civil war brought "Terrible Callamitees Havoke and Distraction" to his door and would soon knock at others. For such early warnings of social destruction, he was called an enemy of the people, an act similar to calling ministers "Enemy's to your Souls for warning you of the Evil Consequences of Sin." He complained that people denigrated both his wartime silence on public issues and his desire for peace. His motives were condemned and he was attacked in speech and sermon even though he grew up in Hanover and was well known by his neighbors. How, he asked rhetorically, could he be an enemy to his country when in his heart he was an enemy to no person in it? when his children were to be left behind to share his country's fate? when he donated to the support of churches to which he did not belong? He had done his Christian duty to the community's poor and defenseless. He knew he could not change the minds of his enemies but merely hoped to soften their "Resentment against those who in their Conscience Cannot think Just as you do." Especially did he beseech them to end the persecution of him and that their hate "not follow my Poor Wife and inocent family when I am gone from them and this is the Chief Design of this Address to you." He concluded with both a prayer and a reminder that "vengance is mine, Saith the Lord I will Repay."

On December 9 Colden left for Fishkill to be banished officially by the committee. And there he waited. For three weeks he remained at Fishkill, and while he awaited the trip to Boston he wrote to friends, seeking reversal of the committee's decree.[17] His letters were rejected by some state bodies and ignored by others until on Monday, January 13, 1777, Colden was brought before the New York Convention, the state legislature. This hearing before the highest tribunal in the state commenced with Gouverneur Morris reading the report of the Committee for Conspiracies and the material taken from Coldengham, and recommending support for the standing committee decision. Then, because "I was far from being endow'd with a faculty for Speaking," Colden read a long defense statement, in which he recounted all that he endured since his first public opposition to the protest movement and then predicted the impending doom of British rights and liberties as a result of the war. He mentioned no desirable results from resisting imperial tyranny. Colden thought he was neutral because he did not fight, recruit, or perform other overt acts to aid the British. Actually the revolutionaries considered him to be an enemy because he undermined their efforts by encouraging dissatisfaction, fostering resignation before an apparently inevitable defeat, increasing loss of confidence, and indirectly stimulating weak-hearted persons to defect. In doing all of these he was more insidious than an open and avowed enemy; he was a viper who used neutrality as camouflage. This interpretation was logical, considering the crises that confronted the new state's leaders. In January 1777 the port area and its wealth were lost to the British. Sir Guy Carleton's invasion from Canada had been repelled but another was imminent. The state was being squeezed to merely the mid-Hudson Valley.

Colden then considered the papers taken at Coldengham that seemed to have impressed the Committee for Conspiracies with his loyalist ties.

First, he dismissed as irrelevant to the question of his allegiance a letter from the Reverend Charles Inglis, even though the divine thanked the defendant for an earlier message, offered news of events in the port area and reports of British troops newly assigned to America. Inglis expressed a definite loyalist point of view but was not belligerent. Another correspondent, Peter DuBois, had written a ten-page letter, describing in detail military conditions about New York City in mid-September 1776, referred to previous messages from Colden, extended good wishes to the Colden family and sprinkled his dispatch with anti-American comments.[18] Certainly a courtroom conviction for treason to the state on the basis of these letters would be impossible, but a man suspected of loyalist activities had avid loyalist friends. In effect, Colden was guilty of loyalty to Britain by association as well as by hearsay.

In his defense before the Convention, the Squire then denied the relevance of a letter from a group of Scots who sought to sell him gold for revolutionary paper, an act hardly worthy of a treason charge. Colden next quickly dismissed the significance of other confiscated papers. Each was either a copy of a published item or had been written to him or by another person in his family. Only the Reverend Annan's sermon and David Pembrooks' affidavit drew his extended comment. Lastly, he explained, "I Did not think in my Conscience, that I was absolved from my Oaths of Allegiance to the King of Great Britain." He could not abjure an oath that was sworn in God's name but he promised any security state leaders desired to insure his absolute neutrality provided he might stay at home. He then told the Convention a bond such as he offered would insure his behavior better than an oath, for by a bond he would be "Bound by every Sacred tye Both as a Gent^n, and as a Christian." If he should take a new vow, which violated a previous one, it would be null because such an oath was not freely made. It was acceded to in order to protect his family. Also, he argued, the sentence of exile to Boston was not capital punishment, but "little inferior to it—For what *Man* would not allmost Rather Dye than to be Draged or Banish'd from his family and Leave Woemen and Children Exposed to Such Eminent Danger of the Worst of Distresses." Here, as in his public letter of the previous month, his plea to remain at home was not based on political or economic arguments. He wanted to stay home with his family. His granddaughters, fifteen-year-old son David, his daughter Jane (who was nearly thirty years old), and his wife Elizabeth were at home, while Cadwallader III and Alexander were working the estate. At this time sons John and Thomas were with the British army, but he would never mention this to the Americans. Except for these two, Coldengham was a most attractive and emotionally secure sanctuary from the turmoil of a revolutionary society. He concluded his appeal to the legislature by presenting the emotional farewell letter originally addressed to his neighbors.

Colden then withdrew from the Assembly, sorry that he "had Discover'd so much Weakness in Delivering my Deffence (for I had let fall a few Tears)." After a week of lolling about Fishkill on an informal parole, he found that the legislature had not come to a resolution. If it reversed the Committee for Conspiracies that had banished him, the ensuing fight would probably cause his imprisonment or exile. For another week he waited in town and then advised the Convention that since the river ice had broken he was going home to his family. The de facto parolee promised to return on the first notice that the body had come to a decision. So he slipped out of town late in January, hoping that no decision was favorable one.[19]

The state leaders' treatment of Colden was not unique; such inconsistencies abounded. The problems of the war effort were too complex and too overwhelming for the revolutionaries to solve efficiently. They nearly drowned in cascades of problems, such as prosecuting the armed struggle, creating state and local governments without adequate manpower, and controlling loyalist subversion. Colden's case was not a major issue for them. The revolutionary leaders knew that they lacked money to imprison him and all other loyalists. Short of management controls, such as bureaucratic staff and low-echelon persons to keep records and files, the leaders sometimes simply did not know which proloyalist neutrals were free or did not have time and energy to pay attention to all such persons. If no complaints came to them from local committees, state politicans often let a questionable individual alone after publicly denouncing the suspect so that future harsh action might be justified. When warned by local committees of new activities or conditions they moved to action, but with many nagging problems (such as military invasion and the severance of communications between areas of the state because of British occupation and loyalist insurrections), they did not seek to create new crises out of old ones that faded away when ignored. Colden now was home because in early 1777 he was being neglected by the revolutionary government, which had more important concerns. Two events contributed to changing this situation.

He may not have been home during the first, which nevertheless cast suspicion on all Coldens. Lady Mary "Polly" Watts Johnson, the beautiful and adept young wife of Sir John Johnson, broke parole and fled to the British. Her husband, the son of Sir William Johnson, had been Tryon County's leading loyalist until he escaped in May 1776, and was soon in New York City. Lady Mary had been arrested when her husband fled and six months later she was paroled to the home of Thomas

Barclay on the Wallkill near Coldengham. Barclay was married to Susan DeLancey, daughter of Elizabeth Colden DeLancey, niece of Cadwallader Colden II, and cousin of Lady Mary Watts Johnson. When the loyalist Barclay and his family fled to the British in early 1776, they went to Flushing; although no evidence linked them to David Colden, it is probable they went to Springhill for refuge. As her place of house arrest Lady Mary selected the former home of her cousin with whom she had spent happy childhood years, near friendly Coldengham.

In the Barclay home she continued her political activities. Lady Mary was reported to have hosted several suspected loyalists and kept up a correspondence with Mohawk Valley sympathizers. In response the Convention warned the Shawangunk Committee to search and apprehend all suspicious persons who approached Lady Mary. In a month she was gone. Cadwallader Colden II was not back from Fishkill to be involved in her activities that had attracted the revolutionaries' attention, but he may have been home when she fled in late January 1777. The state never charged him with complicity, but the Barclay and Colden families had been so close the onus of responsibility must have hung heavy at Coldengham. An important hostage had slipped through the rebels' fingers. Sir John, now free of restraint, was to use Canada as a base to attack the rebels of western New York in savage guerrilla and irregular battles.[20]

The squire was home when three Hudson Valley loyalists unwittingly brought further trouble to the Colden family. John Cumming, a Scot, of Coxackie district in Albany County, just north of Ulster, had come to New York in 1774 with about two hundred retainers and had weathered the revolutionaries' attempts to turn him from the Crown. Cumming responded by encouraging his fifty-seven adult male retainers capable of serving to flee to the royal standard. They agreed on condition he stay and care for their dependents. In the last week of January 1777 he sought counsel in New York City on how to do this. Accompanied by fellow loyalists Alexander Cruikshank and Hugh Denniston, he arrived in the capital only to be told he should care for the families and recruit his neighbors for royal service. The three men took the ferry across the Hudson River from Manhattan Island to Hoboken, New Jersey, and they would have gotten to Albany without involving Colden if they had not met a "Mr. Thompson," who gave them a ride in his sleigh up the Hudson Valley to Ulster, where he left them "pretending business at one Ellison's." On their return home, the three men were arrested and Cumming was told that Thompson was actually the squire's son, Thomas, on leave from his loyalist brigade. By the end of the next month Thomas's relation to the three traveling loyalists and his arrival at Coldengham about the time of Lady Mary's escape were known to the revolutionaries.[21]

Meanwhile Colden was picking up the threads of a squire's life, wisely entertaining such revolutionary friends as Dr. John Jones and William Denning, who owned much land in northern Ulster and lived about four miles south of Little Britain. He was a member of the Convention when visiting Coldengham on the night that Colden's peace was again shattered.[22]

On March 2, just before midnight, Sheriff Egbert Dumond led an armed posse to Coldengham under orders from the Convention to seize Colden, any incriminating papers in the house, and Thomas (who had already secretly returned to New York City). Colden could not acknowledge that his family may have instigated Dumond's enmity for he seemed completely convinced malevolent people sought his destruction. Although the sheriff came from northern Ulster, Colden believed that he "had a principle hand in my being first Sent to Jail and is well known to be a Black guard Character to own me a great Grudge." The squire claimed to have been shocked at being accosted by Dumond, who would have "Insult'd and very Ruffly handled" him if Denning were not present.[23] His surprise at this arrest was probably due to his certainty that he was protected by well-placed revolutionary friends and that his version of neutrality was finally acceptable to state officials. Denning interceded and on the next day brought Colden to the Convention in Kingston, the new state capital. The suspect was questioned by a special three-man committee appointed to investigate his case, and once again Colden thought he gave full satisfaction, for he was not confronted with hostile comments. He explained that Thomas had come home with a message from his other loyalist son, John, when they heard of their father's confinement. The interview was so congenial Colden expected to be freed to return home.

However, on the following day he was put on parole by the Convention, and had to remain in Kingston while the state grappled with a greater problem involving many loyalists. Fearful of their insurrection or collaboration with the British, New Yorkers wrestled with alternatives. Execution of loyalists was unacceptable. Massive imprisonment would reduce conditions in prisons to inhumane levels because the state had limited funds. Banishment behind British lines was humanitarian and therefore was the least objectionable solution. Exiled loyalists who had left their property under New York control were inhibited by what might happen to their wealth, even though these were active men who probably possessed military intelligence. Gouverneur Morris and other moderates carried their policy on March 7, when the Convention resolved that each suspected loyalist or neutral be ordered to take an oath or make an affirmation to "bear true faith and allegiance to the State of New York" and report all loyalist plots. Those who declined to sign this oath within six days would receive a pass to take their families and personal property behind British lines. Those not appearing within six days would be considered to have fled to the British and their personal property would be seized.

Colden, who had been marking time in Kingston since March 3, was made subject to this resolution immediately upon its passage.[24] In response to this choice he organized his thoughts on the oath of the "Pretended Independent States" again tendered to him. Once again he claimed Americans shared the greatest blessings of civil and religious liberty. "Evil and Discontented Spiritts among us" were responsible for the attack on the mother country and the church, a war that would destroy American liberties. This journal entry continued to note that merely for professing these sentiments, Colden was "abus'd, insult'd, threaten'd with destruction of Body & Estate, Imprison'd and Condemn'd to Banishment." Now he was to take an oath of allegiance "to this Imaginary State." Even though such an oath would not bind him, he could not take it. By making this vow he could remain home during the war. *"Temptations* great indeed, (But That I may not be Led into Temptations is my Dayly Prayer.)" God forbid he should be unable to endure "a Little temperary Uneasyness and inconveniency." No! A profession renouncing former oaths to the King and Church would be blasphemous. He concluded this meditation with an excerpt from Psalm 57: "Be Merciful unto me O God, be Merciful unto me, for my soul trusteth in thee Yea in the Shadow of thy Wings will I make my Refuge, Untill the Calamities be overpast." This fervent statement he passed through Denning to some Convention members so the legislature would know that he had resolved to reject the oath.[25]

The sentiment was typical of the man: political action was a religious act. Colden's statement of principle also demonstrated his resolute conservatism, for he would stand fast and be true to his ideals. Emotionally he was neutral and was most comfortable doing nothing in the war, even though intellectually he was a loyalist. Yet he would temper his loyalty to the crown and his hatred of republicanism because of military and political expediency. He was an honest trimmer. Not a pacifist, he was a pacific person. Yet Thomas Palmer and other revolutionaries of southern Ulster continued to think of him as the active loyalist he had been in the early 1770s, not as he was since the fighting began. As late as March 1777 Palmer was certain that Newburgh was "infected with a nest of Tories" and was "greatly satisfied to hear that their leader, the mischievous Major Colden, is apprehended and secured." Palmer still placed Colden at the head of southern Ulster loyalists while state officials, having no evidence on which to convict him, allowed him to amble home after arrests and to remain there on an unofficial parole. To a great extent Colden's threat to the Revolution was based on his being of the class that was leading loyalists in military activities and publishing loyalist propaganda inciting others to take drastic action. However, such behavior was beyond his ability; he had no experience in such roles and demonstrated no proclivity to plan any coordinated loyalist activity. He was not a leader of the demos, and his writing style was too clumsy for popular appeal.

On March 9, 1777, he informed William Denning that he wanted to be sent to New York City by special pass without having to go to Fishkill. He also wanted two favors: permission to take much food to the city and to raise cash there by being allowed to bring some potash (used in making fertilizer, glass, and most important—gunpowder). One may consider Colden audacious in soliciting such privileges, yet his request was the result of his political naivete and open honesty, for he lacked the boldness to be a schemer or smuggler. To Colden's chagrin his appeal was ignored and he was ordered to appear at Fishkill before the new Commission for Conspiracies with all other persons subjected to the resolution. On March 18 he crossed the Hudson, more desirous of a pass to New York City than of refusing the oath, and "Spent that Evening in a sociable manner with the Commissioners without Entering on Politics." The Commission included two politicians of Colden's gentry class: chairman Egbert Benson, Esq., and Jacobus Swarthout. The two other members were Melancton Smith, who worked with aristocratic revolutionaries and was a rapidly rising Dutchess County militant, and Major Joseph Strang, who never achieved prominence. The evening's sociabilities were just a memory on the next day when the Commission told Colden he could not go to the port until the Convention and the commanding American general of the Hudson Valley forts were consulted. This stricture was imposed because of the unanticipated flood of loyalists seeking passes to New York City. John Cumming estimated that on the day the resolution was published, three hundred persons applied for passports and six hundred more sought to go. Therefore, the Commission, the Convention, and the American military leaders embargoed further departures and Colden was given a pass to go home and await further orders.[26]

That evening from Coldengham he wrote to James Duane, the aristocratic merchant who now was a prominent moderate revolutionary. Before the war Duane had criticized Colden's business acumen, and now also denigrated his military sense. Many New Yorkers perceived a recently foiled raid in the lower Hudson Valley to be part of a concerted attempt by the British to move northward from the port. When Colden told him of this, Duane laughed at his "weak and silly" idea. Either ignoring or unaware of Duane's opinion of him, and needing all the help he could get, Colden sought the merchant's advice. He explained how he was psychologically and economically ready to go. He signed over Coldengham, slaves, cattle, and all appurtenances to Cadwallader III. Therefore, since only the Convention could alter the rules concerning what was to be taken to New York City, he informed Duane that he needed its help if he was to survive in exile.[27] Duane advised Colden to keep still, live quietly at home, and make the best of a poor situation. This was most difficult for the squire, for he was not the type of person who could hang in limbo without knowing his official status and live the rest of the war unobtrusively. He was compelled to know what was going to happen to him, for officially he was no longer the owner of Coldengham. Cadwallader II's family continued to live in the house he had built, but Cadwallader Senior's home became the residence of Cadwallader III. This transfer obviously was made to keep the estate safe from seizure, and to avoid paying the great taxes imposed on loyalist owned property. The squire's statement to Duane that he assigned Coldengham to his eldest son is brief and does not consider legal or financial aspects of such a transfer. To the father, the 1777 transfer seemed to have been a temporary expedient while to the son the arrangement was accepted as permanent. In all subsequent statements the father constantly referred to his estate and never again suggested in public that he had given it to his son.

The squire continued to live at home in the spring of 1777 and seems to have undergone no political crisis. His farm work and family relations were always too personal for him to commit to paper. We may infer his tranquility at this time from his sense of outrage when it was once more violated. This occurred on May 1, 1777, when the local militia struck once again, searching the squire's house and removing him to New Windsor. This time the officer in charge was Major Samuel Logan, who had accompanied Palmer on the first arrest and according to Colden was "a fellow who used to make Hatts for me & formerly a Deserter from the King's troops." The squire protested that as a prisoner of the Convention he could not be removed without its authorization, but the major told him Brigadier General George Clinton had ordered him brought to Fort Montgomery.

Since August 1776, when he was appointed by General Washington, Colden's former lawyer had been in charge of the forts on the west side of the river to keep the British from ascending the Hudson Valley. The river forts from Stony Point to West Point were important because there the river was narrowly squeezed by the steep banks of the Highlands and veered at nearly a ninety degree cut. At Fort Montgomery Colden was coolly received by the general and manifested shock at being cast into confinement with several recently convicted loyalists because he had participated in their thwarted attempt to escape to the British.[28]

This episode began on April 23, when Jacob Davis, Jacob Midagh, and a party of loyalists fled the Kingston area toward the port. They were joined by such persons as an American soldier, Jacobus Rosa, and an unidentified British officer who may have been a spy. The band grew to twenty-six men as it pushed its way south through the Ulster forests toward Coldengham. Davis's testimony at his courtmartial averred that a three-man scouting party had stopped at Colden's house. One of the scouts reported that the squire "told them that it was impossible for their Company to get through to the Regulars on Account of the Guards." The band then split up. Soon afterward militiamen captured eleven of the party, but the British officer escaped. By May 1, when Colden was arrested, some of the prisoners were courtmartialed, found guilty, condemned to be hanged, and were about to be sent to Kingston for execution. Because "it might not be prudent to Keep him confined at this post, for many reasons," Clinton also prepared to send the untried Colden, "who stands charged with the like offense, as will appear in the examination of Jacob Davis." In addition to unloading a suspect whom he had known personally Clinton was getting rid of a prisoner for whom he need not accept responsibility. Colden was accountable to the Convention which last had jurisdiction over him. Along with Colden, Clinton sent his opinion of the suspect's situation, "The Evidence against Mr. Colden is but heresay" but it was supported by such great suspicion and resentment of his neighbors that he is "unsafe" at home. Clinton surmised there must be some truth to such widespread and intense hostility, and was sure Colden was somehow involved with the Rosa party, that he somehow befriended the British officer, and that at home he "can do more Mischief than if he was with General [William] Howe." Colden's responses to Clinton's questions were so unsatisfactory Clinton suggested that if the Kingston authorities closely questioned him, the squire would not dare deny his implication, might break down, and might even admit he was an active loyalist.[29]

However, to Colden's face Clinton claimed to fear for the safety of the former county judge. This concern for Colden was to be repeated by other state officials as an excuse for keeping him locked up. Clinton's reason for jailing him, according to Colden was to do "me a great piece of Kindness, for that they did not think my Life was Safe at home from the temper and Disposition of the people." To the prisoner hostile public opinion was manufactured: "There was Great Pains taken to Raise Peoples Pations & Resentments to that Pitch, but . . . it had never given me an hour's uneasyness." Colden wanted the revolutionaries to stop circulating stories that incited the people against him, to respect his personal and civil liberties, and to let him alone. This was impossible in a revolution.

Chapter VI
The Failure of Influence

In March 1777 Colden was a prisoner whose future was bleak, for he was charged with committing overt acts of loyalism that were punishable by imprisonment, confiscation of property, or other drastic measures. He now faced trial by legislature or committee without the legal protection of court procedures. The New York government, meeting in Kingston across the Hudson from Dutchess County, a hot spot of proloyalist hostility, was considering Colden's fate at a most critical time. In addition to the likelihood of Dutchess riots, General John Burgoyne was readying his invasion force. The state was again under seige and its heartland seethed with unrest. The squire had been treated leniently until now, but the future boded severity. Optimistically and perhaps foolhardily, Colden expected to find justice at the hands of the Convention when he arrived at Kingston. However, the legislature's doorkeeper announced that the squire was to be jailed with the other prisoners sent by Clinton. Without a hearing or examination, a dejected Colden was thrust into the facility under the Convention meeting room, where he shared a cell with John Cumming, Alexander Cruikshank, and five other gentlemanly prisoners, "such good company." His mates had also been confined without formal accusations or hearings, some for up to eight weeks. However, these men were not suffering uniquely, for revolutionary authorities had little time, manpower or money to spend on court trials or writs. For example, a year earlier, Henry Van Schaack and two other prisoners had been banished to Hartford, Connecticut, without knowing the charges against them.[1] In the midst of revolutions civil court procedures have been considered luxuries. American revolutionaries used the most efficient means possible to apprehend and isolate suspected enemies. Decisions were made by committees (sometimes called juntas or soviets elsewhere), not by traditional courtroom legal institutions. Loyalists who sought such normal procedures were seeking that which state officials considered necessary in peaceful situations, and which they were to phase in as the fighting wound down. But in 1777 these men considered such techniques to be detrimental to their war goals. Few loyalists were ever indicted by any grand jury or tried in any quarter session court. Nor were revolutionaries tried in court in New York City, which remained under British martial law and was never restored to civil government until after the war. Both sides considered peacetime legal processes superfluous during hostilities.

The morning after he was cast into the cell, Colden informed Gouverneur Morris that Cinton and the Convention claimed they were protecting him from hostile neighbors, but he would rather take his chances at home than in a crowded firetrap of a jail. Morris squelched this appeal by agreeing with Clinton and suggested the prisoner wait for a few days until his case was settled.

Waiting was difficult with an enemy such as Sheriff Dumond. He did not torture the prisoners; he tormented them by denying them special considerations due gentlemen. Cumming complained that the sheriff went through all his mail and confiscated his two violins in spite of pleas that they be left with someone who would appreciate and care for them. To compound his villainy in these gentlemen's eyes, Dumond even destroyed the only pack of playing cards they had. The sheriff was indifferent to entreaties and blustered that he did not care whether the prisoners lived or died, even though he did not deny them the necessities of life. He augmented their discomfort by throwing in six more prisoners, some of whom had been languishing in confinement for over eight months, and removed Charles Gyles, the jailer who had tried to ease prison conditions. The confined gentry feared his replacement would deny them the "Respect, Decency and Humanity which We think Due our Characters." Therefore they asked to be discharged or transferred with the outgoing jailer to the prison ships moored off Kingston at the mouth of Roundout Creek.[2]

The overcrowding of Kingston dungeon was similar to other state jail conditions. To remedy this, on May 2 a prison fleet was created of privateer vessels reassigned from river duty. Begun with two ships others rapidly were added as inmates were sent from Albany and Orange counties, and New York prisoners were returned from New England. A warden, guards, a commissary, a medical doctor, and a victualler (Charles Gyles) were assigned to insure the vessels were sanitary, well served, and secure. The rations allotted by the Convention although adequate for the prisoners' health were not always delivered. On September 3 the commissary was accused in the Convention of neglecting to supply bread to the prisoners and was ordered to remedy the situation before his resignation would be accepted. The usual technique by which the Convention paid for these rations was to assign a fixed amount of money for each prisoner. The responsible official then bought provisions out of these funds. However, inflation reduced the purchasing power of this allotment faster than it was raised, and in order to keep from losing money, the person responsible for feeding the prisoners reduced the quantity and quality of the rations. If a prison supervisor had larcenous ambitions, he would further reduce rations and pocket the difference between monies allotted and spent. All this was in the future. In May, when the prison fleet was being established, it appeared to be a more pleasant facility than the basement dungeon in Kingston under Dumond's control.[3]

That month the creation of the prison fleet was not the only significant event to affect Colden's environment. While a tenant uprising on Livingston Manor across the Hudson from Ulster drove state officials skitterish and news came southward that General John Burgoyne was amassing troops in Canada for the invasion of New York, the state constitution proclaimed by the Convention on April 20 was put into effect. Elections for state officers were authorized for June. For governor, the upstate leaders backed Philip Schuyler; New York City's John Morin Scott was probably the second most popular candidate, and George Clinton, the first choice of few, seemed to have been the second choice of many persons. In the confusion of campaigning without organized parties, and of several candidates in the field, Clinton came off with a victory few had anticipated. In the newly elected state Senate sat such other Colden acquaintances as Arthur Park and Jesse Woodhull of Cornwall, just south of New Windsor.

The eight prison comrades' request for transfer to the prison fleet was still unanswered when on May 12, into their already jammed facility were thrown Jacob Rosa and Jacob Midagh, the only men who did not receive reprieves for leading the attempted flight to the British lines. For their unrepented loyalism they were to be executed. Rosa readily admitted he tried to help his neighbors return to their former allegiance, and if he was to die for this humane act, he would damn his executors. At this point Colden counseled Rosa in a prayer and meditation vigil and convinced the condemned man to accept the imminence of his death as he prayed for his enemies. The prisoner's farewell was a beautiful exhortation to be kind to his memory and to forgive those who caused his death. He died "with the greatest Composure & Resolution," according to Colden. However, another witness claimed the men apparently expected a last minute reprieve and were overcome with emotions as they mounted the gallows.[4]

Meanwhile, over a month passed without any improvement in the living conditions of the eight prisoners, except for Gouverneur Morris' promise that "we would be Soon in a more agreable Situation." Shortly thereafter the inmates were brought news that the four most prestigious men—Colden, Cumming, Cruikshank, and Richard Thurman—would be paroled in Kingston in custody of sturdy revolutionaries. Colden and Cumming were assigned to Colden's friend, Henry Sleght, with whom he shared the bench on the colonial court. This paroling of nonbelligerent prisoners to homes of patriots was not common but certainly was not unique. When short of jail facilities the Americans reasoned that house arrest was not a risk in cases of prisoners such as Colden. A patriot host-keeper could supervise such a parole cheaper than the costs of imprisonment. Expenses were reduced greatly when parolees supported themselves, such as prisoners Matthew Goes and Dirk Gardiner who paid their way when confined to Charles DeWitt's farm. When imprisonment apparently worsened a man's fragile health, the state also extended such a parole as a less stringent means of confinement. Other prisoners who seemed to pose no threat to the new state were allowed home on parole even though they did not take the oath of allegiance. As Colden had been paroled to his home, Benjamin Ludlow of the prominent mercantile family, who refused to take the oath before the Commission for Conspiracies on April 10, 1777, was ordered to "return home till further order of this Board." The revolutionaries did not rigidly enforce the stringent laws against nonbelligerents. Merely to catalog the maximum punishments assigned according to legislation, and to assume that all the extreme penalties were visited on prisoners is to assert that the Americans were conducting a reign of terror. A revolution is by nature not moderate and acts of outrage were committed. However, New York revolutionary officials were moderate in imposing punishments on enemies.

Colden and Cumming spent one pleasant week in Kingston, where they frequently dined and met informally with government officials. There they learned that Charles Gyles, who had left the courthouse prison, was now to leave the fleet prison.[5] Therefore, Colden was again brought low when he heard that the Council of Safety, which governed the state when the Convention adjourned, assigned all eight comrades to the fleet prison. By now it was an overcrowded facility without the attractions it possessed when they had originally applied for a transfer. While preparing to obey this order, which he considered force without right, he was visited by Elizabeth and a son (probably David), with whom he sent a complaint to John Jay. Jay came to see Colden and explained that his recent appeal for release was denied by the Council of Safety. However, he could not answer on what charge Colden was imprisoned, but "surmised" it was for aiding the officer who escaped from the Rosa-Midagh party with dispatches from Canada to General Howe, and for giving Rosa the impression he would be reprieved. The parolee-host did not address the accusation that he had helped the British officer, but defended his aid to Rosa as preparing the inmate for death, an argument which he claimed Jay accepted. Perhaps Jay did not respond for he was too gentlemanly to pursue such a sterile topic. Colden now realized that he had to obey the Council. Then for about fifteen minutes Jay kindly discussed the ramifications of her husband's situation with Elizabeth.[6] On the next day, as Colden was preparing to board, he obtained official permission for the eight comrades to hire their own sloop as a prison, to be attended by one hired servant, and to maintain themselves at their own expense, but he was denied a servant with free access to dock and ship. Even with this largess Colden continued to send unsuccessful pleas for release from the floating prison, drawing from the Council of Safety the retort that,

> The Said Cadwallader Colden hath been apprehended and Detained for Reasons which this Council think Sufficient to justify that Measure, and that it would be improper for this Council at Present to Enumerate or Publish the Same further than to inform the Said Cadwallader Colden that this Council are furnish'd with full Evidence of his being Most Notoriously Disaffected to the American Cause, and that it would be inconsistant with the Peace and Safety of this State to Permitt him to go at Large, or Remain in any Situation which Would enable him to injure the American Cause.

This exasperated Colden. He now realized he was imprisoned for two reasons. The first was for what the Americans claimed he did, but had never proven. The second was for what he may do, "which makes good the Common Saying Viz New Master, New Laws." Such rules, he complained were contrary to English liberty and fully justified disloyalty, if he were so inclined. No legal evidence existed proving he acted for the loyalist cause, he argued, because he was and would remain neutral if freed. He pleaded that contrary to the accusation, if he were at home growing crops, he would be useful to the state. He drew no answer from the Council of Safety and had to submit to imprisonment on the sloop.

Fortunately, before boarding his dungeon Colden had time to shop with Sleght for wine, tea, chocolate, sugar, and other amenities, so that with the sloop's commodious accomodations and with the fresh provisions regularly sent by friends and relatives "we liv'd very Comfortably & very Merry." However, there were inconveniences. Colden reported drinking water was foul because the nearby prison ships "are Continually Emptying their gutts into" the river, "so that it Comes allong side our Vessel like Porige, the very thoughts of it makes me heave allmost on this Paper." After being on board a few days he asked Sleght with friendly, but heavy-handed humor, why he had not delivered the bedsheets Colden's son had let out to be washed. Colden also chided his friend for not sending salt, rum, pepper, a quart mug and "the beer which makes good the Old Saying - Out of Sight, out of Mind." The eight prisoners ate food prepared by their own cook, but they still lacked enough servants to transform the ship into a floating inn. Therefore Colden applied to the Council of Safety for "permission to purchase a negro man, who is confined on board the Fleet prison." With a loyalist slave the sloop's inmates could be transformed into its residents. Unfortunately for the comrades the request was ignored, and the prisoners had to rough it during their confinement.[7] These living conditions were typical of wealthy prisoners' experiences. But poor inmates suffered greatly. In the eighteenth century governmentmaintained prisons provided merely enough sustenance to prevent death. Amenities were to be supplied by prisoners. The eight prison comrades' offer to support themselves and the delivery of specially ordered food to their ship were completely within the prerogatives of incarcerated gentry and was welcomed by the revolutionaries as a saving to the state. Amidst this luxury Colden demonstrated a sense of noblesse oblige, complaining to state officials that because food was not being delivered to other ships less fortunate prisoners "must starve." And they did. Even his ship was without bread for four days. The prompt ameliatory response of the Council when it heard of the shortages, demonstrates poor conditions were not created by state policy. Administrative, economic, and requisition problems hindered revolutionaries' efforts to sustain decent living conditions in prisons. With soldiers and civilians facing food shortages, government was loathe to feed enemy prisoners well. Yet, so luxuriously did the eight prisoners live that after an initial period of adjustment Colden, who constantly complained of his sufferings, no longer protested the conditions. His last comment concerning the life he endured on the sloop was to note the Convention prohibited any of the fleet's prisoners to be on land and forbade other persons free access to both the prison ships and the dock. Yet in spite of this Colden maintained a constant barrage of notes to state officials, seeking his return home or at least a parole so his family could visit him.[8]

Conditions on the fleet became more crowded as a result of the summer military campaign of 1777. When the British forces under General John Burgoyne (invading New York from Canada) reached Fort Ticonderoga on Lake Champlain, eighty Quaker prisoners were assigned to the fleet, twelve of whom were put onto Colden's sloop. Although they crowded the facilities, the Quakers were "good Decent People," with whom the prisoners were happy. Yet in late June Colden continued to concoct plans to get out, such as when he asked Dr. Jones to be taken to Coldengham because of his poor health and need for a doctor's care. The request drew the response that a parole to Coldengham was possible, but it would have to come from the Council of Safety, which did not deign to respond to his plea for a medical parole. Another ploy failed.

More men were confined to the fleet as Burgoyne moved south; now the ships were bursting with prisoners. Undeserved imprisonment rankled. Repeated pleas for parole went unanswered until July when Cadwallader III delivered provisions on board. The squire sent him with a request to the Council meeting in town averring he was needed at home for twenty-four hours "to give Derection about my harvest &c." His request certainly implied that his transfer of Coldengham to his eldest son had been an expediency, and that in this first fall during which he was alienated from the estate, he was needed to bring in the crops.[9] On July 21 prisoner Colden was permitted to leave his ship for five days in the custody of Henry Sleght. The men arrived at Coldengham to find Elizabeth and the teenager David ill. Mrs. Colden was so overjoyed to see her husband, she spent the day outdoors with him, only to worsen her condition.

On the appropriate day Colden and Sleght left Coldengham and returned to Kingston, where the prisoner lodged at a tavern. He then had his friend seek a longer parole and an interview with the Council of Safety. The next day John Jay called on Colden at his rooms. After exchanging pleasantries, each apologizing for inconveniencing the other, Colden asked if he could be paroled at home for several reasons: his wife was ill; he "Lost one of [his] Best Negroes"; no farmhands could be hired, and the estate was going to ruin. Jay answered that he did not know of any gentleman who avowed Colden's sentiments and who was still at liberty. For example, Goldbrow Banyar, an Albany merchant, had been left free by the state because he kept quiet. Also William Smith, Jr., a prominent former Son of Liberty who was drifting toward loyalism, was paroled to his home on pledge he would refrain from making public statements. As for Colden, Jay inferred, too many things happened about him when he was free, so the state could not accept his claim of absolute neutrality. Many gentlemen had violated parole and taken up arms with the British. Since the Convention had "Strong Suspicions" that the squire was of strong "Disaffection," it had no confidence that he would live up to his promise. Jay then added that if Colden thought he was undeservedly punished he should realize it was due to the state's experience with other loyalist gentlemen who reneged on their oaths. In addition, said Jay, Colden was imprisoned for his own good. It was well known to state officials that genteel parolees were made so uncomfortable by neighbors while at home, "they were glad to Come back again." However, if Colden desired, Jay thought he could arrange a parole at John Van Deusen's inn at Hurley, less than five miles from Kingston. Colden answered by repeating his confidence that his neighbors would cause no problems. He was sure three-fourths of them would agree to his return, and added that if he could not be home, he only wanted to be near enough to Coldengham to receive the visits of his beloved family. Jay left, offering to propose Colden's reassignment to the Council of Safety. The host politely thanked him without enthusiasm, "not Being Determin'd in my own Mind wether to Accept the offer or no." The squire then was taken to the prison sloop's dock by Sleght, who was so helpful, kind and cordial, "no one would believe him to be a Dutch man."

Just before Colden's short parole at home ended and he went back to Kingston with Sleght, he had written a petition for his neighbors to endorse. He obviously hoped to circumvent the Americans' claim he was safer in prison than at home. By signing it neighbors would agree to seek his return to Coldengham. But when he returned to prison he heard that the Hanover Committee refused to countenance the plea. In sorrow he wrote to a Hanover committeeman, who was also an elder of the Reverend Annan's church, lamenting the un-Christian attitude of his neighbors. Again he drew no response.[10] Jay seemed correct. Colden's neighbors did not want him home.

At this time the British summer offensive of 1777 severely threatened the state. Rumors were rampant as General John Burgoyne's campaign continued southward from Canada, and as General Barry St. Leger's forces moved from the Great Lakes toward the Hudson River. Colden feared prisoners would be sent far from home because of the imminent threat to the state. Jay's offer of parole at Van Deusen's house in Hurley was better than forced exile, so he reopened negotiations. Without such hopes Cumming and the six other comrades warned the Council of Safety that if they heard of plans to send them far from their homes, they would escape from the fleet. Colden held off the plotters for eight days hoping Jay's response would deliver him from this situation. Instead his twenty-year-old son, Alexander, came with news that General Sir William Howe led his troops southward from New York on his own expedition rather than up the Hudson Valley to rendezvous with Burgoyne and St. Leger. News of the Battle of Bennington, at which Burgoyne's attempt to obtain fresh supplies was repulsed, caused "High Spiritts" on shore and further demonstrated the British seemed unwilling or unable to liberate the Hudson Valley.

By the night of the escape Colden had been informally told that the Council of Safety agreed to Jay's request for his parole. However he was not taken from the sloop until after the flight of the seven prisoners. Moved first to Sleght's house he met Elizabeth and stayed there until September 3, when Charles DeWitt and Gouverneur Morris finished conditions of his parole, which required he disclose all loyalist plots and bound him to the orders of the newly elected Governor George Clinton. Colden and his wife were then driven the short distance to Hurley where the couple remained with the Van Deusens until Cadwallader III arrived to take his mother home on September 7.

Colden was not content with this small victory and in a few days again tried to use influence to get home. This time his means was state Senator Jesse Woodhull, whom he knew since he served as his father's deputy.[11] For Colden Woodhull surveyed opinion in the state legislature, and reported that he had found some legislators who would do their best for him, "but at the Same time found others in the Reverse who were very Violent & Said I had too much indulgence allready." Just be patient Woodhull counselled. However, Colden lost patience in two weeks and appealed directly to Governor Clinton. The squire admitted he was worn down; where he once may have demanded his rights, he now merely solicited permission to go home. In all these pleas for release Colden linked his freedom to love of his home, his wife, his family, or his estate, which needed his expertise. Even though he sought freedom because it was just, the sentimental aspect of his appeals demonstrated he needed Coldengham's residents for his emotional wellbeing as much as, or more than, they needed him.

Obviously torn by his personal sympathies and official duties Clinton sought advice rather than rely on his own judgment. He asked John Nicholson, his New Windsor neighbor and local committeeman, to inquire whether public opinion would accept Colden's return. Nicholson consulted enough people in the greater Hanover area to "find them of different Sentiments." Mr. Birdsal, the first person he encountered in Newburgh, opposed Colden's release because escaped loyalists already were skulking in the woods back of the town. Besides, he added, "if he [Colden] was a poor man he would be kept in Gaol." James Latta of Hanover, a former committeeman and Ulster minuteman, concurred. But all others with whom Nicholson spoke agreed with Clinton's sentiment that if Colden went home and got involved in any other loyalist activity or violated his parole in the least, "it will be a means of accelerating his destruction."[12] The prisoner was still in Hurley and Clinton was still mulling over Nicholson's response when the war intervened. In the crisis of October 1777 Clinton had too many worries even to consider Colden's problems.

In addition to General Burgoyne's climatic battles in the Saratoga area, Governor Clinton was concerned about the British march up the Hudson Valley under General Sir Henry Clinton. This venture was not a major invasion to rescue Burgoyne who was mired down by American troops three times his number. General Sir William Howe had taken most of New York City's garrison by sea to capture Philadelphia, leaving Sir Henry (the British commander in the port) with but seven thousand men. Using only a little more than half that number, Sir Henry plotted a clever diversionary raid. On October 3, proceeding up the east bank of the Hudson River, he feinted the American General Israel "Old Put" Putnam into thinking he would attack Peekskill, but instead he swiftly crossed his men to the west bank of the river and on October 6 routed General and Governor Clinton, who had merely six hundred men to defend Forts Clinton and Montgomery between West Point and New Windsor. The remnants of the American army fled northward and Governor Clinton set up new headquarters at Little Britian, which became the de facto capital of the state.

Unknown to the Americans Sir Henry merely tried to distract American troops and never intended to blast his way northward to relieve Burgoyne. He stopped his advance in order to demolish the forts and then rushed back to New York City to be sure its defenses were strong enough to repulse a possible American attack on the port. Meanwhile, panic spread throughout the New Windsor area as the whipped Americans reeled back from the Highlands forts. As people fled their homes hoping to escape the apparent impending ravage, looters ransacked the area. William Bedlow's family left behind furniture, several boxes of china, and other valuables. When the crisis passed he returned to an empty house. According to local tradition Thomas Ellison was smarter and luckier. He hid his money and silver plate underground in his smokehouse, hung up hams and lit a cob fire. When he returned his meat was gone, but his valuables were safe. George Clinton lost the bed irons from his cot at Mrs. Fall's tavern in Little Britian.[13] Life at Coldengham at this time must have been just as chaotic.

The day after the fall of the Highlands forts Burgoyne lost a major battle of the Saratoga confrontation, unbeknown to the people of Kingston. All they knew was Sir Henry Clinton was forty miles to the south, Burgoyne was eighty miles to the north, and the two seemed to be coverging. On the morning of October 8 the Council of Safety, which governed the state in the military crisis, ordered that all prisoners confined in the Kingston area, both on the prison fleet and on land, be sent to Hartford, Connecticut. Edward Floyd Delancey's brief description of the floating jail asserts it was jammed with prisoners when the British moved against Kingston. He acknowledges the state authorized that the ships be evacuated, but relies on an unnamed witness who claimed many prisoners drowned when the prison fleet was scuttled by New Yorkers. This is contradicted by the attention the state legislature paid to on-board conditions and to Colden's experiences as a result of the October 8 resolution. State officials tried to send prisoners away so as to maintain control of these enemies and prevent them from resuming antirevolutionary activities. Evidence of New York's evacuation of prisoners appeared in the October 13 *New-York Journal* which carried the story of eleven prisoners trying to escape from the group sent to New England for safety. With limited resources mobilized to defend against several invasions and insurrections, New York authorities tried to save their prisoners. If indeed some remained on the prison ships and met tragic ends, their deaths were not New York policy or intent. Their demise was an example of the cruelties of war.

Merely hours after the evacuation resolution was passed an armed militia band broke Colden's peace in Hurley. Colden was having his noon meal at Jacobus Hardenbergh's house along with several friends, one of whom was Roeliff Eltinge, a thirty-seven-year-old merchant from an old Dutch family of New Paltz. In 1774 Eltinge was a deacon of the New Paltz Dutch Reformed Church of the Conferentie faction, the wing of the church in which many future loyalists could be found. He signed the Association, as did Colden, and even cooperated with the New Paltz committee early in the war. His commitment flagged and he fell under the same ban as Colden. On May 21, 1777, he had been assigned to the fleet prison just before Colden was sent there, but the two men were on different ships. On June 17 Jacobus Hardenbergh petitioned the state government that Eltinge had been a model shipboard prisoner and was "moved with compassion" to obtain the prisoner's assignment to his house in Hurley. Early in October the two parolees were becoming friends.[14]

Enroute to Kingston with Colden and Eltinge, the soldiers picked up several other parolees, whom they took to the courthouse. In front of the building the Americans lined up all of the area's prisoners amidst rumors of immediate exile to other states. Colden's indignant protest that he was under parole to the governor was ignored in the tumultuous attempt to get rid of the prisoners as quickly as possible. In this situation the squire resorted to a braggadocio he rarely indulged. Before a group of manacled prisoners he boasted, "in as Chearfull a Manner as I Could telling them that I would be allso" shackled. He added that he would rather be dressed as they were than "to be Dress'd in the Lac'd Cloths & brade Like Some about Us." To ridicule the squire the angered guards tied him to Indian and Negro prisoners, with whom he was found by a group of officials walking to the courthouse. One of them was Colden's former lawyer, Robert R. Livingston, who promised that a message about his condition would be sent to the Commission for Conspiracies then meeting in the building. In an hour the commissioners sent out a list of prisoners to be evacuated, but because Colden and Eltinge were omitted, they were separated from the rest and stood unattended to the side. Eltinge told Colden that since they were not called, "we will walk NOW." Colden advised that they remain on the fringe of the crowd in order to find out what was happening.

His conservatism was again apparent. The prisoner who would not escape from the prison ship and who would not flee from the state authority once again waited to find out what others would do to him. The captain in charge of the prisoner transfer drifted over and told Colden and Eltinge that their names had been on the list, but were crossed off. So the parolees walked to the side of the courthouse and sat on a log to rest. With no one in charge of them Colden suggested they lodge at Sleght's, leaving a message of their whereabouts for the Council. By evening Sleght became nervous and Colden surmised his friend's discomfort: knowing Colden too well could bring reprisals. To relieve his friend, Colden returned to Van Deusen's house in Hurley.[15]

On October 10, 1777, news of the battle which General Burgoyne had lost three days earlier spread throughout the area. His retreat to Canada or his surrender was rumored to be imminent. Three days later, unable to escape encirclement by Americans at Saratoga, Burgoyne asked for cessation of hostilites. On the seventeenth he was to surrender. But on the tenth Sir Henry Clinton was ominously still atop the Highland forts, preparing to send a small raiding party under General John Vaughan to pressure the Americans from the south and thereby help Burgoyne. Sir Henry did not know such aid was already too late. To Colden Burgoyne's rumored retreat and Clinton's inability to move north energetically indicated the British could not destroy the state government headquartered next to his estate. In this situation Colden left Hurley and went home with his son David, justifying his return by reasoning that the Americans had violated his parole when he and Eltinge had been dragged away from his meal at Hardenbergh's.

At home he and Elizabeth agreed, "that We could be under Much more Trouble and apprehensions from my being Supposed to be Concealed in or about my house, then if I was Even Carry'd to New England," with the prisoners sent from Kingston. This decision is all that Colden recorded of their conversations. He never admitted the anguish they underwent in reversing his consistent pleas that he was needed at home and would be safe there. Arrived at with no mention of heart-wrenching arguments, this placid statement is another example of Colden's inability to record more than his actions and the events through which he lived. His decision not to remain at home raises questions. Had he been so enmeshed in his desire to get home he did not consider what would happen after he got there? Was his family working so closely with Governor Clinton's regime that the head of the family would be a burden? Nicholson's recent survey suggested his neighbors would let him come back, but had that opinion changed now that the British were threatening southern Ulster? In spite of Nicholson's survey, Colden's politics may have been so obnoxious to his neighbors in this crisis that Elizabeth and he feared reprisals when they found out he was back on the estate. The decision to leave apparently demonstrated the validity of Jay's comment that men such as Colden could not remain at home easily and often turned themselves in to the American officials because of social pressure. Colden succumbed, sending Cadwallader III with a message to the governor, who was in Little Britain awaiting Sir Henry's move northward. As he delivered the information Cadwallader III also passed on to Clinton anxieties which his father may not have appreciated. His uneasiness led the governor to note that, "Colo. Colden has given his Son great Pain by coming Home, especially at this Time and I believe the Rest of his Family." The estrangement between father and son was obvious.[16] Probably Cadwallader III's identification with the revolutionaries helped maintain the safety of the family more than did the father's pleas.

In the military crisis Colden's note must have seemed trivial to Clinton. Too busy to deal with the problem of his neighbor, the governor did not make a decision but gave to both Cadwalladers a pass to the Council of Safety in Kingston for a determination of the father's case. On their trip north the father turned off at Hurley to stay at Van Deusen's inn while the son went to Kingston, where the Council exploded at him, "in a great Rage & Said they would have Nothing further to do With" the prisoner. Philip Livingston, a Colden acquaintance, and Gouverneur Morris reported to him that John Morin Scott, the former militantly anti-British agitator who had threatened to invade Queens County, carried the Council with a tirade denouncing the squire of Coldengham and thereby squashing all prospects that his status would be changed soon.

At this juncture the British interceded. On the afternoon of October 15 Colden was with his son David in Hurley, relaxing at tea with a friend at Hardenbergh's, when two men rode by broadcasting that the British were at Kingston Landing. Without any information from the north Sir Henry had sent General Vaughan toward Albany after Burgoyne had already asked for surrender terms. Colden ran back to his lodgings, found Van Deusen's house evacuated and the road filled with refugees. The parolee advised Hardenbergh to remain and that his presence at the inn would guarantee protection from the British. Not an admission that he was a loyalist, this advice certainly suggested that he was no friend of the Revolution. The next day, while he and Hardenbergh's slave were bringing his bed up from Van Deusen's, they heard cannonading. From eleven in the morning until four in the afternoon the nearly abandoned and defenseless town was bombarded. Colden and his loyalist friend climbed a hill and saw the pillars of smoke rising from the river port as the British destroyed Kingston. Over three hundred buildings were demolished in the foray and the conflagration. Vaughan's unopposed troops then raided further up the Hudson Valley in Livingston Manor on the day that Burgoyne surrendered.[17]

At this point Colden and his son were in a most precarious situation. With the Americans in Hurley protecting supplies the landlord now considered the Coldens liabilities and asked them to stay concealed in their rooms to keep the American soldiers from becoming suspicious. However, summoning up their nerve they went openly about the town and dissuaded mob action by publicly demonstrating they had nothing to conceal. A man without a country, languishing in a hostile environment without a safe place to retreat, was Cadwallader Colden II. In October 1777 he could not go home, but was not imprisoned or exiled behind British lines. His eldest son legally had control of his estate and cooperated with the revolutionaries whose state government was headquartered next to his home. In this predicament he again turned to George Clinton. On October 19 he sent his son David with a message that he could not remain as he was. He could have fled to the British two days earlier during the chaos of the raid, but "I only want to be with my family and take no part in the present broile." If he were so foolish as to take any part in the war he would "expect to be treated accordingly." He wanted to go home with official permission regardless of the problems awaiting him in Hanover. But Clinton did not want to make a decision and sent the parolee to the Council of Safety in Marbletown, even though Colden did not want to appear there.

Colden was received frostily by the Council which obviously did not want to be bothered with him. Because of Clinton's request, it grudgingly admitted the prisoner for a hearing. Led by John Morin Scott some members favored treating him as having jumped parole when he last went home and wished to send him off to join the prisoners who had been shipped out of the state before the Kingston raid. However, less hostile views prevailed, and he was given an interview. Having been warned he could not later claim he was compelled to take either side, Colden was asked whether he considered himself to be a subject of New York or of the crown of Great Britian. He was told not to plead he wanted to remain neutral, for "no such state of neutrality can be known by the council." This was a clear statement of the cliché, "If you are not with me, you are against me." While the Council recessed for the midday meal, he was given time to frame the answer on which the rest of his life could depend. When called back he posited that he was, "a faithful & true Subject to that State [of New York] from which he receiv'd protection." However, he was bound by his oath of allegiance to the British king. He reconciled this apparent inconsistency by promising "to be a true and faithful Subject to the government of the Said State, So Long as it shall Remain an independent State, and I reside therein."

Obviously Colden did not recognize the legitimacy of the regime created by the revolutionaries. He only accepted the de facto situation that in certain parts of what was once the royal province of New York the crown was no longer obeyed. Coldengham was in one of those parts governed as an independent state. Therefore he acceded to the military situation and would be a subject of the state as long as it remained independent. Yet, he still owed allegiance to the king. In effect he sought a status not unlike a permanent resident alien, obeying New York laws and paying its taxes. The Americans would not accept this in the revolutionary situation of 1777 when the state capital had just been destroyed by the British. Colden wanted to be a disguised loyalist according to the Council. Colden was told that since he was a subject of the king he must be kept a prisoner. However, because of his passive record he would be allowed on parole to part of Jacobus Hardenbergh's property. The Council put itself in charge of the parole so that future appeals would be brought to it rather than to Clinton. Apparently the Council did not trust the govenor's resolve to remain steadfast on Colden's status.[18]

Chapter VII
Banished

Until now Colden suffered only slightly as a prisoner of the revolutionaries. His first stay in the Kingston jail had been uncomfortable, but he paid to cleanse it. On the prison ship he and his comrades had lived well. He had resided as a parolee at homes and country inns, more as a guest than a prisoner. However, he was aware of the greater hardships suffered by poorer prisoners—wallowing in filth, eating merely what was served them, using only utensils and equipment supplied by jailers, and if judged dangerous to the revolution, being confined in irons. By comparison, so easy was his treatment that some impoverished free person may have wished to live as well as he did in prison. To leaders of the state he pleaded for release and drew their personal and individual consideration, yet he complained of their unfairness in confining him without a trial. Poorer prisoners wailed their laments through bars to their jailers and were lucky if their written appeals reached a committee for group decision. By his standards he suffered, but by comparison to the fates of American prisoners on the British *Jersey* prison ship in New York harbor, or loyalists deep in the Simmsbury mine prison of Connecticut, his travail was indeed light.

Why was he treated so mildly? Personally state officials seem to have considered him more of a pest than a dangerous loyalist. However, they phrased their condemnations of him as if he were a threatening enemy because the American revolutionaries could not justify incarcerating him merely for being an annoyance. Perhaps, as fellow gentry, they considered his punishment severe enough. The state lacked men, money, and prison facilities to confine all loyalists, and possibly Colden was punished as severely as limited resources allowed. Regardless of the reasons for the way he was treated, the state leaders wanted men such as Colden removed to a part of the state where they could least harm the war effort. More trouble than they were worth, Colden and Eltinge were thrust from the Council door. On November 5 the two men were exiled to house arrest in the remote Nine Partners district of northeastern Dutchess County, next to the New England border. There revolutionaries were so dominant that Colden's and Eltinge's loyalism would be thoroughly insulated. After the denial of their petitions for reprieve or postponement of their assignment, the prisoners arrived at Nine Partners unbowed, refusing to acknowledge their custodians' interpretation of the document controlling their status. The Council's November 5 order stipulated the two men were under orders of that body or of the state legislature, but the parole document under which the trustees were to supervise the exiles mentioned only the legislature. Colden and Eltinge wanted to accept orders from the Council too, or they might have no agency to which they could appeal should an emergency arise and the legislature not meet.

For two months the parolees' appeals to the state government remained unanswered, and finally on January 1, 1788, isolated and apparently ignored, Colden informed their custodians that he was going to the Council at the temporary capital in Poughkeepsie. If he won an affirmative decision he would go straight home. Irate at his proposed unilateral action the trustees immediately called on Colden, and after a long discussion—which verged on an argument—they agreed that the parolee could go to Governor Clinton with their letter explaining his journey. Clinton probably received Colden with exasperation for he disgustedly said the parolee might as well be free and at Coldengham as where he was. Colden seemed to travel about as easily as any New Yorker.[1]

The Council agreed with the squire that it was in charge of the parole and refused to let him and Eltinge return closer to home in spite of appeals from such members as Robert Harpur, who lodged at Colden's inn in Poughkeepsie. Harpur, an immigrant Presbyterian Scot from Ballybay, Ireland, who had been on the faculty of Anglican King's College, had become an ardent revolutionary. In 1777 he had served in the Provincial Congress, was now a member of the new Assembly and of the Dutchess County Commission for Conspiracies, in addition to being on the Council of Safety. Colden claimed that Harpur, as did other honorable revolutionaries, interceded on his behalf when his plight was explained. However, once again John Morin Scott seemed to be the villain. Scott harangued the Council to deal severely with Colden, even though before the Council meeting the squire obtained the official's promise to present Colden's request for a parole at home. It took six minutes for Egbert Benson, the Council secretary, to report to the parolee that his assignment to Nine Partners stood firm. However, the Council neglected to order him back by a specific date. So Colden once again went to see Clinton, repeating his travails. One may almost picture the busy governor's pique as he again listened to Colden's lamentation. In exasperation Clinton suggested that Colden stay in Poughkeepsie for two or three days to see if the Council might relent and hear his case when Arthur Park arrived from Hanover to represent Ulster.

Five days later, after being hosted by various moderate revolutionaries of the Hudson squirearchy, Colden unsuccessfully sought help from "My old friend Coll [Levi] Pawling." Instead Robert Harpur and Arthur

Park brought him news that the Colden family was well and "Promised to use their Interest to Serve me." Whereupon he pressed on them a letter to the Council in which he again bemoaned that he was denied due process and deserved to be allowed home because other persons who were as neutral as he, were at their residences. Besides, he offered any security or bond demanded to insure his obedience to the new state. Lastly, he wanted his life well ordered and certain. If he was not allowed to go home for the duration of the war, he wanted to know it.[2]

Colden faced a perplexing problem. Even though friendly officials promised to help him, he never was permanently sent home. Since early 1776 he constantly complained of the state's stringent punishment, yet officials told him he was getting off easily by not being sent home. Actually, the state did treat him leniently considering the denunciations of John Morin Scott and other militants who branded him as a leading loyalist. Regardless of Colden's complaints he was not languishing in jail. Perhaps the aristocratic Hudson Valley revolutionaries who knew him introduced resolutions to help him. Disagreements over how to handle Colden may have produced a compromise: his detractors stopped him from going home; his supporters stopped him from suffering imprisonment, banishment, or other severe punishment. Unknown to Colden, inconsistencies in dealing with him may have been the result of such legislative bargaining.

This does not preclude other possibilities. Regularly, Colden was told by friendly legislators that they would try to obtain resolutions to ease his situation. However, because they had more important concerns than due process for Cadwallader Colden II, they may not have pushed hard for his interests. In addition, some persons whom he recorded as his spokesmen might never have ardently supported him. Colden's belief that they promised to help him may have been partially his projection of what he wanted to hear. The speakers may not have promised action, and Colden's misinterpretation of what was said reflected his anxieties more than the sentiments of the politicians.

Harpur and Park returned from the Council to report their unsuccessful effort. The parolee would have to return to Nine Partners. This incident is remarkable in that Robert Harpur, who seemed not to have been closely involved with Colden's case, supposedly commented to the parolee as did others who had known him for many years. At first the Council favored him, but was swayed by the oratory of mischievous members who argued that Colden's neighbors would not allow his return. Therefore, reported Harpur, to do Colden a favor the Council compromised. It did not lock him up and did not let him go home. Now his banishment from Hanover was a positive good according to some councilors. In such high esteem was Colden held, that Harpur predicted the squire would retain Coldengham regardless of the war's outcome.[3]

Life at Nine Partners was eased by Elizabeth and Mrs. Eltinge's visit on January 16, two months after their husbands first settled there. Once again Colden was silent about his personal life and did not comment about events during Elizabeth's visit. He only noted that after four days of living together they resumed his campaign for freedom. On January 20 he wrote two letters to Clinton. One sought his intercession with the legislature which now first met according to the new state constitution of 1777. Colden expressed his fear that since the Convention no longer existed he had no appeal but to the governor. He repeated his tale of sufferings and lamented his wife's wartime problems in managing Coldengham—which were more difficult than those faced by his mother. In addition his sons seemed to have fallen short as managers of the estate—which once again the father referred to as his.

The other letter written on January 20 to George Clinton was more personal and therefore was not recorded in Colden's letterbook. The message offered Colden's thanks for aid given his wife after "Some Insults and abuse she mett with from Som of the Low Class of officers &c." The couple were so happy together, he informed Clinton, they could not refrain from seeking permission to go home together. Colden begged Clinton to ask for his release "and in Case it Dose not Succeed Shall be glad of Your friendly Advice (under Confidence)." Colden reminded him that he had not signed any parole papers under the new constitutional government and he therefore had no legal status.

However, Clinton was out of town when the letters arrived and it took a week for Colden's appeal to reach the state Senate. Eager for an answer, on the 27th the two parolees with permission of the parole trustees left with their wives for Poughkeepsie. There Colden met with Clinton who again promised to intercede with the new state legislature. In the squire's presence Clinton conferred with Senator John Morin Scott and Assemblyman Cornelius Schoonmaker, who, the prisoner claimed, were "two of my greatest enemies." On the next day Clinton sent Colden's petition to the Senate along with the plea of several persons from Coxakie on behalf of John Cumming, who had been recaptured after his escape from the prison fleet. A three man Senate committee, including Levi Pawling, was created to consider these matters.[4]

While they deliberated Clinton advised Elizabeth Colden to lobby for a favorable vote from Scott. She accompanied her husband to the senator's house, but became so nervous she could not summon the courage to engage him in a conversation. Gallantly, Scott said he understood her desire to have her husband back and that the committee report, due the

next day, would settle the matter. At that time "My old friend Coll
[Jesse] Woodhull" brought the decision to the stunned couple who now
heard that the committee recommended the Colden and Cumming cases
fell within the jurisdiction of the reorganized state Commission for Conspiracies. The Senate agreed.

Ironically, the special committee's report had been carried to the
Senate by a man Colden considered his friend, Levi Pawling. The
Senate's approval of the committee report was taken to the Assembly by
Colden's neighbor Arthur Park, another person he considered a supporter. The votes of these proceedings were secret, but the actions of
these men and the rejection of Colden's and Cumming's appeals
demonstrated once again that perhaps Colden deluded himself about his
influence. Legislators seemed to fear that allowing him a parole at home
would set a dangerous precedent. Both houses agreed that he would have
to abide by the normal rules of the state.[5]

Woodhull told Colden that the old commission would be replaced by a
new larger and more powerful thirty-man Commission for Conspiracies,
with three members sufficient for a quorum. Since Colden wanted immediate relief and did not wish to wait until the new body began delibera-
tions, he sought out the two members of the old body still in Poughkeepsie. The two parolees went first to Jacobus Swarthout, who was less antagonistic than the other member, Egbert Benson. Swarthout listened
sympathetically to Colden's plea and suggested they all go to see Benson
who was at Clinton's house. There the three men got Benson to agree
that Colden and Eltinge might have two week paroles at their homes until
the new Commission began to operate. The master of Coldengham was
home the following night.[6]

The squire's account of his revolutionary war experiences are devoted
entirely to his political activities and skip his life at the estate. Nothing
worthy of Colden's recording occurred until February 9, ten days after he
returned home, when he received a one-month extension after informing
Benson and Swarthout that he anticipated being unable to get to
Poughkeepsie on the assigned date because the river had iced over. Once
again Colden's record leaps over his personal life. Immediately after his
copy of the second Benson-Swarthout parole to his home is the following
sentence: "March 13th 1778 Sett out for Poughkeepsey but on account
of Ice, the River, & Badness of the Road, Did not get there till Sunday
Morning the 15th." He repeatedly articulated love for Coldengham but
refrained from writing any impression or feeling for the place. These om-
missions may have been caused by the purpose of his narrative—to
record his sufferings and his political experiences during the conflict. He
omitted from this catalog of adversity that which was dearest to him,

keeping his loved homelife unsullied. Home was his emotional refuge; yet we know almost nothing of what he did there.

As he left his estate on Friday, March 13, his friend William Denning wrote to the Commissioners for Conspiracies requesting that Colden be permitted to remain at home. Denning's letter received no action because Swarthout was out of town and Benson declined to decide the issue. For four days Colden parked himself outside the Assembly door, awaiting his fate until the two men showed up. He was rewarded, perhaps because of his persistence or perhaps because he made a nuisance of himself. The doorkeeper of that body handed him a one sentence note from Benson and Swarthout, "Cadwallader Colden Esq is Permitted to Remain at his Place of Abode in Ulster County until further order."[7]

Again Colden recorded nothing for three and a half months, from mid-March to early July. We may assume he was keenly interested in the political developments about him, for he was home in an area crucial to the revolutionaries' control. The state's legislative capital was in this part of the Hudson Valley, and Little Britain was the governor's headquarters. New Windsor, Newburgh, and Fishkill were depots of stores and ammunition, connected by the Ellison and Colden ferries. With New York City in British hands, much communication between New England and the rest of the United States passed through this neighborhood. In May 1778 five hundred Indian warriors allied to the American cause and accompanied by Continental officers were reported to have crossed at New Windsor on their way to General Washington's camp.[8] Communication and transportation routes extended southwest from Fishkill toward Goshen and on to the northern reaches of the Delaware River. From there the trip to Philadelphia was safe, if the Indians and loyalist soldiers under Joseph Brant and the Butler family were not raiding eastward out of Niagara. Coldengham lay adjacent to this route's linchpin—the Newburgh and New Windsor ferries.

Neutrals as well as loyalists were a threat to this area. The indecisive or would-be neutral persons who held themselves from the war effort or who undermined it with their apathy were considered great problems by the revolutionaries. Failing hard evidence of overt loyalist activities, state officials understood neutrality to be cowardly toryism. They also feared subversion as in the plot emanating from Mamakating on the western slope of the Shawangunk Mountains along a major branch of the Delaware River. This remote region seemed particularly vulnerable because it was isolated from the rest of the county and unintegrated into New York society. On March 31, 1777, a witness before the Mamakating committee told of a scheme to raise three thousand loyalists plus Indians who would raid the fringe of the state, while about four hundred loyalists from Albany and Ulster counties would attack Kingston, capture the state legislature, put prisoners on British men-of-war at a rendezvous with thousands of loyalists near New Windsor, and then call for a general uprising to overthrow the rest of the state's revolutionary regime.[9] It seemed logical that armed loyalists could have been raised in Albany and Ulster in early 1777, for General Burgoyne was then beginning his apparently triumphant march from Canada and emboldened the timid. At the time the Mamakating plot was uncovered a British raid destroyed military stores at Peekskill just below the Highland forts, antirevolutionary tenants were disrupting Livingston Manor, and the Rosa-Midagh escapade broke. A year later the British threat to the state seemed to come from the west led by Joseph Brant, the Iroquois born and English educated loyalist, whose raiders attacked frontier Cobbleskill. Two days later John Butler's raiders hit the Wyoming Valley of northern Pennsylvania. A series of 1778 forays in western New York destroyed German Flats, Unadilla, and Cherry Valley, as semiregular loyalist forces rolled back the state's control to the Catskill and the Shawangunk mountains. Rebel sweeps of the frontier tried to round up loyalists of the area and neutralize the region. Although in mid-1778 the state was safe from invasion by the British army, it was reeling under the staccato jabs of raiding parties. In the last chapter of *Letters from an American Farmer,* Michel-Guillaume St. Jean de Crèvecoeur romantically portrayed the fears and trials of a frontier settler in the Orange County area, just south of Ulster. Attacked by irregulars of both sides, the farmer was pillaged and assaulted without let up. The author's loyalist inclinations are plainly shown in "The American Belisarius" and "American Landscapes" of his *Sketches of Eighteenth Century America,* even though other essays demonstrate he sympathized with rebel victims of harsh fighting. Crèvecoeur's world of burnt farmhouses and barns, defiled women and maimed children ranged through Ulster, and in it lurked the fears of people on each side of the war.[10]

These events hung heavily over the heads of the men who were voting on an act to banish persons who did not support the state. Officials could no longer afford Colden the luxury of remaining neutral at home. On July 1, the day that Brant raided Cobbleskill, Senator Arthur Park came to Colden's gate and handed him a letter from the reconstructed Commission for Conspiracies ordering him to appear in Poughkeepsie. He was in front of the Commission at four in the afternoon of July 3, the day of the Wyoming Valley raid. The Commission lacked a quorum that day, but unofficially its members explained to Colden the oath of allegiance, and gave him a copy of the act and oath under which he was the first person in the state to be questioned. Had the law been entitled with only Colden in mind it would hardly have been more accurately worded. Persons against whom there was no charge of overt hostility to New York were subject to, "An Act More Effectively to Prevent the Mischieffs ariseing from the influence and Example of Persons of Equivocal and Suspected Character in this State." The first type of person covered by the act well described Colden as some Americans saw him: "Certain Persons of Equivocal and Suspected Character . . . affected to Maintain a Neutrality which there is now reason to Suspect was in Many Instances Dictated by Poverty of Spirit and an Undue attachment to Property." The law also cited persons who aided the American cause "till it became Serious." Other Americans considered Colden to be one of those persons who spread hostile rumors and who enticed "Weak Minded Persons from their Duttys they owe their Country." The preamble also condemned persons who refused to support the government that sheltered them. Furthermore it cited those neutrals who at this late stage in the war, after having "Sufficient time to Consider and Determine" their allegiance, still pretended to have "Consciencious Doubts & Scruples." To all of these people a new oath was to be administered. Almost every category of person mentioned in this act was applied to Colden by some group of revolutionary leaders. The suspect was "Solemnly and Without any Mental reservation or Equivocation" to swear (or witness if a Quaker) that New York had a right to be a free and independent state and pledge to do his duty for the state. Any neutral who refused to take this oath would be sent behind enemy lines.[11]

Overnight he "Meditated" and prayed for divine guidance. The next morning, July 4, 1778—exactly two years after he appeared before the Ulster County committee—Colden submitted his answer to the commissioners fulfilling his rational needs, personality, and religiosity. Colden's conscience was insufficient to explain his compulsive behavior. Conscience is not necessarily related to refusing to walk away from the line-up in Kingston or to standing resolutely in front of the legislature's doors until a decision was passed on. His conscience was not the motive for his compulsive behavior.

At nine in the morning of July 4, Colden overtook Benson entering the Commission's meeting rooms. He pressed on the official his written refusal to take the oath, even though the Commission lacked a quorum and no meeting would be held for two hours. After waiting in the anteroom he was called in so that Benson could formally read the oath and law to him. Colden stated he was willing to sign the "obligatory Part," which required he obey the state, but refused to sign the "Creed Part," which required he swear and call on God to witness the state had a right to be free and that he would call on God to deal with him if he reneged on his duty to New York. Because he could not recant his oath of allegiance to King George III, he refused this oath, arguing that it would take the Lord's name in vain. The commissioners "Reply'd I must Either take it as it stood in the Act or they Must Record my Refusal," and so inform Governor Clinton. After considering his situation Colden called attention to the written rejection he had handed to Benson, which was ample explanation of his refusal. He wished this formal declaration filed, per the law, in the Secretary of State's office, so that he "may hereafter have the better oppertunity to appeal to the future justice of my Country." He probably wanted such a document in the office of a rebel official so that if the British won he would be known as a loyalist deserving of "future justice" because of his long career as a prisoner and parolee, and if the Americans won he might use the document to prove he was not a militant loyalist but dissented on an issue of conscience. His legalistic request demonstrated his desire to keep open avenues back into New York, his country, and Ulster, his home county. Finally, Colden agreed he would take an oath "Securing fedelity & obeydience to the present form of government [of New York], and to Preventing my doing any injury to what you Call the American Cause, Either by Example influence or otherwise, Because these things is and will be in My Power to keep and Perform." He could not subscribe to that part of the oath requiring him to call on God. Former oaths of allegiance could not be superceded, for such use of God's name was blasphemy. He was willing to accept "Confiscation of all my Estate" to keep religious integrity, an offer which may have been less brave than the words appear. The chance of Coldengham being taken by the state was remote.[12]

At this July 4 interview the commissioners firmly refused Colden's bargain, avoided face-to-face arguments, and were courteous. After telling him informally that he was to be banished to New York City, they allowed him freedom of the town on parole until their decision was formally announced through Governor Clinton.[13] On the next day Colden went to Clinton's house and discussed with him the Commission's decision. "Mr Benson happening to Come in [,] the governor Told him he Should not Detain me but Leave me with them [the commissioners]. Benson said they knew what to Do." The critical matter was closed, and Colden walked out into the street.

He was free at this point probably because of two reasons. First, officials realized he had nowhere to go and could do nothing but obey the state. He could not flee anywhere in the state, to New York City, or to another state. Second, the state operated inefficiently,—poor bureaucratic follow-up of orders and execution of policies plagued it. Officials procrastinated letting small problems slide by as they concentrated on more complex ones. On Monday, July 6, the commissioners were kept too busy to consider Colden's situation. They were interviewing William Smith, Jr., an in-law of the Livingstons paroled to his family estate. Smith had evolved from a leader of opposition to British policies into a guarded loyalist who was refusing to sign the new oath.

When they met outside of the commission's hearing room, Colden and Smith had long known each other. Smith was six years younger than Colden, but was much more active in public life. His book, *The History of the Late Province of New York From Its Discovery to the Appointment of Governor Colden in 1762* had been sharply critical of the first Cadwallader Colden. Smith was a powerful Assembly politician who later was a councilor, whereas Governor Colden's power was in the prerogative. Smith had also written and argued against an Anglican colonial episcopate and had been a champion of the Presbyterian political faction against the Anglican group on such issues as whether King's College should be an Anglican or nonsectarian institution. When the more secular imperial crises boiled, Smith remained a bulwark of the traditional whig outlook that Assembly power must be maintained against the incursions of the governor. Smith's refusal to accept independence spread a very thin patina of agreement over the deep hostility between him and the defender of the Colden name.

Little wonder that their conversation was not mentioned by Colden, who had never considered himself to be an intellectual. That was Smith's forte. He was an egotist who critically judged others, whereas Colden seemed constantly to be buttressing his poor self-image. Obviously attracted by Smith, Colden may have been wary of his ego and politics. Such a threat to Colden's emotional stability did not appear in his letter-book.[14] In the committee ante-room Colden told Smith that if it were not for the religious aspect of the oath he would have signed the pledge because Governor Clinton had advised that "the Word State in that Clause meant that Part of the Colony not now possessed by the British army." This was arrant nonsense to Smith. Armies' positions in the field did not determine sovereignty. Colden obviously had not thought through the deeper issues of the oath, according to Smith.

On that day Colden called on the commissioners three or four times and was turned away each time. At five in the afternoon, after his conversation with Smith, they finally sent for him and gave him a parole of indefinite duration to an area within eight miles of his home. He thought the Commission had reversed itself, for this was more generous an area than was granted in earlier paroles.[15] His logic seemed correct, but he overestimated the state's ability to coordinate its operations. He was merely being shelved until arrangements could be made to deport him along with Smith and Eltinge. For over two weeks he was home, probably doing whatever he had done previously when sent there.

His life was interrupted on July 27 by an order from the Commission that he report on August 3 to Fishkill to fulfill "his Removal within Ennemy's Lines." He was permitted one week's provisions and as much property as could be fitted into two wagons. This limitation stunned him. He could take no provisions, for he needed two wagons for personal belongings and essential food. How could he live in his exile?

On August 3 the exile-to-be appeared at Fishkill with Cadwallader III and Roeliff Eltinge, who had stopped at Coldengham on his way south. However, no one in town knew what to do with the two men, so they lodged nearby for two days until one of the commissioners showed up. This last incident reaffirmed the inefficiency of the New York state regime. It did not even act systematically to exile supposed enemies. When the official arrived he told Colden and Eltinge that they would go to the port in a sloop obtained by William Smith, Jr. under the guard of Colonel Aaron Burr. For two more days Colden and Eltinge passively awaited the arrival of Burr and the ship. When the party left Fishkill on August 6, the exiles were treated differently. Smith, the possessor of the sloop, closer by experience and marriage to the leaders of the new state, took with him his family, a large cargo of goods, money, a few personal servants, and other possessions. Such a largess was generous by comparison to Colden's allotment, but was much less than Smith had planned to take. Governor Clinton denied his request to bring with him all his slaves and tenants. On August 10 the sloop with its passengers arrived at New York City.[16] There General Sir Henry Clinton, the son of his father's friend, would treat Colden well, and brother David had influence. In the capital Cadwallader Colden II was at his political home.

Chapter VIII
At Home in New York City

The New York to which Colden moved was unlike the colonial city he knew. It still bore the scars of the great fire of September 21, 1776, which swept from the southeast corner of the town, across the island, and up the west shore along the Hudson River, stopping only at the expanse of King's College and vacant lots at the northwest corner of the port. It destroyed about one-quarter of the homes in the city, almost five hundred houses. When Colden arrived two years later, the mile long path of destruction was yet littered with tents and shacks. In addition to the fire damage, the tenor of city life was drastically altered by rapid population growth, from 21,863 inhabitants in 1771 to about 33,000 in 1783. The effect of this overcrowding was aggravated by the turmoil in ownership of urban property. When the Americans controlled the city some ardent loyalists fled, and their property was confiscated. When General Washington's forces were driven from town and the British took over, the reverse occurred.

As the British army evacuated Philadelphia and Charleston, South Carolina, loyalist refugees flocked to the one remaining royal stronghold, swelling the charity rolls and the dole. In addition to this social instability and the growth of the city's population, the condition of housing accomodations remained critical because occupying armies had destroyed nearby forests and quarries that provided building materials. The burgeoning population was further increased by the growth in number of British troops living in or near the city, from 3,341 in 1777 to 17,207 in 1782. These changes occurred as the Americans blockaded the port area by land, making difficult the purchase of supplies from nearby farms and requiring that supplementary goods be brought in by sea. In 1779 and 1780 wholesale prices had risen by three hundred percent over such costs in 1775 and 1776.[1] The rampant inflation of prices in British New York was due to the increase in civilian and military population, to the money brought into the city by refugees and British officials, and to the shortage of goods. This was hardly a city in which Colden could retire from the fray. He lived on credit and had to scramble to survive.

The exile could not enter the competitive commercial world in such an unstable economy and had to seek a position as a gentlemanly government official, the only other occupation to which he was trained. To obtain such a place he had to appeal to the military, for it ran the city. The British commanders governed through their appointed subordinates, leaving Governor William Tryon little power. Under martial law New York struggled to survive its ruling officers. Some officials tried to be fair and generous to supporters, but others thought first of obtaining enough profits in the chaotic situation to retire in Britain as soon as possible. Typically, throughout Anglo-America civilians appointed by the military commanders were not selected because of their qualifications, but because they had influence, a high place in society, or were deserving of favor. This appointment policy caused great hardship; political expertise was needed to govern in wartime crises. Unfortunately, few city officials had it. Lieutenant Governor and Superintendent of Police Andrew Elliot worked hard, but lacked the training and temperament to serve in the embattled capital of the British empire of North America. His assistant was Mayor David Matthews, who used his office to amass great wealth and to throw gala banquets. Police Magistrate Peter DuBois, Colden's old friend, member of the DeLancey political alliance, and vestryman of St. Andrew's of Wallkill, received a salary of £200 per year for performing a job of which he knew little when he was appointed.[2] DuBois denounced the activities of both Elliot and Matthews, especially the corrupt mayor; yet these civilian adjuncts of the military men who governed by martial law formed a three-man judicial panel of distrusting, feuding, and ill-prepared officials. Before them appeared New Yorkers seeking justice without court writs or jury trials.

The diaries and memoirs of loyalists who endured this government were replete with complaints of corruption. Under the guise of wartime need some military officials requisitioned goods and property without adequate payments, pocketing the differences between monies actually paid and the padded officially recorded prices. If the property was later sold at inflated prices, they pocketed more. Wages for illiterate workers who did not know the rates were manipulated, as some officials kept the differences between amounts of money drawn from the treasury and what was given the laborers. Without paying compensation some barrackmasters requisitioned buildings and firewood and kept monies appropriated as payment for these contributions to the British war effort. Commissaries, quartermasters, and barrackmasters became the new rich of the city to the dismay of even staunch loyalists. From Flushing David Colden reported to Thomas Jones in the spring of 1781 when the British and Hessian troops left: "There was not a four-footed animal left in town (a few dogs excepted) nor a wooden fence standing within the township." Armies of all nations have well deserved reputations as voracious forces that supplement deficiencies in their appropriations with whatever can be taken from civilian foes or friends.[3]

When Colden arrived in town he was received "as an old Acquaintance" by Sir Henry Clinton, the son of his father's friend—the old royal governor George Clinton, who gave him the commissary appointment soon after his marriage. The commander and the loyalist knew each other well enough for Colden to complain that after being welcomed by Sir Henry, the busy general "took no more Notice of me." Ironically Colden received short shrift from the British, perhaps because they did not have to pay him heed. In New York he was merely another loyal worthy trying to rely on his name, prestige, social status, and limited abilities in order to obtain a gentlemanly stipend from the meager war chest.

In early September Colden accepted his brother David's invitation to stay at Springhill, where the exile was happily received with "affectionate behavior." Typical of periods when he was removed from strife, his months at Springhill are as secret as are his paroles at Coldengham. However, the brothers did more than just exchange pleasantries or reminiscences, for the exiled Colden brought land deeds and papers for them to consider.[4] Unrecorded by Colden was any psychological uneasiness at his dependence on his younger brother, whom he probably suspected had been favored by his father. Three months after his arrival at David's estate, Colden reembarked on his lifetime journey toward the high status to which he aspired. From Springhill on November 20 he wrote to Lord Jeffrey Amherst, commander-in-chief of the British army, in whose Whitehall office was the seat of British authority in America.

Colden began by seeking Amherst's recognition "that the Sons of that good and faithful Old Servant of the Crown" were worthy loyalists. Amherst had worked well with his father during the French and Indian War and knew the second generation of Coldens. The supplicant emphasized that the Colden family's support of the crown was more consistent, and therefore more valuable than that of persons "who now plume themselves on the Characters of Loyalism." Many of them were only recently to be found on the British side, a none-too-subtle slap at recently converted loyalists, such as William Smith, Jr. However, at the heart of the letter was Colden's effort to obtain rank and position through influence.

Here, and in all his pleas for high office, Colden ignored that the royal government had honored the Colden family in the late colonial period when it had appointed brothers David and Alexander to official positions. That Cadwallader II did not hold a prestigious office was probably caused by a consideration unthinkable to him. He could not admit he was unworthy of high appointment. In his own eyes, when the current senior male Colden lacked prominent public office, the family was being ignored. To him David's status was irrelevant; instead he emphasized his own worthiness. This appeal to Amherst stated that he had been loyal from the first, but had to rely on his land for his position "never enjoying the least post or profit or honour, under the Crown," except for the command in the colonial militia. For his loyality he claimed to have been imprisoned for over two years until he was exiled, the first person in the state to be sent behind British lines under the banishment act of 1777. He did not mention his paroles or the freedom with which he had roamed the Hudson Valley, but gave Amherst the impression that he spent a full two years in prison. His wife, family, and possessions were at the mercy of the Americans he lamented. Colden's plea was typical of most loyalists, for almost every one of them complained of uniquely severe sufferings; each was the most deserving of aid. British authorities however saw the loyalists as a group of people in a similar situation.

Colden also advised Amherst on how to end the war. The British must continue to press the battle. Many loyalist petitioners argued that the rebellion was being conducted merely by a cabal of malcontents, not by the majority of Americans, and could be defeated by greater British efforts. This analysis of the American political situation obviously was supposed to win Amherst's confidence in Colden's judgment, so he concluded the letter with a reaffirmation of its real purpose: He wanted an appointment to a royal office, and flagrantly pleaded that, "If in Honour to the memmory of my Father, Your Lordship would shew any marke of attention to his Sons, it will be most humbly and gratefully acknowledged." The postscript of this letter was yet another partial truth, "I forgot to mention that I have two Sons who from Inherent Principles of Loyalty entered into his Majesties Service on his Troops first Landing in the Province, One is now a Captn the other a Major in the New Corps." In a preliminary version of this letter Colden concluded with, "N.B." followed by the exact same words about Thomas and John Colden. The letter sent to Amherst gave the impression that the comment about his sons was an afterthought, but Colden did not for a moment forget to mention the services of his sons, for his early draft included the statement. He used his sons' military service to buttress his worthiness and the validity of his appeal for a government office. However, he did not mention that he had other sons; Cadwallader III, Alexander, and David never fought with the British army, although they were old enough for service.[5]

As he awaited what was to be Amherst's polite reply, Colden applied again to Sir Henry Clinton, dropping all pretense of having been neutral, admitting that which the Americans had never proven in court. Exiled in the capital, seeking aid from Sir Henry, Colden justified his loyalist pretensions by confessing that he protected the British officer in the Rosa-Midagh group and hired guides to escort him to safety. He was lucky that the rebels, "Could not prove the fact or he would have undoubtedly Suffer'd Death." Instead, he told Sir Henry he was banished, allowing Americans to control his family except for his two loyalist soldier sons. Again he neglected to mention how members of his family at Coldengham were cooperating with the state government. Colden concluded his letter to Sir Henry by pleading he was destitute, and asked that Clinton appoint him to an office so he could aid the royal cause, "and obtain a Suport for the present time when the Necessarys of life are at Such an Exhorbitant Price."[6]

Even though he claimed to have been consistently pro-British he could muster as proof only aid given the British messenger and his sons' military activities. He took no credit for Lady Mary Johnson's or any other loyalist's escape. He did not help the loyalist raids on western New York in 1778 or claim to have aided the royal cause in any clandestine or civilian manner. Nor did he mention his 1775 protest against the Provincial Congress election. In short, Colden did little to document a case for his ardent loyalism. Obviously he had actually been a secret loyalist whose allegiance the rebels had correctly surmised, although it was Colden's good fortune that they had no firm and incontrovertible evidence by which to find him guilty. If, in these letters Colden had invented his loyalism in order to win favors from Sir Henry, he could have enhanced his appeals by linking himself to known loyalist activities in his neighborhood, or he could have fabricated incidents. Instead he told the truth to the British authorities. The basis of his pleas to Sir Henry and to Lord Jeffrey Amherst was his family name, his imprisonment, his suffering, the supposed jeopardy in which his property now hung, and the service of John and Thomas Colden. The help he gave the British officer sneaking through Ulster was no more than corroborating evidence of his loyalism. Colden had always been a conservative man who shied away from performing drastic action; his steadfast loyalism was not based on bravado.

His request elicited from Sir Henry merely a promise of appointment to the first available office. In the meantime, Colden was put on the charity roll for a dollar-a-day subsidy and a small allotment of food. Unable to negotiate a greater stipend from Sir Henry's aide, Captain John André, Colden unsuccessfully tried to bargain for the dollar-a-day retroactively since he left Coldengham. His name and status won him no greater favor than was given to any other worthy loyal refugee. Nothing more could be gained in the city. The stipend was a pittance and no job was imminent, for Clinton had made similar promises to other estimable refugees. So with no better prospects, the squire of Coldengham retired to David's estate in mid-January 1779.

At Springhill he waited in vain until early April for the letter from

Clinton that would appoint him to public office. Impatient, he returned to the city once again to seek his fortune, and on Saturday, April 10, met Colonel Roger Morris, administrator of charity payments to the deserving loyalists. This chance meeting drew from Morris the surprise comment that he had been waiting for Colden to pick up at his home the accumulated fund growing at the rate of a dollar-a-day. But the exile averred he was not sure of the "propriety of Receiving it." He had better make up his mind, Morris told him, and do so by Monday. Claiming to be worth more than Clinton's allotment, he asked Morris to tell the general of his sentiments. One can imagine the immense problem Morris faced in dealing with an arrogant and distrustful Sir Henry and a city full of refugee prima donnas, each of whom considered his hardships to be the most severe and most virtuous. Morris refused the request as inappropriate. If the exile was dissatisfied he should seek out Clinton himself, but he reminded Colden that a dollar per diem since January 1 was awaiting him until noon of that day.[7] Because Colden appealed for aid in mid-January, the January 1 beginning offered him an extra fifteen dollars as a largess. Still dissatisfied Colden picked up his money. Disheartening was the dole of a dollar a day, plus some extra rations from British authorities to whom he remained loyal, to whom he committed his emotional wellbeing, and upon whom rested his bona fide claim to status. He probably remained for a while in New York City rather than at Springhill because there he could continue to lobby for an appointment and for an increase in his stipend. In the city he could meet other prominent loyalists who publicly reinforced each other's pretensions. Privately these exiles gossiped, formed cliques, and tried to undercut the influence of rivals. Colden played this political game hoping to win a large pension, a high government post, and prominence in the reconstituted empire.

Some of the belligerent loyalists served in military units, such as Sir John Johnson's "Royal Greens" regiment and Major General Governor William Tryon's "Provincial Corps." Some civilians under the name "Loyal Refugees," met on September 23, 1778, at Mrs. Montaigne's public house, where one of the group squelched the rumored evacuation of the city and the supposed imminent surrender by the British, claiming that if the perpetrators of the hoax ever fell into his band's hands, the "Loyal Refugees" would cure them of such delusions—with the bayonet. The following year, "Loyal Refugees" was used as the appelation of a military unit under Joseph Sharp, who was authorized by General Sir Henry Clinton to raise a battalion for two years' service. On August 9, 1779, these "Loyal Refugees" attacked the rebels from Connecticut and Long Island who had made life difficult for loyalists living on the outskirts of the city, boasting that they "set out upon the noble plan of supressing rebellion and detecting of Rebels in their secret schemes." The formation of New York's "Loyal Refugees" was followed in 1779 by the creation of other organizations. In accordance with London's order the Board of Directors of the Associated Loyalists was established on December 27, 1780, with William Franklin as president, to raid rebels around the port area.

Meanwhile the politically motivated exiles of each colony met separately to push their pretensions with the military officers in the capital, and through agents, with the men of Whitehall. For example, on August 25, 1779, at six in the evening the refugees from Pennsylvania met at New Tavern on William Street for social and political purposes while those from rebel held sections of New York met at Mrs. Amary's inn, across from the Fields.[8] The refugees of each colony cooperated to apply political pressure, such as on August 18 when representatives of exiles from each province met at Hick's tavern to prepare an address to Major General John Vaughan, the destroyer of Kingston, as he prepared to sail for Great Britain. Three days later this group called the "Loyal Refugees" unanimously accepted a draft of the message. Then from each colony a committee was selected to accompany the "Loyal Refugees" president, Cadwallader Colden II, who was to present the petition to Vaughan. The loyalists' letter offered thanks to the general, King George III, and the mother country. The loyalists were grateful for Vaughan's patronage and aid because, as they lamented, the ministry had represented them in Parliament in ways that hurt their interests and were "contrary to truth."

> You, Sir have been a witness of the transactions of the army since their landing on Long Island and cannot be ignorant of the causes which formerly depressed the spirit of loyalty and prevented it from being so uselessly extended as it otherwise might have been.

This convoluted sentence is typical of Colden, who probably wrote it in his capacity as president of the group. He was certainly aware of the depredations of British troops on Long Island and of the loyalists' complaint that they were suffering under their own protectors. Sir William Howe's refusal to create civilian government on the loyalist western end of Long Island nearest New York City had a crippling effect on loyalist activities. Now the "Loyal Refugees" repeated the complaints of such pro-British victims of the royal army as David Colden.

The loyalists were happy that Vaughan would be their champion to counter "aspersions of which every loyal subject in this country has such just right to complain." British authorities frequently complained that loyalists were laggard in their actions and contributions and that they relied too much on royal officials. Also they were often seen as being more concerned with their own welfare than that of the empire. Mutual antagonism demonstrated such bad faith and jealousy that the British defeat may have become a self-fulfilling prophesy. Each side in the squabble predicted that if its interpretation were not accepted, the empire would sunder. General Vaughan's mission as the loyalists' tribune had no chance to succeed, for the British officials had too great an emotional and political investment in blaming the loyalists for royal defeats, even though the organization of loyalist brigades and associations became an essential element in London's war plan.[9]

In spite of the many former colonial leaders available, the "Loyal Refugees" chose Cadwallader Colden II as its president. Certainly political wisdom would suggest the election of a New Yorker to head the organization. Those from other colonies, such as New Jersey's William Franklin, had less contact with the political life of the city, even though later, when the British were to organize the loyalists, leaders from other colonies served their purpose. However, when first coming together, they apparently wanted to generate leadership from truly loyalist families of New York. Of all the candidates, Colden had a famous name and a father whose services were well known on both sides of the Atlantic and in all colonies. He was certainly more highly respected among loyalists than William Smith, Jr. or the Van Schaack brothers, Henry and Peter, even though they were lawyers and advocates of high repute. Outside of New York the Coldens had a better reputation than had the DeLanceys. In addition, Colden was the first person the rebels called in under provisions of the banishment act, evidence that state officials despised him. Also, coming into New York City with Smith allowed Thomas Jones to depict Colden as a worthy and almost destitute refugee unlike the recent convert who arrived with an entourage. Colden had impeccable Church of England credentials and was related to the Reverend Charles Inglis of Trinity Church. The speed with which Colden sought out General Sir Henry Clinton and wrote to Lord Jeffrey Amherst were other signs of his being well-placed.

In addition to these political endeavors Colden maintained contact with home and occasionally enjoyed his family's company in the city. Elizabeth's several visits to her husband had to be negotiated with the delicacy of international diplomacy. The frequency of her trips indicate she came down river because she wanted to see Cadwallader, not merely because she felt a social obligation to do so. Lacking overt evidence of their affection, the Coldens' desire to be together in this crisis suggests their's was a loving marriage. Her first visit, lasting several weeks, was in September 1779 under a truce flag granted by Governor George Clinton.

To achieve this visit Cadwallader and David Colden had to intercede on behalf of two American officers from Ulster County held by the British on Long Island. One was Lieutenant Colonel James McClaughrey, who was captured when Sir Henry seized the Highland forts in 1777; the other was Major Samuel Logan, the man who had arrested Colden in May 1777 in connection with the Rosa-Midagh episode. If Colden retained any pique against Logan, his former hatter of whom he had nothing good to say at his arrest, it was probably buried under the need to help the officer in order to have Elizabeth visit New York City. The soldiers received permission from royal officials to have their wives come into the city, if Governor Clinton allowed Elizabeth, a daughter, and servants to go into and come out of the British capital. Perhaps the governor wished to aid his captured neighbors more than he wanted to help the embattled Coldens. The exile may have used his position as president of the "Loyal Refugees" to make the arrangement, for the visits occurred when General Vaughan was preparing to sail home. The American prisoners acknowledged they saw their wives "by the interest of Coll. Colden."[10]

Without such political or military reasons Governor Clinton did not allow members of loyalist families to move freely in the state. For example, the day after he allowed Elizabeth to go, he refused to grant permission for her sister Mrs. Margaret Crooke (the Reverend Charles Inglis' mother-in-law), to come up from the port to see her father. At this time Thomas Ellison was living at Coldengham with Elizabeth while General Washington occupied his house in New Windsor. Clinton reasoned Mrs. Crooke's excuse that her father was in poor health was not valid because he had just given Ellison's other daughter permission to leave him for a visit to New York City. "Therefore," he declared, "I conclude your father is not seriously ill." Governor Clinton's logic is obvious. However, life is not logical.

Indeed Thomas Ellison was terminally ill and was to die within the next year. The old revolutionary willed to his son Thomas, Jr., a loyalist in New York City, all monies he had already given him, plus £5, leaving to his revolutionary sons, John and William Ellison, the bulk of his estate. His three daughters shared his lands, but the war widow, Elizabeth, whose husband might never return and who might live a destitute life in exile, seemed to need extra help. Profits from only her land were to be paid annually "for her separate use and maintenance for life." Probably the property was not given to Elizabeth because under eighteenth century law whatever she inherited would be assigned to Cadwallader II, and his holdings were under threat of forfeiture, confiscation, or sequestration by the state. Upon her death, Elizabeth's inheritance was to be sold and the "proceeds and the said dollars and pounds go equally to all her children, then living (except her sons, John and Thomas)." The exclusion of his loyalist son and grandsons from inheritance demonstrated both his concern for Elizabeth and the political ardor of Thomas Ellison. In his will he did not mention Elizabeth's husband whom he had never financially helped. With the exception of Colden's claim that Ellison tried to raise bail for him in 1776, the two men probably did not have a close relationship in the decade before the old man's death.[11]

When Mrs. Colden's party came to the city, Colden's pen once again fell still. The Coldens remained in the port with Captain Thomas for some of the visit and most likely spent some days at Springhill. At the end of her stay the family unsuccessfully requested that Sir Henry allow the old infirm James Umphries, a rebel neighbor who was imprisoned in the city, to go home to Ulster on parole for the winter, to return in the spring if he survived. So the Colden women and the wives of the prisoners on Long Island returned north by themselves. Mrs. Colden tried to bring back goods bought in New York City—clothes, wine, tea, sugar, etc.—but Governor Clinton absolutely refused to let anything come up on a truce vessel unless the material was specified in the negotiations before departure to the city. He told William Denning, who wanted to take possession of Elizabeth's items at New Windsor, that the inflationary and social repercussions of winking at goods so obviously meant for the black market were disastrous. Mrs. Colden was permitted to bring back only "some Family Necessaries."[12]

This first trip established her relationship with Governor Clinton, and she had little trouble when she negotiated three other visits. By then the Ulster County Ellisons and Coldens may have been firmly ensconced in the revolutionary cause. In November 1780, Mrs. Colden came down to see her husband with members of her family, "males capable of bearing arms excepted," and her return was untroubled. The next spring her sloop was seized at West Point where the American General William Heath reported that Mrs. Colden was going south with Mrs. Eltinge, who brought her eighteen-year-old son and too many personal possessions for use on such a trip. Heath sent back the Eltinge boy with what he determined were excess goods and then let the women go. In October 1781 Elizabeth's trip to her husband was complicated by others who sought asylum in the city. A Colden retainer, claiming he did not have long to live, asked for what he thought would be the comfort of the metropolis. Clinton refused unless he negotiated the release of an American prisoner as an exchange. At the end of October a woman also tried to accompany Mrs. Colden to the port for the purpose of seeking payment from her loyalist debtors before they left America. One month after Governor Clinton cleared this trip General Heath sent his permission only for

Elizabeth to pass south. Probably because of his friendship with the
family and because they did not abuse the privilege of a truce flag,
Governor Clinton gave the Coldens scarce passes. They were among a
small group who visited across military lines and thereby retained friendly relations with important persons on both sides. To arrange these trips
Colden had to remain in constant contact with Coldengham, and letters
must have passed regularly. He received at least one message from his
eldest son, via the commanding American officer at Dobbs Ferry on the
Hudson River, whom Cadwallader Colden III asked to forward the letter, promising the officer that if he would send his name back to the
estate, "I shall always be happy to see you at my house."[13] The son was
well established on Coldengham when this letter was written in 1782 even
though his father continued to think of the estate as his. Perhaps his
father's absence and his own security in the new state helped soothe some
of the son's animosities toward his sire.

Colden's continued search for a government office led back to Lord
Amherst's polite reply to his letter. In 1779 Colden sent other pleas for
help to Lord Jeffrey and complained of Sir Henry's botching of the war.
Triumph eluded the government by the fall of 1779, primarily because
the fierce determination which he earlier recommended had not yet been
effected. The British commander continued to fight a typical European
war, amassing troops to attack major centers of rebel sentiment. Lacking
what he considered overwhelming numbers he lapsed into inaction in the
northern theater of war where a stalemate existed after Burgoyne's surrender in 1777. Except for raids out of Canada British military attention
shifted to the South where, supposedly, the majority of the colonists were
loyal. In December 1778 Savannah was captured but throughout the next
year no decisive victories were achieved because the British regulars were
countered by segments of the American army aided by guerrilla forces. It
appeared to loyalists such as Colden that Sir Henry was going after the
branches and was letting his major antagonist remain a martial force just
outside of his reach, for Washington remained unattacked as he paraded
his troops from camp to camp in the middle states. In conclusion Colden
tried to show how sincere he was by presumptuously asking Amherst to
request that Lord George Germain, Secretary of State for America, pass
his letter to King George III who did receive it but did not respond.[14]

Without sufficient income and unable to get a larger allowance from
Roger Morris, the years 1779 and 1780 financially were very difficult for
Colden. These may have been the years in which he borrowed £1,600
from his brother-in-law, Thomas Ellison, Jr., and he may also have ob-
tained money from David when he was at Springhill.[15] However, on
June 21, 1780, he was back in the city again approaching Sir Henry's

aide, the recently promoted Major André. This contact probably was motivated by the letter Colden received on May 3 from Lord Jeffrey's aide, who informed the refugee that Sir Henry was the person to grant him an office, but the lord would support Colden's petition to Clinton, "as far as Consistent with his power." The supplicant now had to gird himself to deal with the aloof general.

Colden's perception of himself in this task is evident in his excessively supplicatory request of André. Colden was worn down by Sir Henry's repeated rejection of his earlier requests, not only for his release but also for merely a pass home. He now pleaded with André to remind Clinton of his promise to appoint him to a government post because he deserved it and then brazenly added that the dollar-a-day stipend was "rather below my Dignity." He was enduring a new financial burden now that Roger Morris cut off his meager food allotment, because he sold some inedible rations to buy "what was more palitable." Colden did not perceive that he performed an illegal act by dabbling in the black market. Instead he complained of receiving a small subsidy, of being dropped by the irresponsible action of the paymaster, and that living in the city was abnormally expensive because he was recently joined by his teenage son, probably David. Then he asked the aide to remind Sir Henry that he hoped the general would have sons as patriotic as had the old lieutenant governor, the close friend of his father.

By July 7 he had not received an appointment and so resorted to using all his influence, informing Sir Henry of Amherst's letter that offered "to embrace any Oppertunity that may offer of Shewing my remembrance of Your Father and of the attention I would wish to pay his sons." He repeated the recommendation of Amherst's aide, that Sir Henry should appoint Colden to office. Now he dealt from the most powerful position in British society: from the influence of a powerful cabinet minister who was Clinton's superior. Nerved to his task Colden asked for a position on the Treasury Board or appointment as secretary of state for the colony, his brother's old office. He even interceded on behalf of Thomas Colden who was recouperating in the city from an illness contracted on duty in Florida and Jamaica. Colden asked Clinton to reassign Thomas to a regular British army regiment in the capital so that both his sons could be nearby; at this time John was serving in the New Jersey Volunteers. Later he was reassigned to his cousin James DeLancey's "Cowboy" brigade where he died.[16]

And the war dragged on. Washington remained in the field with his army keeping the American effort alive as the loyalists fumed over the passage of time that made the return to their homes seem less likely. What was only implied in Colden's advice to Amherst in the previous

year was made explicit in his August 1780 recommendation to Lord
George Germain, which was carried to London by John Cumming who
now fled America. First, the loyalists had to be better integrated into the
war effort. Second, even though many loyalists were already with the
British many others remained outside the lines. "But this is not believed
even by the many here, who say if So D—n them Why don't they Com
in? Why Don't they Shew themselves when We go out?" To answer the
question he reached back into his own motivation. These loyalists did not
come in because to do so they must leave behind, "Wives, family, Property and all that is Dear to them in Life to the Mercy of Rebels." Most
felt too vulnerable to leave these attachments. And what is the reception
of the brave ones who flee within the lines, the refugee asked rhetorically? From his dissatisfaction with Sir Henry's administration came an
answer that many loyalists would have accepted. Most of them thought
they were getting short shrift from Clinton, "Neglected," "disposed,"
and "Scoff'd at," but a prominent rebel who resumes loyalty is
smothered in favors. This may be good policy, he admitted, but it was
very discouraging to men such as he who constantly stood bravely by the
king's standard. And so the British are actually rewarding rebels. As to
why loyalists do not fight with the British troops, "when they go out on
any excurtions, How many thousands have paid dear for this, they and
their familys being afterwards left Expos'd to the unrelenting Crueltye of
the Rebels?" As did generals Howe and Burgoyne, Sir Henry seemed to
believe in 1776, '77, and '78 that the magic touch of the British army as it
passed through a neighborhood rendered the loyalists permanently safe
and dominant in their community. So too did Lord Charles Cornwallis in
1780 and '81 raise the hopes of, and abandon, the Carolina loyalists.
Once the focus of British authority passed through a neighborhood,
argued loyalist commentators, a coterie of American guerrillas and committees often resumed control by sheer force, terror, and organization
advantages.

     The exiles continuously assured the British government that they
represented the majority of Americans and the old whig tradition. The
revolutionaries were members of an evil faction that never spoke or acted
for the people, although its rhetoric might sound whig. The rebels were
actually hostile to the best of the British tradition argued most loyalists,
including Joseph Galloway, the outspoken leader of exiles in London,
who testified before Parliament and published pamphlets announcing the
need for an energetic and aggressive military effort in America.
Whichever side of the ocean or wherever in America loyalist criticisms of
the British war effort were composed they were similar. We may be "Ignorant Countrymen," Colden advised Germain in an unusually sarcastic

tone, but we know that the present military leadership is chasing clouds. "We are so foolish as to think that the deffeating or desperssing Washington's Army, Would do more toward the Settling of Rebellion, than the takeing One Half the Towns on the Contenant, As in that Case we are very Sure, he would never be able to Colect another." Colden's advice was offered by many other loyalists. Stop fighting a European-type war; stop seeking to capture a national capital. There was no locus of power in America, such as France's Paris or Britain's London, which once captured virtually ended all resistance. Capture Philadelphia and Congress ran into exile. American society was as quicksilver; squeeze resistance here and it oozed out there. Washington's army is the key to victory, Colden argued. "Knock up Washingtons Army and the Rebellion is Over,—and had the Loyalists proper Countenance and Encouragement given them from the first arrival of the Kings troops, their Numbers alone by this time would have been Sufficient to have done it."

However, these suggestions were too difficult for the British government to implement. If authorities carried out the loyalists' advice they would be accepting as valid a criticism that the British officers supressed loyalists as mere adjuncts, and would have required that proud generals and ministers, who had defeated the French around the world, revamp strategy and logistics. In short, the loyalists' critique of the British war effort was too critical to be accepted by royal officials, regardless of its validity.

In addition to these problems the British could not focus all their military strength on North America. With the Franco-American alliance and the Spanish declaration of war, the Revolutionary War became a world conflict. The Dutch aid and the League of Armed Neutrality (which brought northern Europe into diplomatic hostility with Great Britain) intensified the mother country's problems. Now the British had to protect Canada from possible French invasion and seek out the Dutch in the Carribean. Its Indian possessions and Gibraltar seemed precarious. On the North American battlefields, Britain had to face the allied power of the French and the Americans, which failed at the seige of Savannah and at Newport, but worked well at Yorktown. In 1780 British public opinion was becoming restive over a war of indefinite duration, which jeopardized the empire all over the world.

Colden's long description of how a more vigorous campaign would win the war was followed by the real reason for this letter to Germain. His father received no reward for his tenacious defense of British policies, but now the sons might be compensated for two generations of loyalty. At the resumption of civilian royal government, Colden wished a seat on the Council to continue the tradition of his father who had long been a councilor. Because such a seat did not carry a large stipend, he requested the more lucrative salaried position of Secretary of New York. A reply from Germain was not needed. Six days after he wrote this letter, on September 1, 1780, Sir Henry appointed Cadwallader Colden II "Commissary to the British Prisoners in the Possession of the Enemy." He would now receive a salary of ten shillings per day, plus five shillings per day for travel, enabling him to live "with Proper Dignity." He fully expected to do the job well because of his political connections on both sides of the Revolution.[17] Satisfied, on the public payroll in a responsible position, not pressured by the desire to achieve, no longer thwarted by others, no longer suffering, Colden felt no compulsion to maintain a letterbook, to describe his activities as a commissary, or to record his achievements. With this appointment he may have afforded living quarters in a nice part of town. In a year he interviewed prospective Latin tutors for David's family at his accommodations in 39 Chapel Street.[18] Chapel was a recently laid short street in the northwest corner of the city, near the open fields beyond the urban tumults, running from Barclay Street along the west side of King's College (between Church Street and the Greenwich Village road and paralleling the Hudson River). Starting where the fire of 1776 ended, Chapel Street would have contained recently built homes, an appropriate location for a person with Colden's pretensions.

His new office was probably similar to one of the responsibilities of Elias Boudinot, Abraham Skinner, and others who served as American commissaries of prisoners. They served under Congress for the welfare of both Americans in British prisons and of British men in American prisons, focusing their efforts on southern New England and the middle states. Their British counterpart for much of the war was Joshua Loring, who concentrated on feeding, housing, and clothing the destitute enemy soldiers held in his prisons. Thus, for most of the war little effort was made by the British to insure that American jailers lived up to Congress' resolutions to care for prisoners of war. Some prisoners endured atrocities, such as those loyalists captured outside New York City on an American raid in September 1779 and thrown into dungeons, chained, and manacled. This was matched by Loring's compliance with the practice of allowing British prison ships anchored in Wallabout Bay of New York harbor to sink to the level of death traps. War led to brutality on both sides.[19]

In June 1780, over two months before Colden's appointment, Loring and Skinner entered long and complicated negotiations to exchange massive numbers of prisoners, at one point bargaining over the means of repatriating five hundred privates on each side. It was not until

November 8, two months after Colden's appointment, that an exchange was worked out. The delicate and time-consuming negotiations may have induced the British to realize they had no systematic knowledge of how their men fared behind enemy lines. While the Skinner-Loring conferences were going on, Colden was appointed with the apparent task of trying to insure the quality of prisoners' life in American confinement. How he did this is unknown, but his travel allowance insinuates he was expected to visit prisons and inspect conditions and probably was empowered to act as did his American counterparts. When poor conditions were discovered and British keepers could not or would not improve them, the Americans themselves sent relief. For example, in 1781 Congress received a report that Americans fared poorly in New York prisons and that it should retaliate against British prisoners. Instead Congress resolved that the various states should supply Skinner with food proportionate to the number of their men held by the British.[20] If Colden was Skinner's British counterpart and supplementary to Loring, he would have been responsible for determining the conditions of British prisoners and for attempting to have Americans remedy deficiencies. If such improvements were not forthcoming he may have been responsible for obtaining relief from Sir Henry's coffers. Colden probably got very little money from his commander, for Clinton constantly complained that he was short of men, money, and equipment. In spite of these difficulties, Colden was probably gratified in his new job, for he was in a humanitarian position, respected by both sides. No doubt he saw himself as effectively helping the British cause in the capacity of a gentleman taking care of less fortunate persons and known to the leaders of both sides.

His sense of noblesse oblige also was apparent in his endorsement of other loyalists' pleas for help. Robert McAndire obtained from Peter DuBois and Colden letters attesting to his imprisonment on the prison fleet with Colden and to his merit as an object of charity. Another recommendation aided Colden's former parishoner, Peter John of New Windsor, who fled with his family to New York City where he lived on provisions issued him by Roger Morris. Colden's neighbor, Thomas Bull, master of the Hill-Hold estate near the Wallkill, wrote to Colden and to Mayor Matthews seeking their efforts to free him from Fishkill jail where the Americans threatened to let him rot unless he arranged a prisoner exchange.[21]

Another of Colden's Hudson Valley neighbors suffering in New York City was Michel-Guillaume St. Jean de Crevecoeur, the French immigrant who gained literary immortality as the author of *Letters from an American Farmer*. Crevecoeur had two farms, one in New Jersey and one in Orange County, New York. When the war began this pacific and conservative loyalist was living on his New York estate, a few miles south of Coldengham. He and a son fled to New York City leaving behind his children and wife who was to die in Westchester County while seeking safety for her young brood. Meanwhile, Crevecoeur applied to Roger Morris for charity based on his loyal attachment and his four years of suffering fines and imprisonments. He worked on Long Island for the British, but was thrown in jail because he was suspected of being in the pay of Governor Clinton. The incriminating evidence was his letter to an American general, written in familiar terms, seeking a pass for temporary passage into the state, probably to get his family to safety. Colden encountered him in prison.

In his July 1779 plea for release on bail, Crevecoeur named both Colden and William Smith, Jr. as character references. Smith told the military commandant of the city that Crevecoeur should be discharged, but also suggested that the general should not take only his word, "Mr. Cadwallader Colden, who was his Neighbor, can give the fullest Evidence of his steady attachment to the King's Cause during the present Troubles." After talking to the officer Smith went to Crevecoeur's cell where he discussed his and Colden's prospective courtroom testimony. Then Smith found Colden and together they went to the superintendent of police to file statements supporting Crevecoeur's plea for release. As they were preparing for the meeting they encountered some loyalists who told them gossip of Crevecoeur's apparent friendship with the Americans and induced the two men to reevaluate the situation. The web of Crevecoeur's predicament became hopelessly tangled when in a later conversation Smith failed to make sense of the account given him by DuBois. Information about the prisoner's incriminating letter came from a close friend of the Isaac Ogden family. "This may be Colden," said DuBois. This twist left Smith with only one conclusion. In such times and circumstances it "is necessary one should keep but little Company and of the best Sort."[22]

Smith's apparent surprise that Colden could not have been a close friend of a neighbor demonstrates that Smith was not aware of the deep animosity that separated the groups of loyalists. By this time Colden was most friendly with those loyalists who disliked Smith and most likely mistrusted whomever he tried to aid. On his part Smith continued to denigrate Colden's and his loyalists friends' intellectual and judgmental pretensions, especially in the William Peartree Smith incident. Peartree Smith was Smith's revolutionary relative, captured at his home in Elizabeth, New Jersey, and brought to New York City where he was paroled within the port. William Smith tried to defend the parolee against the criticisms of avid loyalists. Hugh Wallace, merchant and former tea consignee of the East India Company, thought Peartree Smith "had been in Arms" for the Americans, but William Smith "denied the Charge." Smith also scolded Colden, David Matthews, and Abraham Cuyler, former mayor of Albany, for their distrust of the Jerseyite, and because these leaders of the refugees, "talk suspiciously or utter their Suspicions of others." Matthews thought Peartree Smith should have escaped from the rebels and come in earlier if he were to be considered a loyalist. Cuyler criticized the newcomer, citing rumors that he condemned people since arriving in the port. William Smith responded that "Hints were Nothing, the Accusers should come out and give Proofs." To Colden, who did not understand why Peartree Smith seemed to have been pardoned by Sir Henry's government, William Smith explained the politics of winning support by leniency. Obviously William Smith was sensitive to criticism of his relative who was now in the city and whom he may have hoped to convert to loyalism. Yet political disagreement was only part of the Colden-William Smith estrangement. The haughty Smith remarked on the obstinacy of Colden who had the temerity to disagree with him, "Strange! He was astonished at the Detection of his Error."[23] Colden's devout loyalism, which now ignored his years of professed neutrality, put him on the anti-Smith side of loyalist politics. However, he and William Smith, Jr. would never have been friends, even if they agreed on politics.

The military stalemate became intolerable by March 1782 when the ministry of Lord North was replaced by Lord Rockingham's. The new leadership in Whitehall was so dissatisfied with the accomplishments under Sir Henry that on April 4, 1782, he was replaced by General Sir Guy Carleton who assumed his duties in New York the next month.[24] At that time the Americans controlled New England, and in the middle states most of the countryside and towns, except for the area surrounding New York City. The American victory at Yorktown left only the area around Charleston, South Carolina, under British control in the South. Parliament now realized that after six years of war the United States was virtually independent. As war's ball of string was unravelling, Colden's responsibilities seemed to have increased, and he may have traveled frequently to American prisons. In one three month period, April 1 to June 30, 1782, he received £22.15 as an allowance for travel. Because his commission called for payment of five shillings per day, he may have spent as many as eighty-eight days out of ninety-one away from his residence. His salary for this period was £45.10. For these three months he received £68.5 and was similarly compensated for the next ninety-two days; for the six month period, April 1 to September 30, 1782, he received a total of £137.5. Almost certainly such extensive activity as the war was concluding was going to stand him in good stead. Thirteen months after his last warrant was drawn the British were to evacuate the city and Governor Clinton would administer the entire state. The Revolution would be over.

Colden's services as a type of social worker in the American prisons probably reinforced the image he had earlier presented to the Americans. They knew nothing of his loyal letters to Whitehall. In their eyes he was a gentleman who had claimed to be neutral and had never been a significant military or political threat to the state. He now looked forward to going home, and six months before Sir Guy led the departure from the city, Colden appealed for money to support his return. He sought from the commander one year's salary in advance to pay his expenses in exile, "till I can make my peace here" and return to Coldengham. In spite of his salary for the past two years, he claimed he was deep in debt. In two weeks payment of £100 to Colden was authorized by Deputy Adjutant General Frederick Mackensie.[25]

Sir Guy's reputation for generosity and his popularity with loyalists (and historians) was based on such actions. However, to be fair to Sir Henry, Carleton's problems were not to win the war. A preliminary peace treaty was completed on November 30, 1782, only six months after Carleton's arrival in New York. He merely had to supervise the peaceful dissolution of the British military presence rather than plan invasions, raids, or reprisals. He successfully pulled back, increased rations for prisoners, helped loyalists who wished to flee from the new nation, and prepared such loyalists as Colden to fend for themselves. By the end of April 1783 Carleton supervised the departure of about seven thousand loyalists who did not have Colden's temperament or his connections in America. The remainder of those who were to flee the United States was gone by the end of November.

During the war almost one hundred thousand loyalists left the new nation for Canada and Europe although some were later to return. Others, such as Colden kept all their options and never left. He was not Machiavellian, brilliant, or duplicitous. In a region rife with guerrilla warfare and conflicting allegiances, he was reticent and feared preciptous action. These were his saving characteristics.

Chapter IX

Restoration

Southern Ulster revolutionaries wrestled with their wartime problems as Colden labored with his. New York City was their normal market for produce, and without it Hudson Valley people suffered badly. They sold and bought some products through New England, but the grinding economic stranglehold was wearing. Nor was the situation greatly relieved when Washington located his headquarters in southern Ulster, offering a local market for food and rents for property. By then Continental currency had sunk to its lowest levels. These conditions are demonstrated by the increases in poor rates. In 1778 New Windsor raised its prewar rate fourfold to £80 for the precinct. Newburgh went up 1,600 percent to £800. The economic impact of the Hudson Valley military campaigns is evident in the 1778 vote of the Newburgh meeting, "that donations be collected in the Precinct to be applied to such poor whose husbands or parents were either killed or taken prisoner at Fort Montgomery" when it was captured by the British. Inflation and the maldistribution of wartime profits widened the gulf between people.

As early as 1776 such avaricious Americans as the wife of New Windsor's Captain Jonathan Lawrence were investigated by local committees. The Lawrence family's village store sold salt at eight, rather than the legal maximum of six shillings. Later that year a New Windsor mob broke into William Ellison's store, seizing almost all the salt stored there by a revolutionary colonel who attempted to corner the local market's supply. The mob action led the officer to complain that "from the seemingly disorderly spirit at present prevailing among the common people," property "will be very insecure." In the following July a third incident in New Windsor involved two Albany merchants who stopped in town while taking a load of tea to the upper Hudson Valley. New Windsor men and women seized the cargo and left the state's legal maximum price of six shillings per pound, forcing merely a legal profit on the speculators. The state Council of Safety permitted the merchants to seek restitution in court but they never did, knowing no local jury would favor them.[1] At issue was the right of the community to obtain goods at reasonable prices and the property rights of a merchant. After July 1776 the Colden family on the estate avoided such problems either by keeping their business activities within the bounds of public opinion and state law or by turning the store over to others. Regardless of what they did for a living after the family head left, the Coldens created no antagonism among their neighbors.

Southern Ulster revolutionaries argued among themselves on such other issues as the American currency, sunk in a sea of paper. At Ward's Bridge, where Arthur Park lived, was held a meeting of the disgruntled "principle farmers" from southern Ulster, who presented "capital" grievances to the state. The prices these farmers were paid for goods sold to the army were so high even they were dismayed. They objected to the state and continental policy that granted "unrestricted licences" to traders whose "avaricious practices" bid up prices, causing inflation. The protestors wanted to return to the former practice of supplying produce by contract, believing this had kept money stable. According to these farmers, if prices were fixed by contract and if bidding by procurers were eliminated, at least two problems would be solved. First, prices would drop. Second, civilians who would not be needed to obtain goods for the army would be available for fighting the British. The farmers were determined "to notice the conduct of public servants of every degree," a veiled threat to defeat their political opponents in the revolutionary camp. These protestors' intense concern about complex economic problems demonstrated that currency depreciation was feared by rural folk even though they were not major creditors in society. This complaint was followed in the spring by an argument on the pages of the local newspaper where Robert Boyd, Jr. and Thomas Palmer blasted each other in a series of essays.

Although pitched battles of the Revolution never exploded in Coldengham's immediate neighborhood, by July 1779 Ulster people feared they were under dire threat of raiders, especially when loyalists under Joseph Brant won the bloody skirmish at Minisink. The vital communication route across Ulster to the upper Delaware Valley was jeopardized by this raid. Fear raged through the pessimists, even though Generals James Sullivan and James Clinton led a massive raid that destroyed the Iroquois villages from which the loyalist irregulars obtained aid. As the attacks continued out of Niagara with little interruption the American scorched earth assault seemed to have been successful in that it kept the raids from becoming more severe. So fearful was the state government for this part of New York's safety that it authorized the removal or destruction of vital farm produce left on abandoned Ulster and Orange County frontier farms. For the next two years Tryon County and northwest Ulster were hit several times, and even as General Charles Lord Cornwallis was moving to the York Peninsula in late August 1781, the frontier Ulster precinct of Wawarsing was destroyed by three hundred Indian and ninety white loyalists.[2] Five more skirmishes and raids were visited upon western New York before November 1, 1781. These British and loyalist dangers were never brought to the homes of eastern Ulster as they were to New Yorkers in Westchester and lower Orange counties. Guerrilla, irregular, freebooting, and outlaw bands of both sides pillaged homes and garrisons just above the port. Luckily for Colden's neighbors the British did not pierce the American blockade of the lower Hudson Valley after 1777 and so left them free of the near-chaotic violence that ravaged Westchester and Orange. However, fear of the midnight loyalist bands, which devastated settlements west of the Wallkill and in the lower Hudson Valley, permeated the Newburgh-New Windsor-Hanover area. Thus Ulsterites had much to fear late in the war, even though during November 1778 Washington's troops were scattered about several camps from northeastern New Jersey to western Connecticut near the New York border, and Fishkill was the site of ammunition depots and supply shops. [3] To protect the Hudson Valley and to threaten New York City, Washington set up headquarters at New Windsor in June 1779 where he remained until moving to Morristown. In the winter of 1780-1 he returned to New Windsor where the Yorktown maneuver to capture Cornwallis was planned. After this victory Washington came back to the Highlands and made West Point his camp until he established his last headquarters at Newburgh's Hasbrouck House in March 1782. In addition to his other purposes the presence of Washington's army may have discouraged massive loyalist attacks from the west. Coldengham lay in the heart of this American base of strength.

While Cadwallader Colden II was exiled in New York City, the houses of his father-in-law and brother-in-law served as American headquarters. Just before he died Elizabeth Colden's father let Washington use his house overlooking the Hudson River, while at the house of Elizabeth's brother John, on the main road west from the village, resided General Henry Knox' family and also late in the war occasionally lodged Generals Nathaniel Greene and Horatio Gates. At John Ellison's house an incident occurred that partially explains how the Colden family survived the war at the center of rebel military power. Local tradition in the nineteenth century has linked an etched window at the house to a ball hosted by Mrs. Knox, probably in 1780. Three names were scratched into the glass: Maria Colden, Sallie Jansen, and Gertie Wynkoop. Some flights of fancy declared Washington had the first dance of the ball with Maria Colden, but an Ellison family tradition avers that the general merely entered the festivities with Maria on his arm. Regardless of what she did, the mysterious Maria Colden had never been identified other than as a relative "of John Ellison . . . through his sister's marriage with Cadwallader Colden, Jr.'' Only one Mary could have been involved in this incident; David's daughter—Elizabeth and Cadwallader Colden II's niece—was ten years old in 1780.[4] For this Mary to have been at Coldengham during the war, Elizabeth Colden must have brought her home after one of her trips to New York City, perhaps to be a companion for one of Elizabeth's daughters. The family's relation to the American cause is obvious in this incident, for while Cadwallader II was banished in New York City, his niece and wife attended a gala with his enemy at the home of his in-laws.

Elizabeth Colden's close relation to the revolutionaries was paralleled by her family's bonds of the wedding ceremony. Through two marriages the Coldens were securely tied to the family of John Fell, a prominent merchant and bulwark of the Revolution in Bergen County, New Jersey. Cadwallader III had married his daughter Elizabeth Fell in 1774, but before her death in 1780 Cadwallader III's sister Peggy had probably met Peter Fell, the brother of Elizabeth Fell Colden. During the exile of her father Peggy married Peter, thereby reaffirming the Fell-Colden alliance. The banished father most likely gave his consent to this politically wise marriage; in the Revolution the Ellisons and the Fells were valuable in-laws.

The presence of Governor Clinton's headquarters in Little Britain and of General Washington's troops throughout the area were presumably not small factors in the Colden family's allegiance and no doubt helped Elizabeth obtain passes to the port. As late as 1782 Virginia Continental troops were camped about the farm of Peter DuBois on the Wallkill. On both sides of the swamp between Little Britain and the Hudson River were the New York, New Hampshire, New Jersey, and Massachusetts soldiers; other camps were scattered in the wooded hills of the Newburgh-New Windsor-Wallkill triangle. The Coldens of Coldengham may have cemented their relations with these troops by selling farm produce to them. No bills of sale or requisitions involving the Coldens have survived, but it is unlikely that members of the family would be welcomed at a ball for American generals if they did not cooperate materially in the war effort.

The Colden family's pro-American stand was further solidified by its tax payments. In 1779 New York imposed a statewide real and personal property tax to finance the war effort. Mrs. Colden's and her eldest son's assessment came to over £371.[5] The thirteen taxed tenants on Coldengham paid £158.18.5, including John and Jacob Dunjea who possessed merely twelve acres but had £1,066 in personal property and may have run the store on the estate. Paying less than six percent of Hanover's tax, obviously the Coldens did not dominate the precinct's landed property, yet one could not deny they were a powerful local family. Together the assessment of Elizabeth and Cadwallader III was the greatest in town. In the hands of an ardent loyalist such holdings could be used to harm the new state, but the family was loyal to New York.

Two years after these taxes were paid, the Coldens made further commitments to the American cause. In 1781 New Yorkers still feared the war would shift again northward, and to secure a military force in case the British again attacked from Canada or up from New York City, the state government organized new militia units. Now, with few financial resources to support the bounties that normally rewarded enlistments, the state created land bounty regiments, giving six hundred acres to men who enlisted for three years. Unable to predict the future, but perhaps suspecting the war was winding down, Cadwallader III (a thirty-six-year-old widower) and Alexander Colden (at twenty-four the only son on the estate) enlisted in the Second Ulster Land Bounty Regiment.[6] Meanwhile the father served as commissary of prisoners, Thomas and John were still with the British army, and nineteen-year-old David was in New York City with his father. The Coldens on Coldengham were thoroughly tied to the Revolution.

These relationships in southern Ulster may have eased Cadwallader Colden II's homecoming, yet he could not just sail up the Hudson River at the end of the war and walk into his home. Once banished by law he had to obtain the repeal of the act or his exemption from it. Neither was easy, for the massive entry of loyalists who had departed would have severely dislocated adjustments made since they left. Ardent Americans denounced the peace treaty for envisioning both restitution of loyalists' privileges and property.[7] In the 1780s exloyalists were an important political issue; merely three dozen of those exiled were allowed back into the state in 1784, and in the next eight years, some more were given that privilege. Not until 1792 did New York permit all banished loyalists to return. In the life of a person a decade of delay is a hardship, but considering the bad feelings generated by the war and the hard fate of dissidents in other revolutions, the state was generous in readmitting its recent enemies.

The question of whether to admit loyalists was rigorously argued by New Yorkers when the war ended. Soon after the Continental Congress received the provisional treaty from Paris in March 1783 the New York Senate unanimously rejected seven petitions to allow back "certain Persons sent within the Enemy's lines." Now Colden began his campaign to reenter the state by sending to Governor Clinton a letter written four months before the British completed evacuation of New York City and only three months after he received £100 from Lord Carleton to subsidize his postwar adjustment. To Clinton he recalled their "long and intimate acquaintance, (even from your Childhood)" and mentioned that he heard from loyal gentlemen in the city "that upon all Occasions you make honourable mention of me." From this Colden leaped to conclude that the governor agreed that "in the part (or rather no part)" he took in the war he was motivated solely by principle, conscience and "love of my Country," New York.

With an apparently clear conscience he was pleased America was free, not because Americans deserved to be free, not because Great Britain was evil, not because Great Britain's prewar colonial policies were detrimental to Americans, but because independence made Americans happy. He explained to Clinton that, "I do from my heart & soul pray that the happyness of the Country resulting . . . may exceed the Expectation of the most sanguine Whig." He could now denounce tory baiting; the unforgiving spirit which kept out loyalists "must prove as pernicious to good Policy & happyness of the Country, as it is Contrary to the Laws of Humanity and Christianity." Every person who differed from the whigs could not be driven from the state. Colden admitted he was one of those who had never renounced loyalty to the king. However, such persons as he "would have but little inclination or wish to return to a government that had taken so little care of their interests and so illy requit'd them for their Loyalty." Thus Colden distinguished between his immutable loyalty to King George III and his revocable support of the British government.

He did not mention here the major grievances most loyalists harbored against the British. Loyalists resented what they considered the humiliating treatment received from the British army and government when they fled their homes during the war, and that the government compromised their interests at the peace table.[8] The loyalists condemned the treaty for recognizing the confederate nature of the United States and allowing Congress "earnestly [to] recommend," and not order that state legislatures rescind laws against the losers. That Great Britain created a Loyalist Commission as early as July 1783 to grant compensation for property not returned was proof the former mother country's government knew justice would not be done to her loyal subjects. No wonder Colden absolved himself from allegiance to such a government, even as he continued his fealty to the good and patriotic King George III.

However, Colden promised to be a model citizen of New York. He told Clinton that unless he was warned to stay away by his friends, he would go home and would expect to live decorously and be protected by legal authorities. He was weary of exile and could not go into a neighboring state to renew his life, for persecution continued to hound loyalists who tried such maneuvers. Colden did not expect Clinton to answer him, but asked the governor to send his decision to the Colden estate.[9] The squire did not receive any response to this appeal.

Seven months later, on February 4, 1784, Colden, Henry and David Van Schaack, and Richard Harrison mounted a petition assault on the state legislature to end their exile while they resided outside of New York because after evacuation there was no British power to protect them in the port.[10] Assemblyman John Lamb, a military hero who had served through Yorktown and who was not closely involved in political cliques, moved to table the petition. To counter this outright rejection, Jacob Ford, from Albany County, moved that the petition be sent to a committee. Ford's motion passed 27-12, and the petition of the four loyalists was sent to a special three-man committee. Soon petitions for two Albany loyalists and for David Colden were also received and assigned to the Assembly committee. On the same day in the Senate, David Colden's appeal received shorter shrift; it "was read, and ordered to lie on the Table," destroying his hopes. His elder brother's plea was also rejected when the special Assembly committee on February 10 recommended the house reject all petitions referred to it. The one-sided voice vote of the Assembly concurred. Assemblyman Ford's motion and the floor vote to commit were now to be clearly understood. The house wanted such pleas considered by committee before being rejected; due process was desired, not rehabilitation of loyalists. In four days the Senate voted to postpone consideration of seventeen banished New Yorkers, including Roeliff Eltinge.[11] In early 1784 the wartime policy of the state legislature was still clear and certain.

However, Colden could not accept this. Despite his statement to Clinton in July 1783, he resided in Newark, New Jersey, as he continued seeking admission to New York. He appealed to Ulster's Senator Arthur Park and Assemblyman Nathan Smith, to the Commission for Conspiracies, which was going to be dissolved in late March 1784, and to Senator Philip Schuyler, a leading upstate anti-Clintonian, a large scale landowner, and the father-in-law of Alexander Hamilton. Even though he had never met the Saratogan, Colden wrote him because he had heard the senator had openly supported readmission of a prominent loyalist. To Schuyler the exile explained why he refused to take the "Creed part" of the 1778 oath, rehashed his neutral status, and explained how he was forced to spend the profits of his New York estate in New Jersey, a veiled appeal to the narrow economic interests of his state. He drove hard the point by complaining that if the persecution policy continued, he would have to sell Coldengham and establish residence in another state. Colden concluded with a plea for Schuyler to reopen the subject of his return with his fellow legislators.[12]

This letter was the opening phase of a successful campaign; by the end of April the Senate voted 12-4 to allow eight banished persons from Albany back into the state. This wedge in the solidly hostile antiloyalist front was widened to include Cadwallader Colden II on May 12, 1784, when an apparently exclusionary law was enacted so overwhelmingly that no roll call vote was taken. The seemingly harsh antiloyalist act was acceptable to people of various opinions. For those who wanted to keep out former ardent loyalists, the law maintained the banishment act and described several crimes under which a person could be found guilty of treason, such as those who resided in the state on July 9, 1776, (when the Declaration of Independence was made public in New York) and who subsequently accepted a commission in the British army, fitted out or served on pro-British privateers, or who served as civilian officials for the British. Excepted were persons who were compelled to hold royal offices or help the British.

This one act disfranchised almost all adults in the port area, because any person who lived there during British occupation would have cooperated with the royal government. However, except for such outspoken loyalists as the DeLanceys, Judge Thomas Jones, and David Colden, this prohibition seems not to have been enforced in the southern district of the state, for one could not be sure which of the thousands of port area people were coerced to cooperate with the British occupying forces. Actually harsh state actions under this law were most often visited against northern New York loyalists who had raided their neighbors or were otherwise obnoxious to the state. Therefore, the apparently stringent law of May 12 did not apply where most loyalists had lived. Severe exclusion of upstate loyalists was balanced by allowing back twenty-seven apparently harmless exiles, including Cadwallader Colden II. Still banished were such militant loyalists as members of the Butler and Jessup families, but Colden hardly fit that category.

According to the May 12 act Colden and his group were allowed to reside in the state without being molested by any law already passed, but suffrage or full citizenship was not offered. [13] These twenty-seven men included Roeliff Eltinge; Cornelius Luyster, former inmate of the prison sloop with Colden; Water DuBois, with Colden one of the three men who protested the 1775 election of delegates to the New York Provincial Congress; Colden's three fellow petitioners in February: Richard Harrison, Henry and David Van Schaack; and the eleven other men whose petitions for readmission had previously been shunted aside by the legislature. Thus the state granted all outstanding pleas of mercy from nonbelligerent loyalists at the same time as it slapped down militant ones.

The exclusion of David Colden from among the twenty-seven was probably the result of his adamant loyalism. He was still critical of the new regime as late as September 15, 1783, two months after his elder brother had written to Governor Clinton seeking readmission. To his niece, Henrietta Maria, the widow of Alexander's son Richard Nicholls Colden, David poured out his melancholy, lamenting that the Colden clan was languishing as General Guy Carleton prepared to evacuate the city. John Antill, a Colden in-law, was on half-pay and preparing to leave his wife and children so he could chase after his own welfare in England. David's sister Elizabeth Colden DeLancey lost her property in Westchester and would probably never see her children again; son James was attained and had gone to England; daughter Susan DeLancey Barclay was in Nova Scotia with her husband, living on half-pay; nearly impoverished, son Stephen DeLancey was in Quebec, existing on what he could scrounge there; son Oliver was driven off the family lands, and three other children were also in various stages of preparing to evacuate New York with the British. Another of David's sisters, Alice Colden Willet, was about to be left by her husband without a livelihood as he also readied to sail for England. Property owned by David was taken under the state attainder act by which ardent loyalists' possessions at the end of the war were seized. However, he thought the property belonging to Richard Nicholls Colden's children was safe. "The law is too severe to be continued." This truth of law enforcement could have been an appropriate comment about all antiloyalist legislation. The more severe the act, the less likely it was to be fully enforced.

As David wrote this letter in September 1783, "Cad" was still in New York City preparing to leave the city before state officials entered. Thomas Colden, the war veteran, was too ill to sail for Nova Scotia with his regiment and would have to go into exile with his wife and children at his own expense when he recovered. As for himself, David was condemned to death if found in the state and was soon to seek compensation in London. Perhaps later Cadwallader II eased his mind by assuring that if anything happened to him, there was a place at Coldengham for the Springhill Coldens. In early 1784 David was in London with his fifteen-year-old son Cadwallader D., but was to die in Soho as the British compensated his heirs with £2,720. This money made easier the generosity of Cadwallader II when he welcomed to his home his brother's family, except for Cadwallader D. who did not come to New York until he received his education in the former mother country. On his return the nephew read law and then entered the office of his British guardian's son-in-law, Richard Harrison, a respected member of the New York bar and one of the twenty-seven loyalists allowed to reenter New York with Colden on

May 12.[14]

At Coldengham in May 1784 the squire faced problems of financial readjustment. He had borrowed heavily from his brother-in-law, Thomas Ellison, Jr., probably when both men were loyalists living in the port. Ellison may have been deeply annoyed because the monies were never repaid. In his 1796 will he left only £100 to Elizabeth Colden, and to her and her children he left all debts due him from his brother-in-law, "which is now about one thousand six hundred Pounds, equally to be divided between them." This gift of an unpaid obligation almost cut Elizabeth's family out of his will, just as Thomas Ellison's father had eliminated Cadwallader II by canceling all of his debts.[15] The squire seemed to have avoided paying this debt because he had other pressing accounts and possibly was short of cash.

By July 1784 Colden had been home long enough to settle his immediate personal situation. I have had "a kind reception from my Neighbours when I went home," he wrote David, "and have no reason to fear any further uneasyness." He may not have been persecuted by his neighbours, but they did violate the bounds of his estate. In late 1784 he sought the legal advice of Richard Harrison and Aaron Burr in his complaint against a Newburgh man named Palmer, who may have roughed him up in 1776. Colden complained that Palmer had trespassed on his property and had cut wood without permission.[16] The incident probably occurred during the war when the Coldens were trying to stay on the best possible relations with neighbors; but now that the war was over and he was home, the squire saw no need to placate further his former tormentors.

In mid-1784 Colden felt free enough to leave the estate and visit his sister-in-law Ann, who was running Springhill while David was away. He found ten-year-old Betsy mending her broken hip and hobbling about the house. The slaves were a burden and he would have sold or hired them out, keeping only one married couple for housework; however, he could do nothing and Ann would do nothing without David's instructions. Although the squire could offer no material help, he took all of his brother's papers to his estate, helped in this labor by Josiah Ogden Hoffman, a promising young New York City lawyer, who at this time may have been introduced to David's daughter Mary. Cadwallader offered to move the entire Springhill Colden family to a house he prepared for them at Coldengham, but Ann refused to leave and would not send off any children. The family would stay where it was until David returned.

Cadwallader II wrote all this to his brother and added news of other family members. Cadwallader III and his new wife were with him at Springhill, and nephews and nieces sent their regards. He added that he was off next to visit his despondent sister, Elizabeth Colden DeLancey, whose husband left her without plans to return. Thomas was in Nova Scotia, apparently a permanent exile. He even asked David to find John Cumming, get from him one of his journals so he could gather his papers into one collection, and admonish his old friend for sending only one letter since he left. This message never reached David. He had died on June 10, a month before it was written. When Ann Colden heard of his death she accepted Cadwallader's invitation and moved up to Coldengham where she was to die the next year. Springhill was seized and sold by the state. Instead of inheriting the estate, Colden gained supervision of David's award from the Loyalist Commission and guardianship of his nieces who were then living with him. He also controlled David's frontier property that had not been sold by the state, a situation which was ratified on April 21, 1787, when the state formally vested these lands "in Cadwallader Colden, of the county of Ulster Esquire . . . in trust for the children of the said David Colden."[17] These unconfiscated lands either were part of the two brothers' holdings acquired from their father or were bought by them before the war.

Until he could settle these land ownership problems, he tried to ease his shortage of cash by putting pressure on his debtors. One of them, Abraham Neely, delayed paying Colden because he could not collect personal and state debts due him. Colden's financial problems led him to tell his lawyer, Aaron Burr, that he had to raise money for David's children and took "the Liberty of Drawing on You for £100 Payable in Thirty Days." This loan from Burr may have been used to pay the assessed price of the western lands while David's children were on a trip in Nova Scotia. The uncle's financial guardianship lasted until two years before his death. Cadwallader D. Colden was practicing law in Poughkeepsie (and was to move his profession to New York City the next year) when the state passed a private act on April 8, 1795 finally vesting in him the remainder of his father's estate.[18] At that time Cadwallader D. was twenty-six years old and his sisters Mary (of the etched window glass) was twenty-five, Elizabeth was twenty-one, and Catherine was twenty years old.

Not only did Cadwallader II supervise his brother's estate, he was the only surviving executor of his father's will, which had left an estate still incompletely distributed to heirs. Upon the deaths of most beneficiaries, portions of the wealth were reallocated. For example, he had to apportion property to the heirs of his brothers Alexander and David, and even to the heirs of his nephew, Richard Nicholls Colden and his widow, Henrietta Maria Bethune Colden. The squire's portion of his father's lands and other segments of the estate for which he was responsible continued to be both a boon and a headache. As heir, executor, and guardian he had property to lease, sell, or trade, debts to collect, obligations to pay, and he bore his nephews' and nieces' expenses. On May 26, 1790, Secretary of the Treasury, Alexander Hamilton, acted in a private capacity as an attorney for a Colden creditor. He sought from the squire payment of monies because the creditor was going to Scotland. Hamilton asked Cadwallader D., "do you ever see honest worthy Col. Colden? Be so good as to ask him what we are still to expect from his Father's Estate."[19] Two months later in July, Colden replied he had hoped to send the money due, "but it is not yet in my Power, as that money when I rec'd it I looked to be my own Property and used it accordingly." Subsequently, he realized it had been given him as a bond. He promised Hamilton that when he got to New York City in three or four months he would settle up. He complained, "I have it not in my Power, As I can Receive no moneys Neither of my own nor what is Due to My Father's Estate," and that "the Children of my Brother Alexr have had to the Receipt £530.6.9 More than their Proportion or Eaqual Dividend of the Cash . . . So that they Can Expect no more till the others have an Eaqual Payments." Not only did he care for David's children, but he had to keep track of other relatives' properties. This was a heavy burden for a man who had never been a big-time money or land manipulator.

To maintain his estate life he managed to collect his father's debts over several years. For example, a year before his father died the family sire sold to a farmer of Shawangunk seventy-five acres east of the Wallkill for £105, and on November 1, 1791, Cadwallader II acknowledged in court that he received payment plus interest, finally completing the transaction. On November 12, 1790, he collected a twenty-year debt from Abraham Neely that his father, John Neely, had owed the senior Colden. Complicated financial problems arose as monies owed by other men to the estate of Cadwallader Senior were not paid before critical events removed the debtors from the scene. Cadwallader II tried to straighten out a financial tangle which involved Peter DuBois. Levi Cooper, the brother of William Cooper of Cooperstown and uncle of James Fenimore Cooper, did not receive payment for debts due him. Therefore, he could not make the first payment for parcels he received from the estate of Peter DuBois at the Wallkill. Colden was forced to accept Cooper's I.O.U. as payment of monies due from DuBois' estate's debt to his father's estate. So slow were the resolutions of the problems he inherited from his father that in 1792, sixteen years and a revolution after Cadwallader Senior's death, the son was willing to grab at most any reputable way of ending one aspect of the mess.

This problem of how to resolve prewar obligations vexed more people than Colden. Articles four and five of the 1783 peace treaty stated that no laws could impede creditors' collections of debts in sterling, and that Congress would "earnestly recommend" to the states that all property be restored to prewar owners. However states passed laws that stayed such payment or allowed it in state paper, for sterling hardly existed in rural areas, and wherever found, it was more valuable than it had been before the war. Local courts were crowded with cases over whether prewar debts were still to be paid and if so, in what medium of exchange. Soon after returning to Richmond County, New York, the loyalist Henry Van Schaack complained that his amusements were "clogged" by problems of his "paternal estate." Exacerbating these conflicts was the notoriety of the Rutgers vs. Waddington case in 1784. The loyalist Waddington possessed Rutgers' brewery for nearly five years during British occupation of New York City and was now being sued for unpaid wartime rent. Alexander Hamilton's successful defense of Waddington was based on the primacy of the peace treaty over state law which punished loyalists. This decision intensified antagonism against returned exenemies, who were seen as economic leeches, sucking scarce currency from patriots. That the state Trespass Act was illegal and that Waddington was liable to Rutgers for only one and a half years' rent seemed to be a travesty of justice. The excitement caused by this decision kept the issue of ex-loyalists alive throughout the state, but most heatedly in the southern district.

The good fortune by which Colden retained his estate is most obvious when one considers the fates of the active loyalist DeLanceys, Phillipses, Robinsons, and the wealthy but less opulent Phillip Skeene, John Tabor Kempe, and Isaac Low, all of whose properties were seized by the state. Against such losses must be seen the restitution of such passive loyalists as the Van Schaack brothers and Colden who obtained repayments of prewar debts and resumed their lives.[20] In addition to recouping these arrears, Colden raised money by regularly selling some parcels of real estate. In October 1788 Alexander's daughter Jane and the squire (acting as David's trustee) sold a lot each to James Duane, who had for years tried to build an estate in western New York. Cadwallader II and his niece received £291 and £280 respectively. The repayment of debts and the selling of land kept the Coldengham proprietor financially afloat.

In spite of such sales Colden held some land all his life. The estate's three thousand acres and about a dozen tenants remained his until death. He also owned six thousand untenanted frontier acres of Skinner's Patent in Otsego County, plus almost one thousand acres of a patent between the Wallkill and Shawangunk Kill which were divided into eight lots and produced about £64.9.6 in yearly rents. He held lands by rights

Elizabeth obtained through her father's will, one hundred and seven acres from Peter DuBois' estate (adjacent to St. Andrew's Church on the Wallkill), and one hundred and forty acres from John McClaughry. Finally, from his father's will the squire held three town lots in the original part of Newburgh. Colden probably held many more than these parcels, but this was what he owned when he wrote his will. He was continually selling land within the last two years of his life, according to codicils to his bequest.

In his financial maneuvering he even got the state to help him collect money owed his father. Chancellor Robert R. Livingston certified Colden's claim that his father's estate held a credit of £1,015.11.8 against the estates of loyalists John Weatherhead and John Tabor Kempe, both of whom had fled to Great Britian. Colden's agent in England obtained only £800 so he applied to the state treasurer for the remainder. The official refused to help, claiming Colden had not taken the oath prescribed for those seeking services of that office. Colden then asked the legislature to order the treasurer to pay him the £215.11.8 he claimed was due from the banished loyalists' estates. On December 18, 1792, Colden obtained the law he wanted with the proviso that there were still sufficient treasury funds from the forfeited estates. Thus, nine years after the peace treaty the state was helping a former banished loyalist to recoup monies from loyalists who had not returned. This is one example of the speed with which returned loyalists were integrated into New York society.

Finally, in 1794, when he was seventy-two years old—three years before he was to die—Colden was relieved of the burden of his father's estate. The legislature assigned two trustees to aid him in liquidating what property had not yet been assigned.[21] Thus, ended the obligations of Cadwallader II. For almost all of his postwar life he was to use the estates of his father and brothers as facades behind which he obtained some of the capital for his life as a gentleman.

Chapter X

"The Old Gentleman"

In the mid-1780's New York was more stable than were some other states in the Confederation. At the end of the war political power was in the hands of Hudson Valley agrarians, who until 1785 balanced the state's budget by raising almost half its revenue from import duties levied in New York City. Much of the rest came from the sale of loyalist and Indian property, plus a special tax on the port area counties. Temporarily farmers maintained their prosperity by putting the states financial support on the rival shoulders of port merchants and artisans, ex-loyalists and Indians. In addition, rebuilding the state from the wartime destruction increased the farmers' markets for lumber and produce, especially in the southern district. State paper currency slipped in value, but the frugal Clinton administration kept its value close to par. New York's currency remained strong until 1785 when most of the United States slipped into a delayed postwar depression and money became scarce as British creditors closed their coffers. In 1786 the New York legislature created up to £200,000 in paper loans to ease the financial squeeze. To secure this issue with tangible backing, borrowers were required to put up land or specie as collateral. The state never teetered on bankruptcy or repudiation as did Rhode Island or North Carolina, but eight years of war followed by the economically precarious postwar decade finally caught up with Clinton's administration. The economic repercussions of the war enriched some men, ruined others, and worsened the situation of many men such as Colden.

In his life, as in the lives of his neighbors, the political problems of the United States seemed noncritical. The interstate issues of the Confederation Period directly vexed few Hudson Valley farmers. They may have suffered from the lack of a national currency or great international markets, but they did not blame the Continental Congress operating under the Articles of Confederation. Most of their produce was sold within the state, although some went to the West Indies or New England. Politically the state was secure as Governor Clinton remained in office without organized opposition from the political parties that were to emerge later in the decade. All was not well with all New Yorkers, but conditions were less critical for valley farmers than for port merchants or artisans, or for those with continental dreams for the new nation.

In this situation some old aristocratic prerevolutionaries remained in power, such as the Livingstons and Schuylers. But some new political leaders arose during the war, jarring Colden's sense of a social heirarchy. Clinton, Park, Schoonmaker, and their ilk replaced Coldens and other former provincial grandees. Although his new world was not turned upside down, Colden was forced to adjust to new relations with old friends. One such was Henry Sleght. At issue with Sleght was the money the revolutionary had loaned Colden, probably when he was inprisoned in the Kingston area. The exloyalist acknowledged that he owed Sleght £84, but claimed it was hardly possible for him to owe another £81 to a man who claimed Sleght had borrowed from him in Colden's name. The disagreement over the amount due Sleght would be settled amicably assured Colden, who promised to "retain a due Sence of all your Past favours & to be Your real friend." However, Sleght had lost much property, probably in Vaughan's raid, and was laboring under a load of debts. Colden consoled him, "You are not left alone to Complain . . . You have many fellow Sufferers." The exloyalist had little sympathy for Sleght because he too was hounded by creditors, including the mercantile Beekman family.

At the end of September Colden again disagreed with Sleght, claiming he had a receipt for £36 dated August 25. He asked his friend "Please to look over your books again and inform me how Matters stand." Two years later, in 1786 Colden's debt to Sleght was yet unresolved, for the squire still had trouble raising funds. He sent £80, "which is all I have in the House," and closed by once again wishing, "to take every op[portunity] to Convince you that I am Sensible of Your Past friendship." He seemed genuinely sorry he could not repay what Sleght had done for him in his time of trial.

In late September 1784, only a few months after settling again on his estate, Colden was ordered into county court because a neighbor who owed him money wanted him to accept payment in state currency, which would have netted him about "three Shillings in the pound on a large debt." Prewar debts were contracted in colonial currency or sterling, and postwar payment in state paper was as drastic a solution for the creditor as it was a boon for the debtor. In any case, Colden, because of his conservatism, would have stood against paper money. To avoid such payment Colden refused to appear in court and thereby delayed payment as long as possible.

His poor cash flow may have led him to become delinquent in his tax payment, for on January 3, 1787, he was one of four men who admitted owing £10 each to the state, to be levied against their goods and chattel and paid at the next general sessions court.[1] This obligation may have induced Colden to compose a memorial to the state legislature on behalf of the people who owned lands in what had been the old colonial Evans Patent in southern Ulster and northern Orange counties. The petitioners complained that the law requiring landowners in this area to pay old royal quitrents was unfair. These people would "Pay more for their Poor rough Lands than all the other Inhabitants of the State put together to the Southward of the County of Albany." Certainly he could demonstrate that collecting the quitrents south of Albany was unfair, but claiming that Coldengham and its neighborhood were on "Poor rough Lands" was special pleading. Actually, Colden had a good case; exemption of some rich fertile Hudson Valley lands from such taxes was discriminatory, claimed Colden. Besides, he argued, such colonial taxes were considered one of the "Efficient Causes of the Revolution," by his former enemies. The state policy was actually more onerous than had been Britian's, for the former mother country had not bothered to collect the annoying tax for fifty years, pleaded Colden. The former loyalist even complained,

Now when We have happily got Rid of every other Arbitrary Measure of the Government of Great Britain, to Let the Effects of this one alone to remain in So partial a Manner on so few of the Inhabitants Must appear Still More Arbitrary in Our Government.

Colden considered the maintenance of this tax on one small area to be the outgrowth of the logic by which the state levied a special tax on New York City. The policy of passing taxes which must be paid by parts of the state would lead to drastic retaliation by oppressed groups.

To regain enough income to resume his genteel status, Colden now increasingly turned to selling and leasing his property. Beginning in 1787 he sold four parcels and held the mortgages bringing him an income throughout the last years of his life. One sale was to Arthur Park for a fifty-four acre lot at the bridge over the Wallkill, "whereon the Said Arthur Park now lives." Either Park had been Colden's tenant before buying this land in 1791 or the men owned neighboring lots, which may explain why Park seemed solicitous of Colden's feelings during the Revolution and why Colden expected aid from him.[2]

In addition to these transactions, debts were due Colden from prewar days when he was a merchant of local consequences. One incident exemplifies the problems he faced in collecting these debts. About 1790 Colden found some papers documenting unpaid bills. To collect his due, he retained Judge Matthew Hunter of the county court. Hunter sought payment from several debtors, among whom was John Miller, whose property had been inherited from his father. The younger Miller claimed to have a receipt for having paid, even though he would not show it.

When Colden brought him to the county court he produced his ledger and Miller brought his receipt, which merely noted payment of his grandfather's debt, not his father's. This failing Miller tried a second ploy, asserting that the statute of limitations had expired. The plaintiff and defendant then argued the merits of the case before Judge Hunter, who according to Colden's account, refused to instruct the jury which side had the greater merit. "The jurry went out and Soon Return'd with their Verdict in favour of the Plaintiff," noted Colden.

However, the case did not stop here. On July 12, 1791, Colden complained to his former lawyer, Attorney-General Aaron Burr, that Miller's lawyer obtained a writ of certiorari from a higher court calling for the case records to be sent up for review, perhaps because of Hunter's conflict of interest. To Burr, Colden complained that the amount in dispute was so small the action must have been instigated by a "Pettyfogging Lawyer" who sought to generate unnecessary business. Such an attorney could easily outmaneuver a country judge who "is not supposed to be a lawyer." Miller's attorney operated beyond Colden's ability, he admitted, "for my part I am not Lawyer enough to know in what he had Err'd." Colden bothered Burr with this case over a minor sum because such writs as used in this dispute could subvert law in equity. Many people in Ulster were viewing this case, claimed Colden, in order to perceive the drift of justice. He predicted if the state did not act to stop such lawyers' distortions of what is right, popular support and use of the courts would evaporate.[3]

He brought at least four other cases to court. Just as his debt to Henry Sleght remained to haunt him for years, so too probably did Roeliff Eltinge's debt. Perhaps it went back to their prison days when Colden may have loaned him money, or it may have been incurred by Eltinge's wife, if Elizabeth Colden paid for her expenses when the two women visited their husbands in New York City. Regardless, in the July 1793 session of the county court Colden brought suit against the executors of Eltinge's will, and "On Mo[tion] of Mr. Sleght Atty for the Pltf," the court decided in the squire's favor. Friendship was friendship, but business was business.[4] Colden lost none of his postwar court cases involving debts.

Yet even though he was patching together a solution to his financial problems, neither Colden or any other member of the family ever again became a prominent force in Montgomery town, the postwar name of Hanover. By 1790 all the squire's children were together, for within a few years after moving to Nova Scotia, Thomas and Ann Colden came back to Coldengham to resume their place in the family. Besides the master and mistress of the estate, the family was a veritable clan: Cadwallader

III was forty-five years old; Alice Colden Antill had died in 1776, but her two daughters lived with their grandparents; Jane—"Jennie"—was forty-two; Thomas was thirty-six; Alexander was thirty-three; David was twenty-eight, and Margaret was of a younger, but unknown age. In addition, Coldengham was the home of the two surviving daughters of the squire's brother, David.

In that year the eldest son had been married for seven years to his second wife, Christina Griffith Colden. He had three sons and a daughter from his marriage with Elizabeth Fell Colden and another three sons from his second wife. With the family lived another girl (probably a servant) and three slaves. The third Cadwallader, tired of farm life and to finance his move elsewhere, mortgaged to uncle Thomas Ellison, Jr. two tracts that had been given him by his father four years earlier. The parcels lay in the midst of Coldengham between his father's farm and the one bestowed on Peter and Peggy Colden Fell. With the loan from his uncle in 1789 he bought the grist, fulling, and saw mills at the falls of the Wallkill, where he lived somewhat independently of other Coldens.[5] His father hoped he would "do Well."

Unlike his elder brother, Thomas Colden remained on the estate, happily married to his cousin Ann Willet, and without children. Thomas and Ann delighted in farming and lived on "a fine, Elevated Prospect, with a Quantity of fine mowing ground around it." The father wished the Coldengham farm of his son was "not unprofitable," for in 1790 Thomas had only recently returned from Nova Scotia to work the land. In addition to Thomas and Ann, their farm supported cousin Elizabeth, uncle David's twenty-six year old daughter, who may have been a surrogate daughter for the childless couple. Another adult man and woman plus seven slaves were probably supplied to Thomas by his father, for a person whose farm was not yet profitable and whose only income was the half-pay of a captain in the British army could not afford them.[6]

The squire's favorite daughter, Jane, was still unmarried and too satisfied at Coldengham to leave. She was the first child Colden described in his long letter to his friend Henry Van Schaack. "Jennie is Jennie Still, the Same good girll, too good to Partt with." In 1796 her father reaffirmed their relation: Jennie "is too good to part with, neither can she bear the thought of leaving us, so I am in hopes we shall have her company and affection as long as we live." She was then forty-eight years old and was yet to marry Alexander Murray.[7]

Jennie's younger sister Margaret also lived on the estate with her husband, Peter Fell, and three children. Peter had a "worthy character," Colden noted, but his physical condition was retribution for having been a "Violent Partisan," who commanded a militia unit and spent so many nights on the cold ground he contracted rheumatism. By 1787 Peter was thoroughly crippled and stalwart Peggy, "One of the best and Tenderest of Wives," cared for him. The young Fells lived on his estate supervising construction of their new brick house. The three slaves they possessed were probably gifts from Peggy's father.

Still at home in 1790 were the Coldens' two bachelor sons, Alexander and David. These two young men, Colden complained, he was "going to turn out of My house, to oblidge them to get Wives." When Peter and Peggy Fell vacated their current home to the left of the father's mansion, one of the bachelors moved in and cared for much of his father's farm and stock. The other son took the house on the right and was in charge of the estate's mills, some land, and a little stock. The father kept sufficient land in the middle, "for my own Cultivation and amusement." This decision to keep his children with him by giving each of them part of the estate property marked the effective breakup of Coldengham even though entail was broken when Cadwallader II had been given five hundred acres at his marriage. The squire now surrendered to parental feelings, placing the unity of the family above the unity of the estate. That such a social conservative as he divided his estate among his sons indicates how weak was the institution of entail in New York.

In addition to his children, Colden cared for his eldest daughter Alice's two daughters. The father lamented that in 1771, at age twenty-five she had "married young," to Dr. Lewis Antill and "not much to our satisfaction." When the Antills died they left "nothing behind them but two dear little infants, both girls whom we took to our own bosom (one was but six weeks old) and they knew no other father or Mother."[8] Elizabeth and Alice Antill probably moved into their grandparents home in 1776, when their grandfather was arrested by Thomas Palmer. These two grandchildren may have been playmates of Margaret and Mary Colden, David's daughter (of the window pane). Regardless of his political and economic problems Colden maintained a household that long remained a child's haven. The squire and his wife, well into their sixties, still had an estate full of children. The grandfather's pride in this situation demonstrates his personal life was happy regardless of how he considered his public life.

David's daughter Elizabeth was still on Coldengham by 1790 living with Thomas Colden's family, but another of David's daughters, Alice, died after the war in New York City. There sister Mary had just married the young lawyer Josiah Ogden Hoffman, "a young man of the first character and of professional reputation," her brother assured his tutor, Henry Van Schaack. It was to "My Dear Niece—Late Mary Colden Now Wife of Josiah Ogden Hoffman, Esq." that Cadwallader II wrote a loving blessing on the occasion of her marriage. He had raised David's daughters as his own, commenting that "it is my Wish and has been my endeavours, that the Children of My Dear Brother, Should feel as little as Possible their great Loss of the best of Fathers at an Early Period of their Lives, and the Dutifull and affectionate Return I have hitherto met with from them Verifyss" the validity of the efforts. The bride's uncle was proud to have given his niece to a groom worthy of her and to have done all that her natural father could have done. Mary's fifteen-year-old sister Catherine was at school in New York City at this time.[9]

In 1790 a tired Elizabeth Colden had raised her husband's relatives as her children and had labored to keep the family together. To her goes much of the credit for the family's survival in the war. These efforts were expended at an age when most women retired to become grandmothers. In her sixty-fourth year her husband appraised her as being, "Much as Usual, Some times complaining & realy ill, but Allways about the house." Her strong spirit is evident in his description of her physical condition. We know of her only through her husband's comments and may presume (without surviving letters) she could sign her name but was not comfortable with a pen in her hand. We do not know her opinions, but can recognize her as a competent, practical, enduring, strong-willed, and sympathetic woman.

The arrangement of Colden's comments about his family members in his 1790 letter to Henry Van Schaack is significant in understanding his sentiments. After considering his situation he described his wife's condition in less than optimistic tones. Then he discussed Jennie, whose love lifted his spirits, and continued by describing his children's situations, anticipating that they would make their own way. As he ended he seemed to lose confidence and feared his offspring would not succeed. Hiding around the edges of his letter is his and Elizabeth's fatigue. Yet, in spite of her illness she was to survive him for eighteen years, dying at the age of eighty-nine.[10] She had physical infirmities, but emotional strength.

To his friend Van Schaack, Colden laconically revealed, "Know then, that in Body and Mind I am Well." However, his nephew, Cadwallader D., disagreed.

> My uncle lives perfectly retired on his old place near New Windsor. He seems to have taken a disgust to all parties and politics, and endeavors to make himself contented by finding employment on his farm. However, he cannot forget his disappointment. His spirits are low and I think he breaks very fast, but when he can meet with an old friend you may see what had been.[11]

Cadwallader D. accurately gauged his emotional situation, but may not have fully fathomed his uncle's continuing hope to be a force in his neighborhood even though the old loyalist still resented the results of the war. Six years after returning home he asserted, "I am as Industrious Active and Strong as Ever I was in my Life." However, the immensity of his labors seemed to sap his energy, for he also noted he "had as it were the World to begin a New Again." Obviously he was ambivalent. Happy to be home again on his estate, he enjoyed periods of intense activity followed by the letdowns normal to a sixty-year-old man. His optimism flagged—"I fear I Shall not Retreve the time and other losses Occasion'd by that [A word here is lined out completely.]—I allmost Said Cursed Rebellion, Now Calld Glorious Revolution." Here were the sentiments of an old man striving to be at peace with a new world to which he was not emotionally reconciled. What he wrote—and crossed out in such heavy lines as to be illegible—is impossible to decipher. The stark obliterating marks are significant because normally when he wished to make changes in his letters he merely ran his pen once or twice through the omitted words. The expunging of this word suggests the emphatic emotions this topic raised.

The best he could say about the Revolution was that out of great evil God sometimes does produce good. He now wished that independence would benefit all, "tho' I Can't Yet help thinking that we might have been happyer at this Day had we remain'd as we were." But nature forbade continual happiness, so perhaps the change came at a good time, if not for his generation then for his posterity who might enjoy its fruits. God, seeing farther than man, "offten makes Use of Bad Men and Wicked Designs to bring about good Purposes, that is tho he does not turn their Hearts, Yet he makes their Wicked Deeds Subservient to good Ends. Witness the Treatment that Joseph, of old, Mett with from his Brothers." This topic, so often on his mind, spilled forth whenever he considered a related issue. "But where am I a Rambleing, I did not mean to touch upon this Disagreable Topic which brings things to Mind which I wish to be forgot, I satt Down to Answer your kind inquirys after the Wellfare of my Family." His experiences in the Revolution still were too easily remembered, and he wished for less tumultuous times, believing that more change could only produce more calamities. He wanted to be as good a citizen as "any other Man can be. I wish no more changes least we should be still changing for the worse." At the age of sixty-eight Colden wanted no more revolutions.

He had been raised to believe political power went to the virtuous, a euphemism for the socially worthy. Now successful politicians seemed to be corrupt men. In 1788 he composed an essay to express his concern about his state's new political scene, beginning with the linkage of political problems to a major religious maxim, "What is a Man Profitted if he gain the Whole World and losses [his] own Soul." The rich man is

"More interested in the Prosperity of his Country than the Poor, for where there is nothing to Loose there is nothing to fear." He did not consider how this situation developed, but merely recorded it. Obviously he was troubled by his sons' standards of living, blaming the war and the postwar crises for the destruction of the Colden position in society. He did not consider that the economic and political genius of the family lay in other Coldens or that his sons may not have been as brilliant or ambitious as his nephew. By opposing the Revolution he had lost his prestige, but he could survive even though the expansive world of Cadwallader, Sr. became the contracting world of 1788. When this analysis was written Cadwallader III had not yet mortgaged the farm he disliked for the mills that he hoped would make him happy; Thomas was just starting life at Coldengham; David and Alexander were still at home and not demonstrating the ambition to succeed beyond the estate, and the postwar depression had barely been survived. For Cadwallader II the family's mundane future could not have been caused by family or personal shortcomings. Therefore, the cause would be found in that infernal Revolution which produced the chaos that smashed his dreams.

From this attitude he reasoned that the affairs of state are safer when left to "Men of fortune & Family than in those who have none." As most conservative persons Colden would not accept all persons of "Fortune & family" as capable of governing well, but wanted power for those whose wealth was equal to their "Probity and understanding." In his world so many revolutionaries rose quickly to powerful stations that corrupt men, not the incapable sons of wealth, were his country's worst enemies. A wealthy person from a good family could resist temptations of malefaction or corruption, whereas a poor man in politics was so concerned with his private interests that to be honest he needed a double portion of a rich man's virture and integrity.

To prove this he suggested, "Look back to the former Situations of Many of our Boasting Patriots, and See whether the Country has risen in proportion to their own accumulated Fortunes." Because many revolutionaries advanced socially during and after the war they must have put their welfare ahead of society's. Colden's own experience could have shown some contrary tendencies, for Henry Sleght was hardpressed and did not improve his status. Some patriots did not advance; some loyalists or their families did. Brother David may have died during the war, but his son had the ability and ambition to become prestigious. Had Colden been more acute and more objective he might have realized that with permanently exiled loyalists and the dead of war removed from the political scene, their places would have to be filled. Among its many effects the Revolution reduced societal pressure, sucking up into positions of power persons of less than genteel origins. To Colden in 1788, New York's liberty and welfare, of which men talked incessantly, were in greater danger than before because of who held power: The undeserving waxed great. This view of the political world was a logical result of the war's effect on a disillusioned conservative who managed to survive the turmoil only to witness his deserving family of rank shouldered aside by the ambitious rabble.[12]

Newburgh's 1790-1 religious strife to control the Episcopal glebe may have justified these opinions in Colden's mind. It began for him when he realized that with his family settled about him the Coldens were a little congregation. He sought an Anglican minister and found the Reverend George Spierin, from Ireland by way of Perth Amboy, New Jersey, who rejected Colden's offer and took the dormant pulpit of St. George's Church in Newburgh. Colden accepted the need to maintain the parish and moved into St. George's political life, becoming a trustee by a thirty to six vote on June 4, 1790. Colden immediately tried to reform the parish policies by objecting to paying the schoolteacher with glebe rents. He also proposed that the minister receive this money so that he might conduct a proper Episcopal academy.

For almost a generation Dissenters were a majority of the Newburgh population and therefore often dominated meetings of the parish. As when the English had outnumbered Germans in 1749, the postwar St. George's parish was controlled by its enemies. The Dissenter-elected trustees had been free to use the glebe income for an elementary school until Colden, the outsider, proposed that funds be diverted to a new purpose. As a property owner in Newburgh, Colden was a freeholder even though he was not an inhabitant. The Newburghers who opposed the squire and a revitalized Episcopal Church manifested their opposition on the technical issue that his election as trustee was illegal because he did not live on the patent land. By their objecting, they sought to end the colonial practice that allowed a person to partake in elections in whatever locality he owned property. Colden responded, proposing that the trustees seek changes in the patent from the legislature. The first modification would permit election of trustees if they lived up to twelve miles from Newburgh, not coincidentally the distance from Coldengham to the parish. The second would define precisely how much money from the glebe rents should support the school and how much the minister. The third recommendation sought modification of the old royal charter's wording conformable to republican institutions, hopefully lessening the antagonism of republicans and Dissenters against the church. The trustees agreed to this package of reforms.

Opponents of the church immediately asked the legislature not to act until "the collected sense of the Parish be taken." They obtained so many signatures that the trustees were induced to call a meeting of the parish. On the afternoon of February 10, 1791, at Martin Wygant's inn, they gathered to consider the charter and heard Colden review his election as trustee and the rise of opposition to his glebe proposal. He sought the advice of attorneys in New York, who counseled him to draft the amendments that were adopted by the trustees and "signed by sundrey inhabitants" before being sent to the legislature. Colden then made the argument a personal issue by remarking that the many criticisms of him only serve "to gratify the few designing persons."

Phineas Howell, a Dissenter, interrupted the squire whose "Character as a gentleman and Citizen" was not under question. These subjects were "foreign from the business of the day," claimed Howell, who moved the question of whether "Col Colden shall undertake to vindicate his character." The vote was "that he shall not." The meeting then voted that Colden be allowed to speak on the issues of the second petition, which demanded a parish vote. He resumed his address, asserting "That falsehoods were contained in the last mentioned petition; and denied the charges held up therein. He was again interrupted, so he said no more." Then the parish voted against changing the charter. The vote kept monies raised by the glebe for use of a local school controlled by Dissenters. Colden's aborted attempt to vindicate his character and citizenship indicates that he identified himself as a crucial part of the argument. To Newburghers also he may have been, even though they denied it.

Three months later, on May 3 at another parish meeting, Colden admitted the trustee's difficulties would continue as long as he held office. Therefore in order "to restore peace and harmony" in the parish he resigned. At this point the Rev. Spierin offered "not to have anything to do with the Glebe school any further, which the trustees agreed to." If the meeting had adjourned after this act, the issue may have been understood as a defeat for a joint Colden-Spierin venture. However, Spierin was not the issue, for the trustees agreed to split glebe income between the minister and a schoolmaster, and three weeks later they elected him schoolmaster. His further service in the parish, where he would always have remained pastor to a minority, was over by the end of 1794. In that year two militant Dissenter trustees voted that glebe rents should be paid to them to do with as they saw fit. This produced an uproar that led to the resignation of all trustees and formation of a newly elected body that was just as antagonistic to Episcopalians, although it was less autocratic.[13]

In 1792, when the state recognized full citizenship for ex-loyalists and while the church fight was still unresolved, Colden partook in gubernatorial election politics. At that time federal elections were important when they coincided with already existing local rivalries; the House of Representatives and the federal Senate were remote bodies. Presidential politics in that year was as foreign to many Americans as is today's political maneuvering to choose a secretary-general of the United Nations. Much more significant and locally powerful were the state governors; therefore, election to that office was most heated. Since 1777 Governor Clinton had served New York, basing his power on several factors. He was able to prevent military and political calamities and economic disaster during the war. After 1783, with loyalist and western Indian lands for sale to land hungry New Yorkers, Clintonian politicians had a positive reward for supporters. Government costs were kept to a minimum after the war, producing a treasury surplus for many years between the late 1780s and 1796. Most of Clinton's support rested heavily on the middling farmers and petty bourgeoisie of the Hudson Valley attracted by this fiscal policy and his democratic rhetoric. Opponents were found among ex-New Englanders in northern and eastern parts of the state, who resented Clinton's adamant assertion of New York's pretensions against New Englanders' demands for territorial and other concessions. Other anti-Clintonians were among the middling class of New York City and among the many gentlemanly conservatives from all over the state. These "Federalists" in 1792 found a most attractive candidate to oppose Clinton: United States Chief Justice, John Jay. Cadwallader Colden II also supported Jay in this most hotly contested campaign in the state's history.

In Ulster, even though the Clintonian majority was solid, the Federalists fought hard. In the heat of the spring campaign Solomon Sleght gloated to the locally prominent Federalist Peter Van Gaasbeck that only five men showed up at his public house for a meeting of the Ulster Clinton committee. This led Sleght to report optimistically that Jay partisans were winning the local campaign. At Coldengham were ardent Jay supporters, claimed Sleght.

> The Colden Family have ordered their Horses to be fed & their Boots & Spurs to be cleaned. The old Gentleman [Cadwallader Colden II] had promised me a Visit this afternoon which has prevented me from going out [;] we shall Consult probably on the Subject of Ways & Means to turn George Clinton *Out*, & to put John Jay *In*.

Sleght's letter was ill-founded, for Clintonians were not having great difficulties in Ulster. The seventy-two-year-old Cadwallader II was again part of the county's political minority, again a loser. He certainly was closer to the aristocratic rhetoric of the Federalists than to the democratic tone of the Clintonians.

As the votes came in from the various counties, the race tightened significantly. On June 3, Colden informed Van Gaasbeck he had just spent an evening with Benjamin Sears, "a Warm Clintonian," who had just come up from New York City. Sears reported that Jay had a narrow majority of two or three hundred votes in the port area; Staten Island was expected to bring Clinton even, and Orange and Ulster counties were to give Clinton such a large vote that even the solidly federalistic Otsego County ballots would not pull out a Jay victory. This Clintonian scenario was barely correct. Only by interpreting election laws so that some ballots from Otsego County were not counted could Clinton's supporters create a statewide victory of 108 votes, a maneuver as unethical as those performed by Federalist Judge William Cooper, the county boss of Otsego. As with the presidential Hayes-Tilden contest of 1876, local election irregularities were excuses used by the party in office to justify sophisticated counting procedures that did not tabulate crucial votes.[14] From now until his death Colden entered no more contests.

Yet the Colden name continued to have some prestige among the social and mercantile leaders of New York City. In 1793 he sent to the city's Chamber of Commerce a portrait of Lieutenant Governor Colden, which he was pleased to know would hang in a room dedicated to the Chamber's founders. Colden's desire for respect is apparent in his superfluous letter to the Chamber. On May 8 he had received the acknowledgment of his gift from the Chamber's president. The following day he thanked that officer for his note of appreciation. One does not normally offer thanks for a thank you, unless one is deeply in need of acceptance.[15]

The recognition he sought among his neighbors could only come through church affairs. Squeezed out of St. George's Colden concentrated on St. Andrew's at the Wallkill, for which he had been a vestryman and warden since 1775. He now helped St. Andrew's be the leading Episcopal Church in the region, donating an acre of land so the parishoners could build a parsonage. When the Reverend Frederick Van Horne came to minister at St. Andrew's in December 1793, two years after Colden's resignation at St. George's, the squire outflanked his enemies. His power at the Wallkill parish was firmed by the marriage of his granddaughter Elizabeth Antill to Van Horne, who now reversed the journey of his Anglican predecessors by traveling to Newburgh to serve Episcopalians there. Colden had won his place of prestige without a fight. In 1796, the year before he died, Colden generously wrote off St. Andrew's £500 debt to him and Andrew Graham voided the I.O.U. due him. Colden and Graham had advanced money for the construction of the church before the war. This gift removed a heavy financial burden from the parish.

Colden's gift to his grandchildren, the Van Hornes, was of a different sort. In 1793 through his will he gave to the young married couple the six lots he purchased from Peter DuBois' estate, hoping in vain that the minister's father would build a house for them. Disappointed, Colden revoked the gift in a codicil and instead gave them possession and the rents of the land as long as they remained at St. Andrew's.[16] Colden's purpose was realized; he kept his beloved granddaughter nearby and his church was ministered by his grandson-in-law. This was a major achievement in his life.

As he approached death Cadwallader Colden II reached out to correspond with a cousin in Scotland who inquired about the family in America. He recalled to his relative that his father had emerged as a magnificent ornament of colonial society from a moderate Lowland Scottish background. His mother received his warmest accolades, and his deceased siblings were all duly mentioned. When considering his father's long and arduous service to the crown, he dropped into one of his melancholic moods; "He was the only one that government did not recompense for his loyalty during the American war, while others less deserving have recovered more than they lost."[17] Very few loyalists who applied for compensation to the Loyalist Commission received what they sought and most complained of being given short shrift by the government. The prominence of this complaint in this letter demonstrates that Colden was a grieving loyalist until he died. Colden was actually describing his own dissatisfaction by mentioning his father's fate. The difference between what Colden thought his status should be and what he perceived it was could only be explained as a result of the war. His hatred of the Revolution followed him to the grave.

His description of the Colden family in America also considered the grandchildren of his eldest brother, Alexander. In January 1796 two who were living in the Caribbean inquired of Colden whether they had any funds due them through their father's portion of their grandfather's will. Two others, the children of Henrietta Maria and the late Richard Nicholls Colden, had excellent abilities, which were not realized even though the mother "seem'd ambitious to have them shine in Congress." Colden also brought the lives of David's children down to 1796. Cadwallader D. married the daughter of Episcopal Bishop Samuel Provost, "and is likely to become one of our first lawyers"; two of his three sisters were "well-married, and the other is a fair way for it."[18] Colden's sister Elizabeth Colden DeLancey died after the war, having been left a widow. Her husband's death was "not much regretted." His other sisters, Jane and Alice, died leaving surviving children scattered, except for Alice Colden Willet's youngest daughter, Ann, the wife of his son Thomas, who was still childless.

At this point he turned to his immediate family, beginning with himself, his love of farming, and his good fortune to have Elizabeth as a wife. No hint of his personal suffering, real or imagined, dimmed his assertion that for the past fifty years he and his wife were the happiest of couples. He then tripped lightly through his children's experiences, noting only one dark spot: Cadwallader III had two wives, a houseful of children, and "has been rather unfortunate" in his situation. Obviously his attempt to become a miller was not financially successful. Because the situations of the old man's other children were not described, it is probable Cadwallader III's station was uniquely unsatisfactory or else the father had unique satisfaction in noting it. In general the Colden family seemed serene, except for a passage describing the suffering of the old governor and the wasting of his wealth. The only members of the American Colden family who had immediate prospects of social prominence were his nephews: Cadwallader D. and Alice Colden Willet's orphaned son, Gilbert Colden Willet, who married the daughter of a rich Quaker and was waxing wealthy. With its mediocrity the family returned to the mass of people from whom the first Cadwallader Colden had emerged, and upon whom Cadwallader II looked down. Its future attainments would be due to the abilities of its members, not to the status or estate left by the first two generations of Coldens.

On February 18, 1797, Cadwallader Colden II died. Six days later his will with two codicils was filed.[19] By it Elizabeth received £500, all his slaves, livestock, furniture, and silver, plus the lands her father left her, which her husband had managed. She was also given for her lifetime the use of their mansion, the farm, and the meadow. To his eldest daughter, Jennie, a forty-nine-year-old spinster, Colden left two estate lots leased for £29 per year, and if she remained unmarried and lived with her mother, the balance of the estate left to his wife. If she married all this property would go to her brother, David, who would give her £25 per year for life. Cadwallader III now was to own a five hundred acre farm plus the house in which the original Cadwallader Colden lived, ratifying the son's use of land he had been given years before. For this gift the eldest son was to give up claim to all Coldengham lots willed to his brothers. So estranged was the father's namesake, the old man stipulated that if the son refused to obey this will and pressed his demand for all of the estate, he would be cut out completely with no inheritance. The father did not presume the third Cadwallader would relinquish claim to all of Coldengham.

To Thomas, the father left the one hundred seventy acre estate farm he was already using. Alexander was given ownership of Coldengham's mills and adjoining lands, all of which he possessed for years. David received ownership of about four hundred acres he also had farmed for years. Margaret, the widow of Peter Fell and the current wife of Peter Galatian, was given three leased lots of Coldengham and another one hundred forty acre farm off the estate. Alice Colden Antill's orphaned daughters, who had been raised as Colden children, were also remembered. Elizabeth Colden Antill Van Horne was left with Wallkill land, and the unmarried Alice Antill received three tenanted lots on the estate. Nor were other grandchildren forgotten. Cadwallader III's son, Cadwallader IV inherited three town lots in Newburgh, the last of the patrimony which came down from Cadwallader, Sr., but in a codicil the grandfather repossessed the lots because he had improved them and awarded the grandchild £500 for them. In addition, Cadwallader II distributed a few lots on the frontier to each child and grandchild, and to each son he left two lots on a tenanted Wallkill patent, producing for each heir about £19 per year. Cadwallader Colden, Sr. had left to Cadwallader II enough to live on for most of his life, consuming the capital he inherited. However, the third generation of Coldens could not do this, for Cadwallader II left each only a small inheritance. The wealth of Cadwallader II was sufficient for one family to live well. Its division consigned the heirs to standards of living lower than their father's unless they had acquisitive abilities to rebuild their fortunes. Colden left his children enough on which to create a stable future if they labored hard, but not enough to be of the gentry.

What then is the meaning of a life spent enduring so much? On the family level Colden demonstrated almost an ideal virtue. He longed to remain a family man, loving his wife and children, albeit he was not close with his eldest son. Financially, he was not a catastrophic failure, but he was less than successful. Emotionally he was a conservative person who sought the recognition he thought, felt, and believed his name and public status deserved. Such an attitude was probably the product of his youthful and early adult relations with his father. The son seemed to yearn for the elder Colden's aid and resented his father's apparent inclination to favor brother Alexander. He never rose to the political level achieved by brothers who were appointed to provincial office by their father, and he had to settle for a seat on the county court. His use of this station to bring suits in his own court, his influence in local Anglican Church affairs, the operation of his country store and his local militia offices, demonstrate that he played the role of influential squire in southern Ulster, though he dreamed of higher provincial status. However, his personality could not appeal to his neighbors in elections, for he was too remote to be one of them and not sufficiently intelligent or intellectually acute to impress them with his superior abilities. His pretensions had the ring of hollowness, which denoted that Colden was of a superior class but was not a social leader. Before the Revolutionary War he relied on his father's patronage and seemed not to have thought of succeeding on his own. Had he tried he would have been unique, for gentry status deserved such special aid, according to the generally accepted standards of almost all European cultures. Only poor persons or outcast children of wealthy parents succeeded on their own. Colden's search for patronage was normal in eighteenth century America. Yet when thrust into a situation that could only be solved by his own resources, he endured, although he did not prosper. He probably never considered himself to be a dependent person; his station required that he be one.

The Revolutionary War occurred when he was in his fifties and most likely did not change the financial outcome of his life severely, for he had long lived off capital rather than profits. The costs of the war merely aggravated his economic problems; it did not create them. Nor did the war bring him any closer to his family; it only enhanced his pre-existing affection for the clan living on the estate. And the war cannot be blamed for his political separation from his southern Ulster neighbors; it was the effect of that separation. Without the war Colden would have become what he became—a disappointed old man out of step with a new America.

The squire successfully hid his one secret act as a loyalist, but did not hide his opinion that the war was a social calamity. His professed neutral stance fooled few revolutionaries, but he clung to that position and relied on influence to avoid physical harm and loss of his property. Officials rightly believed he was a loyalist and that he would remain passive. With crises constantly breaking on the state leaders, and with demonstrative loyalists threatening their work and crowding their prisons, Colden was considered merely a limited threat to the state. He benefited from this attitude by being able to travel through the mid-Hudson Valley with several paroles and even obtained one on the eve of his banishment. To receive such lax treatment even though he was several times called before state tribunals and was the first person exiled under the Banishing Act demonstrates the inefficiency of the revolutionaries. In the British headquarters he was only one of many exiles and achieved a public office after obtaining the patronage of his father's friends. Meanwhile his family at Coldengham cemented ties with the revolutionaries and kept the family property safe. The favors he obtained from the British were unknown to the Americans, who allowed him back into the state along with other passive loyalists just one year after the war ended.

Colden escaped the postwar vengeance of militants; few undemonstrative loyalists were maltreated while wartime emotions still ran high. Neither he nor his son Thomas were subjected to indignities similar to that visited on a former enemy in 1783 when he returned to the "Wallkill, in order to tarry with his parents, where he was taken into custody immediately; his head and eyebrows were shaved, tarred and feathered, a hog yoke put on his neck and a cowbell thereon; upon his head a very high cap of feathers was set, well plum'd with soft tar." Colden had feared such molestation as he prepared to return home, but was received by neighbors without incident. Of a prominent family, he could have been singled out for harsh retribution, but his advanced age and personality precluded drastic punishment. He had been a nuisance to the Americans and was too meek to have aroused the ire of any but the most militant revolutionaries. The moderate policy of forgiving ex-loyalists if they lived quietly and avoided prominence served Colden as it did many other loyalists. Even the well-connected William Smith, Jr. (later to be Chief Justice of Quebec) kept his Vermont holdings, just as Peter Van Schaack, whose friendship with John Jay, Egbert Benson, Gouverneur Morris, and Theodore Sedgwick of Massachusetts helped pave his reentry into New York in 1785, also maintained his possessions. About one-third of the postwar founding members of the New York City Chamber of Commerce had been loyalists who reestablished their American lives after the peace. This New York experience was similar to that in Massachusetts where the antiloyalist fervor created legislation to keep out former enemies. However, as early as April 1784 Samuel Adams, a former leader of the antiloyalist forces, supported the return of ex-enemies "who would be useful & good Citizens," but not the "Highly dangerous" former loyalists. Once the evaluation of the quality and utility of the exiles became the criteria for readmission (and all banished tories were not excluded by definition of their status) the trickle of returnees could become a tide. In 1786 antiloyalist sentiment had so abated in Boston that exiled Frederick William Geyer was told by Governor Bowdoin he did not need the prescribed licence to reside in Massachusetts. Geyer then sued for prewar debts and rented his former home, which had been confiscated.[20]

So too did Colden return to Coldengham. However, his fondly remembered Hanover was no longer the same; even its name would change in honor of the revolutionary martyr—Montgomery. New men rose to leadership and old friends were gone. His Newburgh mission of the Anglican Church was controlled by its enemies and political life was dominated by johnnies-come-lately. Yet he endured. Cadwallader Colden II was a survivor. Some great men lived through the trauma of the period, dying in prison or in questionable legal situations. In a revolutionary age he constantly advocated the losing sides of arguments. Yet he won the battle to outlive the war, its calamities, and his enemies' animosities. The ordeal of living left him scarred. Cadwallader II was not at home in his postwar world, and he lived long to complain about his situation.

NOTE

The reader should recognize that in quotations I have not modernized the vagaries of eighteenth century spelling, and that only errors of logic or fact are noted. In addition, the footnotes refer to "NYHS". This is an abbreviation for The New York Historical Society, the publications and holdings of which were used extensively in this study.

Notes for Chapter I

[1] Cadwallader Colden II to unknown cousin in Scotland, April 27, 1796, Cadwallader Colden Papers, The New-York Historical Society; Samuel W. Eager, *An Outline History of Orange County* (Newburgh: S.T. Callahan, 1846-7), 245-8.

[2] New York and Richmond counties compose Manhattan and Staten islands which have 22.3 and 50 square miles respectively, and their populations in 1771 were 21,863 and 2,847. Without substantiation, Stella Sutherland, *Population Distribution in Colonial America* (New York: Columbia University Press, 1936), 83, states Ulster had a population density in 1775 of 30 persons per square mile. See also Evarts B. Greene and Virginia D. Harrington, *American Population Before the Federal Census of 1790* (New York: Columbia University Press, 1932), 102.

[3] Russel Headley, ed., *The History of Orange County, New York* (Middletown: Van Deusen and Elms, 1908), 303, 305; E. Wilder Spaulding, *His Excellency George Clinton: Critic of the Constitution* (New York: Macmillan, 1938), 9; Eager, *Orange County*, 257; Edward M. Ruttenber and L.H. Clark, *History of Orange County, New York* (Philadelphia: Evarts and Peck, 1881), 106, 374, 389-91.

[4] In 1790, under the name of Montgomery the town had 3,563 inhabitants, Wallkill had 2,571; New Windsor had 1,819, and Newburgh had 2,365. Ruttenber and Clark, *Orange County*, 24, 28, 376; Headley, *Orange County*, 20; copy of contract between Cadwallader Colden and Jacobus Bruyn, April 2, 1732, copy made by Benjamin Wynkoop, July 12, 1810, Senate House Historic Site, Kingston, N.Y.

[5] Edward M. Ruttenber, *History of the Town of Newburgh* (Newburgh: E.M. Ruttenber, 1859), 94; "Colonel Thomas Ellison," The Historical Society of Newburgh Bay and the Highlands, *Publications,* XVIII (1919), 9-12; Edmund B. O'Callaghan, ed., *Documentary History of the State of New York,* 4 vols. (Albany: Weed, Parsons, 1849-51), III (1850), 362.

[6] Surveys of Charles Clinton for Cadwallader Colden, September 26, 1730 and October 17, 1736; Cadwallader Colden, *The Letters and Papers of Cadwallader Colden,* The New-York Historical Society, *Collections* (New York) LI (1919), 43, 155; correspondence of Cadwallader Colden and Governor George Clinton, April 9, 25, and May 9, 1748, ibid., LIII (1921), 47, 60-2; ibid., LIV (1923), 66, 76, 254.

[7] Ruttenber and Clark, *Orange County,* 380; Headley, *Orange County,* 250; Historical Records Survey, New York (State), *Records of the Road Commissioners of Ulster County,* 3 vols. (Albany: Historical Records Survey, W.P.A., 1940), I, vii, x, xi, 51; Cadwallader Colden, manuscript maps of Ulster and Orange counties, Henry E. Huntington Library, San Marino, CA., HM 15442, LO 5512; Miscellaneous Papers, including Common Pleas and General Sessions Papers, Jury Lists and Recognizances of Ulster County, Historical Documents Collection, Queens College, Flushing, N.Y., reel UC-27, frame 53.

[8] These figures are derived from U.S., Bureau of the Census, *Heads of Families at the First Census . . . 1790, New York* (Washington, DC: G.P.O., 1908), 10. In 1790 Hanover had 528 heads of families and a white population of 3,327. Therefore there

were over 6 members in each family, a figure which was probably consistent throughout the agrarian, preindustrial eighteenth century. The 1779 tax assessment list shows 409 taxpayers. Some of these taxpayers lived in the homes of other taxpayers and were not heads of families. Some heads of families may have been so destitute they paid no taxes. If these two groups were the same size, then the 409 figure may have approximated the number of families in 1779. Therefore the number of families in 1779, eleven years before 1790 was about 77 percent of the later figure. Eleven years before 1779, the same 77 percent ratio produced 315 families and a population of 1,973. These figures do not include slaves.

Ruttenber and Clark, *Orange County,* 212, 286; Eager, *Orange County,* 93; Ruttenber, *Newburgh,* 141. Miscellaneous Court Records, Ulster County, Historical Documents Collection, Queens College, reel UC-31, frames 437, 439, 485.

[9]Cadwallader Colden II, Day Book, August 11, 1767 - November, 1768, The New-York Historical Society. Miscellaneous Court Records, Historical Documents Collection, Queens College, reel UC-32, frame 121.

[10]Greene and Harrington, *Population,* 58-61, 67, 98-103; Carol M. Meyers, ed., *Early New York Census Records, 1663-1772,* 2nd ed. (Gardena, CA.: RAM, 1965), 96, 167. Kenneth Scott, comp., "Ulster County, New York, Court Records, 1767-1775," *National Genealogical Society Quarterly,* LXI (1973), 299; Cadwallader Colden II to Cadwallader Colden, September 25, 1758, dated September 26, 1758, Washington Headquarters Museum, Newburgh. Ruttenber and Clark, *Orange County,* 215. Edgar J. McManus, *A History of Negro Slavery in New York* (Syracuse: Syracuse University Press, 1966). Cadwallader Colden to Dr. Home, December 7, 1721, *Papers of Colden,* NYHS *Collections,* L (1918), 51. Cadwallader Colden to Mrs. John Hill, April 13, 1725 and Alice Colden to idem, September 8, 1732, ibid., LXVII (1937), 180, 202.

[11]Cadwallader Colden to Alice Colden, September, 1744, ibid., 307.

[12]Alice Mapelsden Keys, *Cadwallader Colden, A Representative Eighteenth Century Official* (New York: Columbia University Press, 1906), 91; Edward Porter Alexander, "The Provencial Aristocracy and the Land," in *History of the State of New York,* ed. by Alexander C. Flick, 10 vols. (New York: Columbia University Press, 1933-37, III, 157; Sung Bok Kim, "A New Look at the Great Landlords of Eighteenth Century New York," *The William and Mary Quarterly,* Third Series, XXVII (1970), 586-7; Ann Grant, *Memoirs of An American Lady* (Freeport, NY: Books for Libraries Press, 1972, repr.), II, 6.

[13]Kim, "Great Landlords," 599; Colden-Bruyn contract, April 2, 1732, Senate House Site; Eager, *Orange County,* 109; New York (State), Secretary of State, *Calendar of New York Colonial Manuscripts, Indorsed Land Papers, . . . 1643-1803* (Albany: Weed, Parsons, 1864), 126, 128, 236; Ruttenber and Clark, *Orange County,* 16, 215, 370, and map following page 16; Headley, *Orange County,* 37, 385; Keys, *Colden,* 87, 95. *Calendar of Council Minutes, 1668-1783,* in University of the State of New York, *New York State Library Bulletin,* LVIII (1902), 332-33. At the end of his letter to Cadwallader Colden, John Lindesay told the surveyor-general he paid the purchase price, the charges and the survey costs. He added that as soon as he got all the accounts arranged he would "State your Sons part to your Debite." November 21, 1738, *Papers of Colden,* NYHS *Collections,* LVII (1937), 260. Note at end of the abstract of Helena Cooper's will, *Abstracts of Wills on File in the Surrogate's Office, City of New York,* NYHS *Collections* XXXV (1902), 76. E. Alfred Jones, ed., "Letter of David Colden, Loyalist, 1783," *American Historical Review,* XXV (1919), 82-3; abstract of Catherine Colden's will, NYHS *Collections,* XXX (1897), 23.

[14]Edwin Purple, "Notes Biographical and Genealogical of the Colden Family, and Some of Its Collateral Branches in America," *The New York Genealogical and Biographical Record,* IV, (1873), 170-1; C. M. Woolsey, *History of the Town of Marlborough, Ulster, County, New York* (Albany: J. B. Lyon, 1908), 141, 216; Rut-

tenber and Clark, *Orange County,* 106, 218, 249-50, 295; Nutt, *Newburgh,* 22, 24; Minutes of the Ulster County Court of Common Pleas, May, 1742 session, Historical Documents Collection, Queens College, reel UC-50, passim. Edwin M. Ruttenber, *Obstructions to the Navigation of Hudson's River* (Albany: J. Munsell, 1860), 162, note 1; Ruttenber, *Newburgh,* 97, 132.

15Ibid., Ruttenber and Clark, *Orange County,* 280; Ruttenber, *Obstructions,* 162, note 1. New York (Colony), *Calendar of New York Colonial Commissions, 1680-1770,* abstracted by Edmund B. O'Callaghan (New York: The New-York Historical Society, 1929), 31, 58. Cadwallader Colden to Captain Cunningham, December 6, 1756, Henry E. Huntington Library; petition of January 17, 1761, *Papers of Colden,* NYHS *Collections,* LV (1923), 7. For death of John Colden, Ibid., LXVIII (1937), 3. Jones, "David Colden," 83; Brooke Hindle, "A Colonial Governor's Family: The Coldens of Coldengham," *The New-York Historical Society Quarterly,* XLV (1961), 239, 244-4; Purple, "Colden Family," 178.

16Jane Colden, *Botanic Manuscript,* ed. by H.W. Richett and Elizabeth C. Hall (New York [?]: Garden Club of Orange and Dutchess Counties, 1963). Purple, "Colden Family," 171, 178; Alexander, "Aristocracy," 148; New York, *Colonial Commissions,* 78. Abstract of Isaac Willet's will, January 30, 1770, NYHS *Collections,* XXXIV (1901), 117.

Notes for Chapter II

1Purple, "Colden Family," 166; Eager, *Orange County,* 237; Headley, *Orange County,* 317; Ruttenber and Clark, *Orange County,* 382. John Eager, "An Early Canal," *Historical Magazine,* VIII (1864), 114-5; Margaret V.S. Wallace, " 'Big' Little Britain: Cadwallader Colden and His Canal," *Orange County Post,* February 20, 1960.

2Cadwallader Colden II to unknown cousin in Scotland, April 27, 1796, Colden Papers. Cadwallader Colden to Dr. John Fothergill, October 18, 1757, *Papers of Colden,* NYHS *Collections,* LIV (1923), 202. Cadwallader Colden to Elizabeth Colden DeLancey, undated, ibid., LIII, (1921), 339-40; Alexander Colden to Katy Colden, April 25, 1759, ibid., LXVIII (1937), 174. Cadwallader Colden to Peter Collinson, June 3, 1755 and [October, 1755], ibid., LIV, (1921), 13, 36; Cadwallader Colden to Dr. John Bard, July 5, 1758, ibid., 234-6. David Colden to Benjamin Franklin [September 18, 1757], to Alexander Colden, September 23, 1757, and to Cadwallader Colden, Sr., March 2, 1758, ibid., 184, 185, 220. Hindle, "Governor's Family," 239.

3Cadwallader Colden II to unknown cousin in Scotland, April 27, 1796, Colden Papers. Cadwallader Colden to Alice Colden, May 22, 1741, *Papers of Colden,* NYHS *Collections,* LI (1918), 223, and July 12, 1743, ibid., 340; Cadwallader Colden to Alice Colden, August 29, 1744, ibid., 305-6.

4Cadwallader Colden II to unknown cousin in Scotland, April 27, 1796, Colden Papers; Cadwallader Colden to John Colden, February 5, 1749-50, *Papers of Colden,* NYHS *Collections,* LXVIII (1937), 64; Hindle, "Governor's Family," 239.

5Joseph Bragdon, "Cadwallader Colden, Second: An Ulster County Tory," *New York History,* XIV (1933), 415; Cadwallader Colden to Alice Colden, April 18, 1747; *Papers of Colden,* NYHS *Collections,* LVII (1937), 345; Cadwallader Colden to John Colden, February 5, 1749-50, ibid., LXVIII (1937), 64-5. Cadwallader Colden to John Aimett, [October, 1743?], ibid., LVII (1937), 302; certificate dated June 29, 1743, Van Schaack Family Papers, Columbia University; John R. Bleecker to Philip Livingston, March 1, 1786 recalls how Cadwallader Colden II surveyed a site on the frontier in 1743. Miscellaneous Manuscripts. NYHS.

[6] The commission problem is reconstructed from letters in *Papers of Colden,* NYHS *Collections,* LII (1920), 239, 261-2, 277, 280, 378, 383, 384, 389, 395, 401.

[7] Cadwallader Colden to John Rutherford, undated, ibid., 311-2. Cadwallader Colden to Alice Colden, April 18, 1747, ibid., LXVII (1937), 345. Cadwallader Colden to Governor George Clinton, January 29, 1747/8, ibid., LIII, 9.

[8] Ulster County Clerk's Office, Title of Record-Deeds, Liber DD, 555, March 22, 1743, Kingston, New York; Cadwallader Colden to unknown cousin in Scotland, April 27, 1796, Colden Papers. Purple "Colden Family," 174-5, 183; Eager, *Orange County,* 616; Headley, *Orange County,* 388. Elizabeth Colden DeLancey to Alice Colden, undated, but suggested as late 1750s by the editor of *Papers of Colden,* NYHS *Collections,* LIV (1923), 409-10.

[9] Ruttenber and Clark, *Orange County,* 370; New York, *Council Minutes,* 332, 333, 386, 402. New York *Indorsed Land Papers,* 298, 300. David Colden to William Cockburn, August 12, 1773, *Papers of Colden,* NYHS *Collections,* LVI (1923), 187. Assessment Record, February 12, 1744/5, Senate House Site. Letters addressed to Cadwallader Colden, dated 1749-1753, *Papers of Colden,* NYHS *Collections,* LIII (1921), 178, 222, 223, 229, 329.

[10] Return of a survey dated June 29, 1743, Manuscript Collections, Columbia University; John R. Bleecker to Philip Livingston, March 1, 1786, Miscellaneous Manuscripts, The New-York Historical Society. Cadwallader Colden to John Colden, May 17, 1750, *Papers of Colden,* NYHS *Collections,* LXVII (1937), 71.

[11] Ruttenber and Clark, *Orange County,* 142. Elizabeth Colden to Cadwallader Colden, August 14, 1753, *Papers of Colden,* NYHS *Collections,* LIII (1921), 403; Cadwallader Colden to James Alexander, August, 1754, ibid., LXVIII (1937), 140. Charles Clinton to David Colden, June 28, 1762, ibid., 185-6.

[12] Cadwallader Colden II to James MacDonald, September 18, 1765, ibid., 201-4; James Duane to Cadwallader Colden II, April 4, 1768, ibid., 211. Elizabeth Colden DeLancey to Alice Colden, undated but suggested as late 1750s by the editor of ibid., LIV (1923), 409-10.

[13] Bragdon, "Cadwallader Colden, Second," 414. John Catherwood to Cadwallader Colden II, August 22, 1748, George Clinton Papers, William E. Clements Library, University of Michigan. Cadwallader Colden to Governor George Clinton, May 10, 1753, ibid. Petition of December 22, 1755, *Papers of Colden,* NYHS *Collections,* LIV (1923), Alexander Colden to Cadwallader Colden, August 21, 1757, ibid., 173-4. Headley, *Orange County,* 56.

[14] Letter of November 1, 1757 in unsigned article, *Olde Ulster,* III (1907), 107. Deposition of Archibald Brown and Daniel McNeal taken before Charles Clinton, October 3, 1757, Huntington Library; Cadwallader Colden to [Alexander Colden], October 3, 1757, ibid.; Charles Clinton and Cadwallader Colden II to Lieutenant Governor James DeLancey, October 3, 1757, ibid; Cadwallader Colden, Cadwallader Colden II Thomas Ellison to Lt. Gov. DeLancey, October 10, 1757, ibid,; Cadwallader Colden to Lt. Gov. DeLancey, October 16, 1757, ibid.

[15] Cadwallader Colden, maps of Ulster County, ibid. Cadwallader Colden II to unknown addressee, enclosed with his father's letter to Earl of Loudoun, October 22, 1757, ibid. Cadwallader Colden to James DeLancey, October 21, 1757, ibid. Ruttenber and Clark, *Orange County,* 54. Cadwallader Colden II to Cadwallader Colden, September 25, 1758, Washington Headquarters.

[16] Cadwallader Colden II to Captain James Clinton, May 17, 1760, *Papers of Colden,* NYHS *Collections,* LIV (1923), 319. New York (Colony), Laws, Statutes, etc., *The Colonial Laws of New York,* 5 vols. (Albany: J.B. Lyon, 1894), IV, 445, 793. Commission from Governor William Tryon, March 14, 1774, Colden Family Papers, Library of Congress.

Notes for Chapter III

[1] In his will the father confirmed ownership had been given to his son when he assumed the governorship of New York. Abstract of Cadwallader Colden's will, May 20, 1775, NYHS *Collections,* XXXIII (1900), 56. Springhill was leased on May 12, 1761 from John and Thomas Willet of Flushing. Eleven years later Colden bought it for £2,000. Purple, "Colden Family," 166.

[2] Eager, *Orange County,* 238, states, "This old mansion was long known as the 'Colden Academy.'" Mr. Robert Eurich, Curator of "Hill-Hold" concurs. Letter from Robert Eurich to author, June 3, 1977.
The Reverend Samuel Auchmuty to Sir William Johnson, November 19, 1767, Sir William Johnson, *The Papers of Sir William Johnson,* 13 vols. (Albany: University of the State of New York Press, 1921-1962), V, 801.

[3] The date stone bears the inscription, "J., W. and G. Many." Mildred Parker Seese, *Old Orange Houses,* 3 vols. (Middletown: the author, 1943), II, 64; Gladys deFreitas, "Colden Mansion: Sturdy Relic of Pre-Revolutionary Days," *Middletown Times Herald,* [New York] May 14, 1938; Vincent Connolly, "Colden House Recalls Area's Heritage," *The Evening News,* [Newburgh] December 16, 1968. R.T. H. Halsey and Charles O. Cornelius, *Handbook of the American Wing* (New York: Metropolitan Museum of Art, 1942), 7th ed., 200-208, describes the Verplanck Drawing Room of the Metropolitan Museum of Art, lined by Coldengham woodwork. Considered a classic example of Georgian decoration, it was stripped from the mansion and placed into the museum's display. See museum photographs, MM 15367B, MM 16175B, and MM 20492, Metropolitan Museum of Art, New York.

[4] Cadwallader Colden II to James Duane, March 20, 1777, Cadwallader Colden II, Letterbook, Henry E. Huntington Library, San Marino, CA "Hannover [sic] Tax List, December 1779," New York (State), Treasurer Tax Assessment List, 1779, 1780, 1786, 1788, New York State Library, Albany.

[5] Ulster County Clerk's Office, Title of Record - Mortgages, Kingston, New York, II, 20-1, 39-40, 64-7, 180-1; III, 108-109, 110-1, 167-8.

[6] Cadwallader Colden II, Day Book, passim, and entry for October 3, 1767, NYHS. Eager, *Orange County,* 236, 251.

[7] Proceedings of the Ulster County Court of Common Pleas, May 1762 to September 1773, Historical Documents Collection, reel UC-50.

[8] Miscellaneous Papers, Ulster County, Historical Documents Collection, reel UC-26, frame 256. Court of Common Pleas, session of September 1765, ibid., reel UC-50; George Clinton Papers, session of September 1765, ibid., reel UC-2; also sessions of September 1771 and May 1772.

[9] Cadwallader Colden to the Secretary of the Board of Trade, December 6, 1765, *Cadwallader Colden Letter Books,* NYHS *Collections,* x (1877), 71; Cadwallader Colden to Lord Mansfield, January 29, 1768, and to George Grenville, ibid., 155, 158.

[10] Milton M. Klein, "Democracy and Politics in Colonial New York," *New York History,* XL (1959), 237; Patricia U. Bonomi, *A Factious People: Politics and Society in Colonial New York* (New York: Columbia University Press, 1971), 239-40. Roger Champagne, "Family Politics versus Constitutional Principles: The New York Assembly Elections of 1768 and 1769," *The William and Mary Quarterly,* Third Series, XX (1963), 57-99, especially p. 61. Bernard Friedman, "The New York Assembly Elections of 1768 and 1769," *New York History,* XLVI (1965). 3-24

[11] Senate House Site. The essay is in Colden's hand. With Colden's original is a newspaper clipping which inaccurately reproduces the "confession" and incorrectly cites the author as "Mayor Colden." The only mayor in the Colden family was not

Cadwallader Colden II. This error is worthy of special note. Colden held the rank of major in 1768. He lived in New York City only as a refugee during the Revolution, and never was its mayor. The word "major" and the first name "Cadwallader" has confused almost all historians who consider descendants of Cadwallader Colden, Sr. The mayor of New York City in the early nineteenth century was not the son of the lieutenant governor, but was Cadwallader D. Colden, son of David Colden and therefore the grandson of the family sire and the nephew of the second squire of Coldengham.

12 Carl Bridenbaugh, *Mitre and Sceptre* (New York: Oxford University Press, 1962), chapters 10 and 11. Although Bridenbaugh's argument has limited applicabilty to Ulster, the Revolution in New York was not akin to a religious war. Michael Kammen, *Colonial New York - A History* (New York: Scribners, 1975), 289. Alice Kenney, "Albany Dutch: Loyalists and Patriots," *New York History,* XLII (1961), 331-50; *The Gansevoorts of Albany* (Syracuse: Syracuse University Press, 1969), and *Stubborn for Liberty* (Syracuse: Syracuse University Press, 1975).

13 Marius Schoonmaker, *The History of Kingston, New York* (New York: Burr Printing House, 1888), 54.

14 Cadwallader Colden to Sir William Johnson, February 26, 1769, as quoted in Jean Paul Jordan, "The Anglican Establishment in Colonial New York, 1693-1783," (Ph.D. dissertation, Columbia University, 1971), 468. John Sayre to the Society for the Propagation of the Gospel, January 30, 1769, S. P. G. Letters, University of California, Los Angeles, microfilm, XVIII, 124; Letters (Series B), II, 432. Ruttenber and Clark, *Orange County,* 129. Great Britain, Historical Manuscripts Commission, *The Manuscripts of the Earl of Dartmouth,* 3 vols. (London: H. M. S. O., 1887-96), II, 330.

15 Carl L. Becker, "Nominations in Colonial New York," *American Historical Review,* VI (1900-1901), 268n. According to Becker this letter was written to George Clinton, but it could not have been, considering the date it bears: January 11, 1769. George was then thirty years old and could not have been the father referred to in the letter.

16 Spaulding, *George Clinton,* 24.

17 Eager, *Orange County,* 230-1; Ruttenber and Clark, *Orange County,* 383. Wallkill records before 1768 are lost. New York, *Colonial Commissions,* 76, concludes with 1770 and should be supplemented with Kenneth Scott, comp., *Calendar of New York Colonial Commissions: Book II (1770-1776)* (New York: National Society of Colonial Dames in the State of New York, 1972).

18 Court of Common Pleas, sessions of May 1771 and September 1774, Historical Documents Collection, reel UC-50.

19 George Clinton Papers, sessions of 1774 and 1775, Ibid., reel UC-2. Court of Common Pleas, session of September 1773, ibid., reel UC-50.

20 Patricia U. Bonomi, "Local Government in Colonial New York: A Base for Republicanism," in *Aspects of Early New York Society and Politics,* ed. by Jacob Judd and Irwin H. Polishook (Tarrytown: Sleepy Hollow Restorations, 1974), 37-8, and chart in appendix, pp. 118-30.

21 Kenneth Scott, comp. "Ulster County, New York Court Records, 1693-1775," *National Genealogical Society Quarterly,* LXI (1973), 295. Miscellaneous Papers, Ulster County, Historical Documents Collection, reel UC-27, frames 1-169 contain minutes of the colonial session court. Scott's article reproduces much of these minutes. Ibid., reel UC-28 contains court orders.
   This series of violent incidents caused severe injuries, such as those infliced on Alexander Trimble who nearly died from the attacks. Ibid., reel UC-27, frame 162. Scott, "Ulster Court Records," 298-300. Warrants and affidavits involving Mary Denniston are in Miscellaneous Papers, Historical Documents Collection, reel UC-27, frame 157 and reel UC-28, frame 362.

[22] Hezekiah Watkins to S. P. G., S. P. G. Letters, (Series B), III (pt. 2), 767, 773-80, 783-7. 791-5, 796-800, 802-806. See also Watkins to S. P. G., S. P. G. Letters, XV, 77; XVI, 64, 171-2, 300, 386.

[23] Samuel Auchmuty to S. P. G., undated, read at S. P. G. meeting of February 11, 1765, S. P. G. Letters (Series B), II, 58-9. Resolution of S. P. G., Letters, XVI, 297; Auchmuty to S. P. G., May 3, 1765, S. P. G. Letters (Series B), II, 34-5.

[24] Samuel Auchmuty to Cadwallader Colden II, June 4, 1768, *Papers of Colden,* NYHS *Collections,* LVI (1923), 138. Cadwallader Colden II to S. P. G., June 10, 1769, S. P. G. Letters (Series B), II, 441-2; S. P. G. Letters, XVII, 226; John Sayre to S. P. G., December 12, 1772, ibid., IX, 452. Sayre's story is sketched briefly in Jordan, "Anglican Establishment," 468.

[25] O'Callaghan, *Documentary History,* III, 363, 364; New York (State), State Historian, *Ecclesiastical Records of the State of New York,* under supervision of Hugh Hastings, 7 vols. (Albany: J. B. Lyon, 1901-16), VI, 4172; Ruttenber, *Newburgh,* 44; Ruttenber and Clark, *Orange County,* 253, 254. "Royal Charter of Incorporation of St. George's Church, Newburgh, N.Y.," Historical Society of Newburgh Bay and the Highlands, *Publications,* XVI (1914), 21-6.

John Sayre to S. P. G., December 22, 1772, S. P. G. Letters, XIX, 449-52 and September 5, 1774, ibid., XX, 244. For letters which discuss Sayre's career in Fairfield, see indexes to subsequent volumes. Ruttenber and Clark, *Orange County,* 129-30, 392, states Sayre "resigned his position in 1775, through attachment to the crown." He did not once mention his problems in the Newburgh mission as being the least related to the imperial crisis. His move to a congregation with less extensive responsibilities and in an area where the number of Anglicans were growing, were significant motives.

John W. Lydekker, *The Life and Letters of Charles Inglis* (London: Society for Promoting Christian Knowledge, 1936), 39, 55, 56. Reginald V. Harris, *Charles Inglis, Missionary, Loyalists, Bishop (1734-1816)* (Toronto: General Board of Religious Education, 1937), 164.

Notes for Chapter IV

[1] Hugh M. Flick, "The Rise of the Revolutionary Committee System," in *History of the State of New York,* III, 230-2; Jordan, "Anglican Establishment," 521; [Thomas Ellison, Jr.,] "New York Pending the Revolution," *Magazine of American History,* VIII (1882), 279-86. Alexander C. Flick, *Loyalism in New York During the American Revolution* (New York: Columbia University Press, 1901), chapt. 2. David Ammerman, *In the Common Cause* (New York: Norton, 1974) stresses the conservatism of New York sentiment and claims the number and size of its committees were small. The minimum number of committeemen in New York, claims Ammerman, exclusive of the port, was 150. See pp. 106-07. This figure for the colony is so low as to be grossly inadequate. Albany alone had a county committee of 154 persons.

[2] Distribution of Assessed Property Among Hanover's Revolutionary Leaders in 1779.

Value of Assessed Property	Number of Leaders
-£50	0
51-100	2
101-150	0
151-200	1
201-250	3
251-500	10
501-750	4

Value of Assessed Property	Number of Leaders
751-1,000	2
1,000+	0

Militia officers' rosters in New York (State), Secretary of State, *Calendar of Historical Manuscripts Relating to the War of the Revolution*, 2 vols. (Albany: Weed, Parsons, 1868), I, 163; committeemen in Peter Force, ed., *American Archives*, 9 vols. (Washington, D. C.: M. St. Clair Clarke and Peter Force, 1837-53), Series 4, I, 1192. The names were compared to "Hannover [sic] Tax List, December the 29th 1779," Assessment Lists, 1779.

These twenty-seven positions of protest leadership early in the war were filled by twenty-six persons. Arthur Park served in the militia and the precinct committee.

³ Valuable introductions to New York committees and commissions are Dorothy C. Barck, "Introduction," in New York (State), Commission for Detecting and Defeating Conspiracies, *1777-1778, Minutes of the Committee and of the First Commission* . . . , NYHS *Collections*, LVII (1924), xi-xix; Victor H. Paltsits, "Introduction," in New York (State), Commission for Detecting and Defeating Conspiracies, 1777, *Minutes of the Commissioners* . . . *Albany County Sessions*, 3 vols. (Albany: J. B. Lyon, 1909-10), I, 9-61. Flick, *Loyalism*, chapter 6 considers these bodies.

⁴ *American Archives*, Series 4, I, 1191-2; Becker, *Political Parties*, 237-8. William Tryon to Earl of Dartmouth, December 6, 1775, O'Callaghan, *Documents Relative*, VIII, 646; New York, *Calendar of Historical Manuscripts*, I, 340-1.

⁵ David Colden to William Tryon, October 21, 1776 and Tryon to David Colden, November 12, 1776, *American Archives*, Series 5, II, 1164.

⁶ David Colden to Cadwallader Colden II, May 17, 1768, *Papers of Colden*, NYHS *Collections*, LXVIII (1937), 212. Scott, *Colonial Commissions: Book II*, 19. *Abstracts of Wills*, NYHS *Collections*, XXXIII (1900), 56-7.

⁷ *American Archives*, Series 4, I, 322, 326, 1100. Becker, *Political Parties*, 141, quoting *New York Mercury*, September 5, 1774. Schoonmaker, *Kingston*, 164.

⁸ *American Archives*, Series 4, I, 1183, 1191, 1202; Edward M. Ruttenber, *History of the County of Orange: With a History of Newburgh* (Newburgh: the author, 1875), 134; Ruttenber and Clark, *Orange County*, 256, 383; *Road Commissioners of Ulster County*, II, 49; Scott, *Colonial Commissions: Book II*, 17. Alphonso T. Clearwater, ed., *The History of Ulster County, New York* (Kingston: W. J. Van Deusen, 1907), 142.

⁹ *American Archives*, Series 4, I, 1202.

¹⁰ Ibid., II, 131-2.

¹¹ Ibid., 298. Petition of Cadwallader Colden II, Peter DuBois and Walter DuBois, April 14, 1775, Washington Headquarters, Newburgh; New York, *Calendar of Historical Manuscripts*, I, 21-3. Robert Boyd, Jr. to New York Convention, August 6, 1776, *American Archives*, Series 5, I, 792.

¹² Headley, *Orange County*, 82, 308; *American Archives*, Series 4, II, 833; New York, *Calendar of Historical Manuscripts*, I, 23-4.

¹³ Cadwallader Colden II to Myles Cooper, July 15, 1775, *Manuscripts of the Earl of Dartmouth*, II, 330. Cadwallader Colden II to New York Convention, December 26, 1776, Colden II Letterbook. Ruttenber, *Orange: Newburgh*, 134ff.

¹⁴ "Records of the Reformed Dutch Church of Shawangunk, New York," *Year Book of the Holland Society of New York, 1928-1929* (New York: The Society, 1931), 8. *American Archives*, Series 4, II, 833; New York, *Calendar of Historical Manuscripts*, I, 23-4. *Olde Ulster*, I (1909), 179; Nathaniel Sylvester, *History of Ulster County, N.Y.*, 2 vols. (Philadelphia: Evarts & Peck, 1880), I, 98.

¹⁵ New York (State), University, *New York in Revolution*, I, ed. by Berthold Fernow as vol. 15 of *Documents Relative*, 299, cites Colden's command of the seventh company (Hanover Precinct); Clearwater, *Ulster County*, 158 accepts this. However, Headley, *Orange County*, 58 and Ruttenber and Clark, *Orange County*, 48, state he commanded the third company.

¹⁶ *American Archives*, Series 4, III, 983; VI, 156. New York, *Calendar of Historical Manuscripts*, I, 163, 227. New York (State) University, *New York in the Revolution*, I, 299; Schoonmaker, *Kingston*, 177. New York (State), Legislature, *Journals of the Provincial Congress, Provincial Convention, Committee of Safety and Council of Safety of New York*, 2 vols. (Albany: Tweed, 1842), I, 277. New York (State), Governor, *Public Papers of George Clinton*, 10 vols. (New York and Albany: State of New York, 1899-1914), I, 218.

Purple, "Colden Family," 177, 182; Helen Jordan, "Colonel Elias Boudinot in New York City, February, 1778," *Pennsylvania Magazine of History and Biography*, XXIV (1900), 454, note 3 says John Fell was "the greatest Tory hunter." He was called a "zealous Whig" by Larry R. Gerlach, *Prologue to Independence: New Jersey in the Coming of the American Revolution* (New Brunswick: Rutgers University Press, 1976),287, 300, 466, note 22.

¹⁷ Ruttenber and Clark, *Orange County*, 58, 654-5; "Colonel Thomas Ellison," 9; Henry Cruger Van Schaack, *Memoirs of the Life of Henry Van Schaack Embracing Selections from His Correspondence during the American Revolution* (Chicago: McClurg, 1892), 55 note. John Jay, *John Jay: The Making of a Revolutionary, Unpublished Papers, 1745-1780*, ed. by Richard B. Morris (New York: Harper & Row, 1975), 33, 73, 138, 528; Richard B. Morris, *Seven Who Shaped our Destiny* (New York: Harper & Row, 1973), 154-71.

¹⁸ Spaulding, *George Clinton*, 36. Ruttenber and Clark, *Orange County*, 64, 70, 229; Eager, *Orange County*, 636-7; "Robert Annan" in the section "Associated Reformed," p. 12 of William B. Sprague, ed. *Annals of the American Pulpit*, 9 vols. (New York: R. Carter, 1869), IX. Each section in the volume is paged separately. Margaret V. S. Wallace, " 'Big' Little Britain: The Rev. Robert Annan," *Orange County Post*, December 1, 1966. Clearwater, *Ulster County*, 158-9; Headley, *Orange County*, 58-9. New York, *Calendar of Historical Manuscripts*, I, 18, 264-6. Ruttenber, *Orange: Newburgh*, 138-40; *American Archives*, Series 4, V, 1409-10; New York *Journals of the Provincial Congress*, II, 303. Woolsey, *Marlborough*, 114. Ruttenber, *Newburgh*, 59 note.

¹⁹ Flick, *Loyalism*, 63. Division of Archives and History, *Revolution in New York*, 212. New York, *Calendar of Historical Manuscripts*, I, 651. Frank Moore, ed., *The Diary of the American Revolution*, 2 vols. (New York: Scribner's, 1860), I, 117-9. *American Archives*, Series 4, VI, 1054-5, 1111-2, 1153, 1415, 1418, 1442; Series 5, II, 697.

Notes for Chapter V

¹ Wallace Brown, *The Good Americans* (New York: William Morrow, 1969), 228 and 231, asserts New York had three or four times as many loyalists as any other colony and that half of the loyalists fighting with the British army came from that province. Paul H. Smith, "The American Loyalists: Notes on their Organization and Numerical Strength," *William and Mary Quarterly*, Third Series, XXV (1968), 260, accepts the estimate of William Nelson, *The American Tory* (Oxford: Oxford University Press, 1961), 92, that half of the New Yorkers were loyalists.

Exceptions to the generalization about the power of the British navy exist. For example, Rhode Island and eastern Long Island were also vulnerable to naval power but were not loyalist strongholds.

[2] Ulster County Clerk's Office, Mortgages, III, 202-203. Colden II, Day Book, contains several entries for Dr. Hill. *American Archives,* Series 4, IV, 1532.

[3] Robert Boyd, Jr., to the New York Convention, August 6, 1776, New York, *Journals of the Provincial Congress,* II, 303; *American Archives,* Series 5, I, 791-93. Robert Boyd, Jr. to George Clinton, July 3, 1776, *Papers of George Clinton,* I, 246-47.

[4] Letter of June 27, 1776, New York, *Journals of the Provincial Congress,* II, 245; *American Archives,* Series 5, I, 1097.

[5] Petition of Cadwallader Colden II to the New York Convention, August 21, 1776, *American Archives,* Series 5, I, 1097; statement of January 13, 1776, Colden II, Letterbook.

[6] In Jay, *John Jay,* 354, Richard B. Morris considers Colden, "one of the most influential and articulate Loyalists imprisoned by the New York authorities." If left at large, he could have become a leader of a loyalist uprising. In addition, Morris suggests Colden was so aristocratic he demanded special treatment when confined in prison. These are not entirely supported by close reading of the Colden letterbook and his requests for aid. Colden may have come from a most influential colonial family, but he was not a political leader in the Revolutionary War. In addition, his writing style was pompous and clumsy, not suited to pamphleteering. He admitted he did not speak well when he defended himself before the state legislature. He did not disseminate his opinions in published form. He wrote copious letters only after he was imprisoned. Then he bombarded New York officials with appeals. Considering his life to this point it is highly improbable that he could have or would have led insurrections against the new state. Finally, the living standards of gentlemen in prison during the era were consistently better than those of common prisoners. Deferential treatment was offered by captors. Supposed demands were often little more than requests for privileges readily advanced.

[7] Cadwallader Colden II to New York Provincial Congress, July 6, 1776, written from the Ulster County jail. New York, *Journals of the Provincial Congress,* II, 245, 306; *American Archives,* Series 4, VI, 1111-12; Series 5, I, 1097, 1404. New York, *Calendar of Historical Manuscripts,* I, 456-57. Colonel James Clinton informed General George Washington of his old superior officer's arrest "on suspicion of being an enemy to the liberties of America."

[8] New York, *Journals of the Provincial Congress,* II, 245, 303; *American Archives,* Series 4, VI, 1112, 1272-73. New York (State) University, *New York in the Revolution.* 146.

[9] *American Archives,* Series 5, I, 1404; New York, *Journals of the Provincial Congress,* II, 306.

[10] New York, *Journals of the Provincial Congress,* II, 303; *American Archives,* Series 4, VI, 1273; Series 5, I, 793.

[11] New York, *Journals of the Provincial Congress,* I, 231, 842. Edward Floyd DeLancey, Note LXV in Thomas Jones, *History of New York During the Revolutionary War,* 2 vols. (New York: NYHS, 1879), I, 705-707. Testimony of John Cumming in the Transcripts of the Manuscripts, Books and Papers of the Commission of Enquiry into the Losses and Services of the American Loyalists, New York Public Library, XLII, 61.

[12] Oral testimony of Cadwallader Colden II before New York Convention, January 13, 1777, Colden II, Letterbook; U.S., *Journals of the Continental Congress,* 34 vols. (Washington, DC: G. P. O., 1904-37), VI, 896; "Inscriptions in Colden Cemetery, Coldengham, N.Y." The Historical Society of Newburgh Bay and the Highlands, *Publications,* XVI (1914), 32.

[13] Cadwallader Colden II to New York Convention, December 26, 1776, Colden II, Letterbook. The documents taken at Colden's arrest were:
  1. A letter to Colden from "I.[?] Colden" of Long Island.
  2. A letter to Colden from Charles Inglis.

3. Two messages sent as one letter to Colden from Peter DuBois.
4. Two letters to "Major Colden" from "Mr. DuBois."
5. A note to "Mr. Colden" from unnamed Scottish gentlemen.
6. A small note criticizing the Rev. Annan's sermon on politics.
7. A list of American and British ships and guns on Lake Champlin.
8. A copy of September 19, 1776, declaration by the brothers Lord and General Howe.
9. A protest against the measures of Congress.
10. A piece of poetry commenting adversely on the revolutionaries' policies.

New York, *Minutes of the Committee for Conspiracies*, 14-5; New York, *Journals of the Provincial Congress*, I, 762; New York, *Calendar of Historical Manuscripts*, I, 662. Surviving copies of material taken from Coldengham are in John McKesson Papers, numbers 7, 8, 9, 20, 25, 28, 29, in The New-York Historical Society.

14 Undated letter of Cadwallader Colden II, Colden II, Letterbook. This citation is taken from the first and second pages of the statement read to the Convention by Colden.

15 Rick J. Ashton, "The Loyalist Experience: New York, 1763-1789," (Ph.D. dissertation, Northwestern University, 1973), 119-37, "A Note on the Persecutors" is a critique of the men who operated the antiloyalist state machinery.

16 Cadwallader Colden II to New York Convention, January 13, 1777, Colden II, Letterbook; committee minutes, November 28, 1776, New York, *Minutes of the Committee for Conspiracies*, 15-16.

17 Public letter of Cadwallader Colden II, December 8, 1776, Colden II, letterbook. Catherine Snell Crary, "Cadwallader Colden II: True Lover of his Country or Enemy of the State?" *Journal of Long Island History*, X (1973), 7-13, claims this letter is proof of his love for his country. One cannot deny he did love it, but the letter's avowed purpose was to save his family from persecution and to get himself out of a predicament. Letters of December 26, 1776, and January 3, 1777, and undated narrative following letter of January 3, 1777, Colden II, Letterbook. Colden to Committee of Safety, January 8, 1777, and Colden to president of Convention, January 10, 1777, in New York, *Journals of the Provincial Congress*, I, 763, 768; II, 389. New York, *Minutes of the Committee for Conspiracies*, 83; New York, *Calendar of Historical Manuscripts*, I, 662.

18 New York, *Calendar of Historical Manuscripts*, I, 555. The letter to Colden dated at Long Island, February 20, 1776, from "I. Colden" and taken from Coldengham, was not considered by the defendant and has not survived. Neither has one of the four letters sent by DuBois. An exerpt of one of the DuBois letters is in Catherine Snell Crary, ed., *The Price of Loyalty: Tory Writings from the Revolutionary Era* (New York: McGraw-Hill, 1973), 298-99.

19 Undated narratives following the resolution of January 6, 1777, and the public letter of December 8, 1776, Colden II, Letterbook; Colden to James Livingston, January 15 and 23, 1777, New York, *Journals of the Provincial Congress*, I, 784; II, 389. Colden's copy of the January 23 letter is included in his letterbook.

20 New York, *Calendar of Historical Manuscripts*, I, 556, 617-18, 671; II, 148. Jones, *New York*, I, 79-80; note, 591
Other material concerning this incident may be found in: John Watts dePeyster, Introduction to *The Life and Misfortunes and the Military Career of Brigadier-General Sir John Johnson, Bart.* (New York: C.H. Ludwig, 1882); *Letterbook of John Watts, Merchant and Councillor of New York*, NYHS Collections, LXI (1928); Flick, *Loyalism*, 86; Schuyler to Dayton, May 25, 1776, *American Archives*, Series 4, VI, 647; Thomas Barclay, *Selections from the Correspondence of Thomas Barclay: Formerly British Counsel-General at New York*, ed. George Lockhard River (New York: Harper, 1894), 16, 23, 117; New York, *Journals of the Provincial Congress*, I, 721; New York, *Calendar of Historical Manuscripts*, II, 127.

²¹ In his deposition made before New York authorities, Cumming stated he thought this was the same sleigh on which Lady Mary Johnson escaped. Such a claim linked Colden to her flight, but since the state officials never accused the squire of being involved directly with her trip, it is unlikely there was proof of the story. American Loyalists, Transcripts of the Manuscripts, XLII, 55-87, especially 57; depositions of Cumming and Cruikshank, March 8 and 10, 1777, New York, *Calendar of Historical Manuscripts*, I, 672-75.

After Colden was banished to New York City, he was to become a friend of the exiled New Jersey governor, William Franklin. When Cumming was in London, he sought compensation from the British government for property lost to the revolutionaries and got ex-Governor Franklin to endorse his claim. Franklin admitted he did not know Cumming but knew Colden well, and Colden had spoken so highly of Cumming, that Franklin felt obliged to endorse the claim. See also Cumming's claim for temporary support. American Loyalists, Transcripts of Manuscripts, I, 151-52; XLII, 83. For other parts of Cumming's story see the index to the *Papers of George Clinton* which cites many letters.

George Clinton to Levi Pauling, February 24, 1777, *Papers of George Clinton*, I, 624, denounced the ease with which these three men and Thomas Colden moved about the lower Hudson Valley, and planned to have the state increase surveillance over travel in the region. According to Christopher Tappan the Committee of Safety would question closely the travelers, including Thompson "Alias C---." Tappan to George Clinton, February 28, 1777, *Papers of Clinton*, I, 637.

²² Dr. Jones's father was of the same generation as Cadwallader Colden, Sr. and Charles Clinton. John Jones married into the Livingston family early in the war. Later he was to be at the call of Governor George Clinton, who summoned him to treat Alexander Hamilton when the young aide of General Washington fell ill while stopping at Little Britain. Ruttenber and Clark, *Orange County*, 162; *Olde Ulster*, IV, (1908), 335. Colden to John Jones and William Denning, February 8, 1777, Colden II, Letterbook. Becker, *Political Parties*, 168, 197, 232, 257-58; Sylvester, *Ulster County*, 331. After the war, Denning bought portions of DeLancey's confiscated New York City property. Harry B. Yoshpe, *The Disposition of Loyalist Estate in the Southern District of the State of New York* (New York: Columbia University Press, 1939), 28, map facing 28, 68 note. Simeon DeWitt's map, "The Last Cantonment of the Continental Army, at New Windsor," in Peter J. Guthorn, *American Maps and Map Makers of the Revolution* (Monmouth, NJ: P. Freneau Press, 1956), 16.

²³ Undated narrative following letter of February 8, 1777, Colden II, Letterbook.

²⁴ American Loyalists, Transcripts of Manuscripts, XLII, 59. New York, *Journals of the Provincial Congress*, I, 826. New York, *Calendar of Historical Manuscripts*, I, 662-63.

²⁵ March 10, 1777, Colden II, Letterbook.

²⁶ Thomas Palmer to unknown addressee, March 11, 1777, Ruttenber and Clark, *Orange County*, 70. Letter dated March 12 in Colden II, Letterbook and March 9 in New York, *Journals of the Provincial Congress*, II, 403-404. See also undated narrative following private thoughts, March 10, 1777, and undated narrative following letter of March 29, 1777, Colden II, Letterbook. New York, *Journals of the Provincial Congress*, I, 829. American Loyalists, Transcripts of Manuscripts, XLII, 59; Commission for Conspiracies to Colden, March 19, 1777, New York, *Minutes of the Committee for Conspiracies*, I, 205.

²⁷ Letter of March 20, 1777, Colden II, Letterbook. William Smith, Jr., *Historical Memoirs from 12 July 1776 to 25 July 1778*, ed., William H. W. Sabine (Hollis, NY: Colburn & Tegg, 1958), 101.

²⁸ Major Logan's supposed villainy had not kept Colden from lending him money on a town lot in New Windsor. "Samuel Logan (Hatter of New Windsor)" owed £50 on a mortgage to Colden "Merchant of Hanover," and was to pay by August 29, 1773.

Ulster Clerk's Office, Mortgages, III 138-39. Undated narrative following letter of
April 2, 1777, Colden II, Letterbook.

²⁹ Schoonmaker, *Kingston,* 252-55. From the *Papers of George Clinton* see: record of
courtmartial of Jacob Davis, May 2, 1777, I, 764; George Clinton to president of the
Convention, May 2 and May 4, 1777, I, 784 and 796.

Notes for Chapter VI

¹Petition, May 11, 1777, New York, *Journals of the Provincial Congress,* II, 448:
Henry Cruger Van Schaack, *Memoirs of the Life of Henry Van Schaack* (Chicago:
McClurg, 1892), 59.

²Letter of May 5, 1777, Colden II, Letterbook. Petition of John Cumming, et al. to
Provincial Convention, May 5, 1777, New York, *Calendar of Historical Manuscripts,*
II, 130. Cadwallader Colden II to Provincial Convention, May 11, 1777, ibid.; New
York, *Journals of the Provincial Congress,* II, 448.

³There is no adequate study of this prison. A short note by Edward Floyd DeLancey
appears in Jones, *New York,* I, 705-10. Also, "The Fleet Prison," *Olde Ulster,* II,
40-5.

Rations were assigned by a three-man Convention committee. At first the prisoners
were given a diet with more calories than that enjoyed by many free poor New
Yorkers. This may have reflected what these three gentlemen considered necessary in-
take, based on their experiences. They assigned daily, one pound of bread, three-
fourths pound of pork or half pint of peas and one pound of beef. This was a diet of
over four thousand calories per day! On September 1 a revised daily diet was in-
stituted. It contained one-fourth pound of meat, half pound of fish, and one and a
half pounds of bread. Every ten days each prisoner would get half pint of vinegar,
one ounce of salt and two quarts of peas.

⁴Letter of May 12, 1777, and following undated narrative, Colden II, Letterbook.
Documents relating Colden to the Rosa-Midagh executions are gathered in Crary,
Price of Loyalty, 226-30. Note the letter on page 228 should be dated May 12, 1777.
This letter may also be found in Jay, *John Jay,* 355-6.

⁵Letter, May 13, 1777 and following narrative, Colden II, Letterbook. Schoonmaker,
Kingston, 256. Resolution of February 24, 1777, New York, *Committee for Conspiracies,* 153, 235. New York, *Calendar of Historical Manuscripts,* II, 161.

⁶Colden to Dr. Jones, May 28, 1777, and following narrative, and Colden to John
Jay, May 31, 1777, and following narrative, Colden II, Letterbook; Jay, *John Jay,*
357.

⁷Letter of June 3, 1777, and resolution of the Council of Safety, following letter of
June 3; Colden to Pierre Van Cortlandt, June 14, 1777; undated narrative following
letter of June 3, 1777, Colden II, Letterbook. Colden to Henry Sleght, June 8, 1777,
Senate House Site. Colden to Council of Safety, June 21, 1777, New York, *Journals
of the Provincial Congress,* I, 973.

⁸Colden to Pierre Van Cortland, June 14, 177, ibid., II, 468. Narrative of June 18,
following letter of June 14, 1777, Colden II, Letterbook. American Loyalist,
Transcripts of Manuscripts, XLII, 62. Colden to Pierre Van Courtland, July 3, 1777,
New York, *Journals of the Provincial Congress,* II, 516.

⁹Narrative dated June 29 and letters of July 3 and 20, 1777, Colden II, Letterbook.
Schoonmaker, *Kingston,* 267; Colden to Pierre Van Cortland, July 3, 1777, New
York, *Journals of the Provincial Congress,* II, 516.

¹⁰ Jay, *John Jay,* 358: undated narrative following Council of Safety resolution of July

21, 1777, Colden II, Letterbook. Colden does not mention that anyone else received permission to visit home. In his petition to the British government, Cumming stated that John Jay "Thro' the intercession of Colonel Colden agreed to permit your Memorialist to visit Mrs. Cumming, who was then in childbed." Cumming found an American to whom he was paroled for three days. American Loyalists, Transcripts of Manuscripts, XLII, 62. Letter of August 6, 1777, Colden II, Letterbook.

[11] Letter of August 21, 1777, New York, *Journals of the Provincial Congress,* II, 493. American Loyalists, Transcripts of Manuscripts, XLII, 64; undated narrative following letter of August 25, 1777, Colden II, Letterbook; New York, *Calendar of Historical Manuscripts,* II, 277, lists the seven men who escaped.

Gouverneur Morris to Colden August 30 and resolution of August 27, 1777, and Colden to Gouverneur Morris, September 3, 1777 and following undated narrative, Colden II, Letterbook. Parole dated September 3, 1777, ibid; *Papers of George Clinton,* II, 274-5. Colden to Henry Sleght, September 8, 1777, Senate House Site. Becker, *Political Parties,* 209 and 215, note 127; Ruttenber and Clark, *Orange County,* 631.

[12] Letters of September 9, following undated narrative and letter of September 22, 1777, Colden II, Letterbook. Ruttenber and Clark, *Orange County,* 63, 280 and 327. John Nicholson to George Clinton, September 23, 1777, *Papers of George Clinton,* II, 343 and 339.

[13] Christopher Ward, *The War of the Revolution,* 2 vols. (New York: Macmillan, 1952), II, chapter 41, succinctly describes the battle for the Highlands forts. Gerald C. Stowe and Jac Weller, "Revolutionary West Point: 'Key to the Continent'." *Military Analysis of the Revolutionary War,* ed. by Editors of *Military Affairs* (Millwood, N.J.: KTO Press, 1977), 151-71. See also Spaulding, *George Clinton,* 65-76 and William B. Willcox, *Portrait of a General: Sir Henry Clinton in the War of Independence* (New York: Knopf, 1964), 169-96. Ruttenber and Clark, *Orange County,* 22.

[14] New York, *Journals of the Provincial Congress,* I, 1063. DeLancey, note LXV in Jones, *New York,* I, 710.

New York, *Journals of the Provincial Congress,* I, 1105. *New-York Journal and the Genral Advertiser,* October 13, 1777, p. 2, col. 3. *Olde Ulster,* III, 176; LeFevre, *New Paltz,* 95, 100, 127, 168, 172, 487, 491; resolution of May 21, 1777, New York, *Committee for Conspiracies,* 299, and resolution of October 6, 1777, ibid., 394; New York, Calendar of Historical Manuscripts, II, 186.

[15] Undated narrative following the entry for Tuesday, October 7, 1777, Colden II, Letterbook.

[16] George Clinton to Council of Safety, October 12, 1777, *Papers of George Clinton,* II, 426.

[17] The destruction of Kingston is filiopietistically told in Schoonmaker, *Kingston.* For an honor roll of local heroes who lost property in the raid, see p. 522. Spaulding, *George Clinton,* 82-4; Willis G. Nash, "The Burning of Kingston," *Proceedings of the Ulster County Historical Society for 1933-34,* 51-60.

[18] Undated narrative following letter of September 21, 1777; letter of October 19, 1777; undated narrative following letter of October 19, 1777, and parole dated October 21, 1777, Colden II, Letterbook. Letters of October 21, 1777, *Papers of George Clinton,* II, 468, note. October 21, 1777, New York, *Journals of the Provincial Congress,* I, 1071; New York, *Calendar of Historical Manuscripts,* II, 299.

Notes for Chapter VII

[1] Colden to Pierre Van Cortlandt, October 31, 1777, and following undated narrative; narrative dated November 8, 1777, and following undated letter of Colden to Council of Safety; order of November 5, 1777; Colden to Robert Harpur, November 10, 1777, Colden II, Letterbook. New York, *Journals of the Provincial Congress,* II, 492. New York, *Calendar of Historical Manuscripts,* II, 304, 306.

[2] Colden to Council of Safety, January 6, 1778, Colden II, Letterbook.

[3] Undated narrative following letter of January 6, 1778, ibid.

[4] Colden to George Clinton, January 20, 1778, ibid.; Colden to George Clinton, January 20, 1778, Miscellaneous Papers, New York Public Library.
    A New York militant, Brigadier-General Scott was elected associate justice of the state court, but he declined the honor. Instead he served on the Council of Safety and in various legislative offices. In October 1777, when Colden refused to take the oath to the state and was assigned to Hardenbergh's house in Hurley, Scott was an active member of the legislature. At that time, Colden noted it was Scott, at the beginning of the discussion, "who was the Chief Speaker & who Seem'd to have Sway and . . . appear'd inclin'd to favour me." However, when the question of his allegiance was posed to Colden, Scott was the legislator who "took pains to tell" the prisoner that he had to answer and could not claim he was forced to respond. Colden quickly became aware of Scott's antagonism.
    Schoonmaker was a member of the Dutch family of Wallkill, the town in which St. Andrew's Church was located. Schoonmaker emerged from the Revolution a major influence in Ulster affairs. He had limited schooling, was a farmer, and worked as a surveyor to supplement his income. An avid revolutionary, Schoonmaker served on various Ulster committees and was in the new Assembly.

[5] New York (State), Assembly, *Journals,* January 30, 1778; *Papers of George Clinton,* II, 698: New York (State), Governor, *Messages from the Governors,* ed. by Charles Z. Lincoln, 11 vols. (Albany: J.B. Lyon, 1909), II, 20.

[6] Undated narrative following letter of January 20, 1778; Colden II, Letterbook; Colden to Egbert Benson and Jacobus Swarthout, February 9, 1778, and pass signed by Benson and Swarthout, February 13, 1778, ibid.

[7] Undated narrative following pass written by Benson and Swarthout, February 13, 1778, ibid.; Benson and Swarthout to Colden, March 17, 1778, ibid.

[8] Nutt, *Newburgh,* 23; *New-York Journal,* May 11, 1778, p. 2, col. 3.

[9] *Papers of George Clinton,* I, 693-7, 716-9.

[10] Michel-Guillaume St. Jean de Crèvecoeur, *Letters from an American Farmers* (New York: E.P. Dutton, 1957) and *Sketches of Eighteenth Century America* (New Haven: Yale University Press, 1925).

[11] Teunis Tappan to Colden, July 1, 1778, and undated narrative following letter of July 1, 1778, Colden II, Letterbook.

[12] Ibid. Colden to Commission for Conspiracies, July 4, 1778, ibid. There is no book-length scholarly discussion of oaths in the revolutionary period. Harold M. Hyman, *To Try Men's Souls: Loyalty Tests in American History* (Berkeley and Los Angeles: University of California Press, 1959), especially chapter four, considers this period, but is a survey and makes generalizations too readily. Flick, *Loyalism,* fits the oaths into the context of the loyalists' experiences. However, he considers them as but one of several persecutory actions by the state and ignores oaths enforced by the British. Michael Kammen, "The American Revolution as Crisé de Conscience: the Case of New York," in *Society, Freedom and Conscience,* ed. by Richard M. Jellison (New York: Norton, 1976), 125-89 is the best consideration of oaths and conscientious

scruples in the context of early modern English and colonial history. Yet one may differ from Kammen's conclusions about conscience as the motive force behind Colden's behavior. In the squire's life his affection for family and for his social position, his theology, his need for a stable environment, and his feelings of inadequacy were all significant reasons for his refusal to take oaths Americans tendered him after 1775. Kammen's close reading of the letterbook has produced an analysis of Colden not completely consistent with other sources of information about him. However, Kammen's brilliant sixty-five page essay is meant to be suggestive, and its conclusions should be tested by further research.

13 Comissioners for Conspiracies to George Clinton, July 4, 1778, Papers of George Clinton, III, 520; narrative following letter of July 4, 1778, Colden II, Letterbook.

14 Smith, *Memoirs, 1776-1778,* 412-3, 416. See also Smith, *Memoirs, 1778-1783,* 2, 51. Jones, *New York,* I, 146-8.

Jones, *New York* is severly critical of Smith. He first thought Smith was sent behind the British lines to spy for the Americans. As a recent convert to loyalism Smith was lionized by British authorities at the expense of more steadfast loyalists, according to Jones. Colden was not prominent enough to merit lengthly consideration by Jones in his history, but by extolling Colden's continuous adherence to the crown and sufferings in comparison to his companion's treatment by Americans and British, the loyalist judge and author created the squire of Coldengham as an ardent loyalist in order to denigrate Smith. See L.F.S. Upton, *The Loyal Whig: William Smith of New York and Quebec* (Toronto: University of Toronto Press, 1969), for a sympathetic view.

15 Teunis Tappan to Colden, July 6, 1778, Colden II, Letterbook.

16 Jones, *New York,* I, 146-8; undated narrative following letter of July 28, 1778, Colden II, Letterbook. Colden did not complain about the amount of Smith's cargo; Jones made the point to show the special treatment accorded Smith. Spaulding, *George Clinton,* 109.

When the Commission arranged for Colonel Burr to meet one of its members in Fishkill it told him the passengers were the squires Smith and Colden. Eltinge had no rank. Zepha Platt, Robert Harpur, Peter Cantine, Jr. to Aaron Burr, August 3, 1778, Emmet Collection, New York Public Library; Teunis Tappan to Burr, August 3, 1778, Matthew Davis, *Memoirs of Aaron Burr,* 2 vols. (New York: Da Capo Press, 1971 repr.), I, 132-3. The Robert Harpur who was a member of the Commission that exiled Colden was the same man who had called Colden a lucky man, according to Colden's notes.

Brief accounts of Colden's arrival in New York are in the *New-York Gazette,* August 17, 1778, as recorded in Moore, *Diary,* II, 83-4, and John Montresor, *Journals of Captain John Montresor,* August 11, 1778, NYHS *Collection* XIV (1882), 509

Notes for Chapter VIII

1 Estimates vary but all agree there were many British troops in the port area. Approximately 5,000 were stationed on Manhattan on November 5, 1779, and on Long Island were 8,371; the total being 13,371. *New Records of the American Revolution: The Letters, Manuscripts and Documents Sent by Lt. General Sir Charles Stuart . . . During the Revolution, 1779-81* (London: L. Kashnor, 1927), 98. Thomas Hughes, *A Journal by Thomas Hughes* (Cambridge: Cambridge University Press, 1947), 55, estimates that on December 4, 1778, 20,000 British, German and loyalist troops were in the entire port area.

Arthur Harrison Cole, *Wholesale Prices in the United States, 1700-1861* (Cambridge, MA: Harvard University Press, 1938), 15.

² Elliot is described favorably in Robert Ernst, "Andrew Elliot, Forgotten Loyalist of Occupied New York," *New York History* LVIII (1976), 285-320. Jones, *New York,* II, 162 is more critical.

³ Ibid., I, 363. Oscar Theodore Barck, *New York City During the War for Independence* (Port Washington, NY: I.J. Friedman, 1966, repr.) was written before the Sir Henry Clinton papers were available at the William E. Clements Library, University of Michigan. Thomas Jefferson Wertenbaker, *Father Knickerbocker Rebels* (New York: Scribner's, 1948) considers the Clinton papers, but its tone is anecdotal and does not focus on the British occupation as does Barck's volume. Wilbur C. Abbott, *New York in the American Revolution* (New York: Scribner's, 1929) considers British occupied New York City in less than ten percent of its text, and adds little to other volumes. As do many writers, Abbott confuses the many Coldens named Cadwallader, claiming that Cadwallader Colden, Sr. "was the father of a future Senator of the United States.", p. 15. U.S., Congress, House, *Biographical Directory of the American Congress, 1774-1961,* House Document 442, 85th Cong., 2nd sess., 1961, p. 718 cites only Cadwallader David Colden as a representative from New York. Not only were no Coldens in the Senate, Cadwallader David, the son of David and the grandson of the senior Colden, served in the New York Assembly and state Senate. James Rivington, *Rivington's New York Newspaper: Excerpts from a Loyalist Press, 1733-1783* (New York: NYHS, 1973) is a compilation of local news items, with an incomplete index of names. Much valuable primary material, especially from newspapers and official documents, is gathered in I. N. Phelps Stokes, *The Iconography of Manhattan Island, 1498-1909,* 6 vols. (New York: Arno, 1967, repr.).

⁴ Undated narrative following letter dated July 28, 1778, Colden II, Letterbook; NYHS *Collections,* LXVIII (1937), 374.

⁵ Cadwallader Colden to Lord Jeffrey Amherst, November 20, 1778, Lord Jeffrey Amherst Papers, Public Record Office, London (microfilm copy in Library of Congress). Colden's draft in Colden Family Papers, Library of Congress. A copy of Library of Congress manuscripts is in the Senate House Site, Kingston.
Jeffrey Amherst to Colden, January 9, 1779, Colden Family Papers, Library of Congress; copy in Senate House Site.

⁶ Letter of January 13, 1779, Colden II, Letterbook. Kammen, *"Crisé de Conscience,"* 165-7. Kammen's conclusion that Colden can accurately be considered a neutral whose conscience refused to let him take sides, seems to be based on a reading of letterbook statements written in 1777 and '78. At that time Colden had an important stake in having the Americans believe he was absolutely neutral. "The Memorial of Cadwallader Colden Esq Son of the Late Lt Governour of New York" to Sir Henry, written on January 13, 1779, near the end of the letterbook, among other letters he wrote while in New York City, clearly shows that Colden did not consider himself to have been neutral, but to have outsmarted the Americans.

⁷ Colden to Roger Morris and Roger Morris to Colden, April 12, 1779, Colden II, Letterbook.

⁸ *Royal Gazette,* September 23, 1778, p. 2, col. 2; October 7, 1778, p. 3, col. 3; July 31, 1779, p. 4, col. 1; August 14, 1779, p. 3, col. 2; August 25, 1779, p. 2, col. 2.
The "Loyal Refugees" was also used by other loyalist exiles, such as Deputy Superintendent of Indian Affairs in East Florida, Moses Kirkland, who called his military unit by that name. Philip R.N. Katcher, *Encyclopedia of British, Provincial, and German Army Units, 1775-1783* (Harrisburg, PA.: Stackpole, 1973), 92. See also Flick, *Loyalism,* 114-5.
Gatherings of exiles in New York were similar to the meetings held by loyalist refugees in England. Men from each colony met separately in a favored London club to raise their spirits and their political influence as they sought pensions, compensations for losses, and appointments to offices. Mary Beth Norton, *The British-Americans: The Loyalist Exiles in England, 1774-1789* (Boston: Little, Brown, 1972), chap. 3.

[9] Royal Gazette, August 25, p. 3 and September 1, 1779, p. 2, col. 2. Paul H. Smith, *Loyalists and Redcoats: A Study in British Revolutionary Policy* (New York: Norton, 1972) studies the role of loyal provincial troops in the British war effort, and his essay, "The American Loyalists: Notes on Their Organization and Numerical Strength," *William and Mary Quarterly,* Third Series, XXV (1968), 259-77, is a sophisticated estimate of their numbers.

[10] Ruttenber, *Orange County,* 58; New York, *Calendar of Historical Manuscripts,* I, 264-6; James McClaughry and Samuel Logan to George Clinton, August 16, 17, 1779, *Papers of George Clinton,* V, 214-6.

[11] George Clinton to Mrs. Margaret Crooke, September 24, 1779, ibid., 281. "Colonel Thomas Ellison," 12; will of Thomas Ellison, *Abstracts of Wills,* NYHS, *Collections,* XXXVI (1903), 235-6.

[12] Colden to John André, November 16, 1779, Clinton Papers, Clements Library; permit granted to Major General James Pattison, November 16, 1779, *Papers of George Clinton,* V, 360; letters by Governor Clinton, November 28 and 29, 1779, ibid., 375-7; Tench Tilghman to Captain Cartwright, November 22, 1779, George Washington Papers, Library of Congress.

[13] Order of George Clinton, November 12, 1779, *Papers of George Clinton,* IV, 409; William Heath to George Clinton, April 7, 1781, ibid., V, 755; Clinton to William Heath, October 3, 1781, ibid., VII, 454-5; Joseph Sackett to George Clinton, October 7, 1781, ibid., 382; Mrs. Keziah Townshend to George Clinton, October 30, 1781, ibid., 460; William Heath to George Clinton, November 1, 1781, ibid., 468; ibid., V, 159.

Cadwallader Colden III to unnamed officer, July 24, 1782, Miscellaneous Papers, New York Public Library.

[14] Colden to Jeffrey Amherst, May 5 and October 28, 1779, Amherst Papers, Library of Congress.

[15] Will of Thomas Ellison, Jr. filed February 1, 1796, in Ulster County, Surrogate's Office, Kingston, New York, Wills and Inventories, XLI (1792-1795), 634-43.

[16] Colden to John André, June 21 and July 7, 1780, and Colden to Henry Clinton, July 7, 1780, Sir Henry Clinton Papers, Clements Library. Rivington, *Rivington's Newspaper,* 307.

[17] Colden to George Germain, August 24, 1780, Lord George Germain Papers, Clements Library. The war is discussed as the men of Whitehall understood it, in Piers Mackesy, *The War for America, 1775-1783* (Cambridge, MA: Harvard University Press, 1964). A critique of the British effort is R. Arthur Bowler, *Logistics and the Failure of the British Army in America, 1775-1783* (Princeton: Princeton University Press, 1975). The best overview of the loyalist experience is, Wallace Brown, *The Good Americans* (New York: Morrow, 1969).

Appointed by August 31, 1780, Colden officially started his duties when he received his commission. See Commission, Sir Henry Clinton to Colden, September 1, 1780, Colden Family Papers, Library of Congress; Colden to John André, August 31, 1780, Sir Henry Clinton Papers, Clements library. In spite of Colden's complaints Sir Henry gave him an office, and two months earlier David Colden had been appointed Assistant Superintendent of Police on Long Island with a salary of £200 per year. Jones, *New York,* II, 162.

[18] Rivington, *Rivington's Newspaper,* 176. The existence of Chapel Street in this northwest corner is certain, but when it became a thoroughfare, its course, and its extent are uncertain. On the 1755 Maerschalk map of the city, a short unnamed street appears where later the name Chapel Street is applied. The 1766 Montresor map of New York did not show a street in this corner of town. However, the Ratzer city map of 1767 showed it running northward, sliding west around the college and continuing northward beyond it. In 1783 at 31 Chapel Street lived the Reverend Mr. Lymon and

Dr. Henry Micanon, who had recently opened his office in that building. *Royal Gazette,* September 3, 1783, p. 2, col. 3. The newness of of the street and the advertisements of these two professional men suggest life on Chapel Street was fashionable late in the war and soon after.

¹⁹ LC, *Journals of the Continental Congress,* IV, 95; XVI, 51. Charles H. Metzger, *The Prisoner in the American Revolution* (Chicago: Loyola University Press, 1971), 179-80, and Albert Greene, *Recollections of the Jersey Prison Ship* (New York: Corinth, 1961, repr.).

²⁰ Metzger, *The Prisoner,* 213-4; LC, *Journals of the Continental Congress,* XIX, 1912; *Papers of George Clinton,* VI, 283-8; VII, 239-40, 740.

²¹ Headquarters Papers of the British Army in America, Public Record Office, London (microfilm copy in Library of Congress), reel 6, document 1915, April 13, 1779 and reel 11, documents 4046 and 4048. The Headquarters Papers are also known as the Sir Guy Carleton Papers and the Lord Dorchester Papers.
Letter of September 6, 1780, Sir Henry Clinton Papers, Clements Library.

²² Smith, *Memoirs, 1778-1783,* 127. 129, 134, 147. Crèvecoeur eventually was released from prison and lived impoverished in the city until September 1, 1780, when he sailed for Great Britain. There he published *Letters from an American Farmer* in 1782. He returned to his native Normandy, and in 1783 came back to New York City as the French consul. In 1790 he left for France, never again to see the society he loved and the country whose birth he resisted.

²³ For William Peartree Smith's relation to the emerging revolutionary movement in New Jersey, see Gerlach, *Prologue,* citations in index on p. 530. In 1778 the Jerseyite was using his influence with Elias Boudinot to obtain for his son the position of deputy secretary of the Continental Congress. J.J. Boudinot, *The Life, Public Services, Addresses, and Letters of Elias Boudinot,* 2 vols. (New York: Da Capo Press, 1971, repr.), I, 167. Smith, *Memoirs, 1778-1783,* 276-8.

²⁴ Colden to Jeffrey Amherst, January 28, 1781, Amherst Papers, is his final complaint about Sir Henry's refusal to pay his salary and the general's strategy.

²⁵ Pay warrants, June 30, July 27, and November 4, 1782, Headquarters Papers, reel 14, documents 4971 and 5149; reel 16, document 6095. Except for these pay warrants there is no information about or description of his obligations, expenses, routines, or the types of services he performed. In addition, these warrants of 1782 cited Colden's services as "Resident Commissary of Prisoners within rebel lines." The commission of September 1 did not mention "Resident." The meaning of the word in the warrant is not clear. It is assumed that Colden resided in New York City and traveled to American prisons for inspections and may have temporarily stayed at or near these facilities, but did not maintain a permanent residence behind American lines. Letter of March 29, 1783, ibid., reel 19, document 7243; order of April 8, 1783, ibid., documents 1361 and 7243.

Notes for Chapter IX

¹ Ruttenber and Clark, *Orange County,* 212, 228, 286; Eager, *Orange County,* 93; Ruttenber, *Newburgh,* 141; Miscellaneous Court Records of Ulster County, Historical Documents Collection, Queens College, reel UC-31, frames 437, 439, 485.

² Timothy Colmon to George Clinton, undated, *Papers of George Clinton,* V, 341. Colonels Pawling and Willet to George Clinton, August 22, 1781, ibid., VII, 190-2, 195-9. *New-York Journal and General Advertiser,* November 1, 1779, p. 2, col. 2.

³ Ibid., February 15, 1779, p. 2, col. 2; April 10, 1780, p. 1, col. 2; April 17, p. 2, col. 2; April 24, p. 2, col. 2; May 8, 1780, p. 2, col. 3; November 30, 1778, p. 2, col. 2; Ward, *Revolution,* II, 594; Nutt, *Newburgh,* 29.

[4] Incidents involving the American headquarters in New Windsor and Newburgh are considered in many local histories. See especially: "Some Facts and Traditions in Regard to the 'Knox Headquarters' in the Town of New Windsor . . .," Historical Society of Newburgh Bay and the Highlands, *Publications*, XVIII (1919), 13-9, and Moffat, *Orange County*, 17 which quotes Robert R. Ellison as the source of Maria's relation to Elizabeth Colden by marriage.

[5] Cadwallader Colden to Henry Van Schaack, June 13, 1790, Peter Van Schaack Papers, Library of Congress; Purple, "The Colden Family," 177; "Inscriptions in Colden Cemetary, Coldengham, N.Y.," Historical Society of Newburgh Bay and the Highlands, *Publications*, XVI (1914), 32-5.

DeWitt, "Last Cantonment," 16; Nutt, *Newburgh*, 32-3; Eager, *Orange County*, 262; Ruttenber and Clark, *Orange County*, 373. Major Edward C. Boynton, *General Orders of George Washington . . . Issued at Newburgh on the Hudson, 1782-1783* (Harrison, NY: Harbor Hill Books, 1973, repr.).

"Hannover [sic] Tax List, December 29, 1779," Assessment List.

[6] New York, *New York in the Revolution*, I, 12, 14, 261.

[7] The loyalists' role in the peacemaking is in Richard B. Morris, *The Peace-Makers* (New York: Harper & Row, 1965). Beardian-Beckerian analyses are Oscar Zeichner, "The Loyalist Problem in New York After the Revolution," *New York History*, XXI (1940), 284-302 and E. Wilder Spaulding, *New York in the Critical Period, 1784-1789* (New York: Columbia University Press, 1932). Jackson Turner Main, *Political Parties Before the Constitution* (Chapel Hill: University of North Carolina Press, 1973) discusses the problem of returning loyalists in the contexts of other postwar political issues. For Main's discussion of New York, see especially chapters 3 and 5.

[8] New York (State), Legislature, Senate, Journal, March 13, 1783; Zeichner, "Loyalist Problem," 297-8, claims the petitions sought permission for fourteen persons to return.

The Royal Gazette, August 27, 1783, p. 2, col. 3 and September 17, 1783, p. 3, col. 2, presents arguments on each side of the readmission issue.

In addition to Morris, *Peace-Makers*, loyalists figure prominently in Norton, *The British-Americans* and Charles Ritcheson, *Aftermath of Revolution* (New York, Norton: 1971), in which they are considered pawns in diplomacy.

[9] Colden to George Clinton, July 26, 1783, *Papers of George Clinton*, VIII, 221-4. This letter is erroneously attributed by the editor to "Former Lieutenant Governor Colden." This is an example of errors by historians who do not realize that the family sire died in 1776, and who attribute all statements by "Cadwallader Colden" to Colden, Sr.

[10] The petition of Cadwallader Colden II, Henry Van Schaack, David Van Schaack, and Richard Harrison to New York Assembly. New York (State), Legislature, *Assembly*, Journal, February 4, 1784.

[11] The Assembly votes on Ford's motion were not grouped by clique or party as later in the decade. Voting to refer were ten persons who in the later 1780s were generally to support policies frequently described by historians as "Clintonian" (or "Localist" by Jackson Turner Main). Such politicians often came from rural areas, had little formal education and often viewed the world from the interests of parochial constituents and their values. Agreeing with them on this vote were five others, who on most questions often opposed the other ten. These five assemblymen were frequently to vote with the bloc often called by historians "Anti-Clintonian" or "Federalist" (or "Cosmopolitan" by Jackson Turner Main). Twelve other "yes" votes came from men who were either neutral or had unrecognizable voting trends. Of those who voted to table the petition, six were Clintonians and six were Anti-Clintonians. Main, *Political Parties*, 32-3, defines his "Localist" and "Cosmopolitan" labels. Assembly, *Journal*, February 2, 5, and 10, 1783; Senate, *Journal*, February 2, 13, and 16, 1784.

¹² Cadwallader Colden to Philip Schuyler, March 5, 1784, Philip Schuyler Papers, New York Public Library.

¹³ Senate, *Journal,* April 29, 1784; Assembly, *Journal,* May 12, 1784. New York (State), Laws, Statutes, etc., *Laws of the State of New York Passed at the . . . First Seven Sessions,* 5 vols. (Albany: Weed, Parsons, 1866-7), I, 772-4. Zeichner, "The Loyalist Problem," 294, suggests the law was executed forcefully. Flick, *Loyalism,* 164-8 suggests it was hardly enforced in southern New York.

¹⁴ David Colden to Henrietta Colden, September 15, 1783, in Jones, "David Colden," 79-86. David's estate was bought by William Cornwell for £800 on July 30, 1784. Harry B. Yoshpe, *The Disposition of Loyalist Estates in the Southern District of the State of New York* (New York: Columbia University Press, 1939), 137. In England David claimed the loss of a three hundred acre estate valued at £2,531, plus land in Albany, Ulster and Tryon Counties. All his property was valued at nearly £12,000. Each of his daughters received £460 and Cadwallader D. won £800 from the British government. American Loyalists, Transcripts of Manuscripts, X, 141, 143, 145, 151; XI, 204; XIX, 413; XXIX, 451. See also Cadwallader D.'s request for money to return to America in order to regain his property. Ibid., VII, 366. George Duncan Ludlow, the family lawyer, guardian, and representative of David's children before the Loyalist Commission, sought temporary relief for David's widow, ibid., VI, 602.

¹⁵ Will of Thomas Ellison, Jr., *Abstracts of Wills,* NYHS *Collections,* XXXVIII (1905), 330-1. Even though Ellison was a vestryman of Trinity Church from 1781 to 1784, Colden never mentioned him during his exile. Purple, "The Colden Family," 182. The only property left to any Colden child was the house on Queen Street in the port, given to Cadwallader III's son, Thomas Ellison Colden - his namesake.

¹⁶ Cadwallader Colden to David Colden, July 7, 1784, Colden Papers, NYHS. Aaron Burr to Cadwallader Colden, December 21, 1784, Colden Family Papers, Library of Congress; Cadwallader Colden to Aaron Burr, April 5, 1785, Aaron Burr Papers, NYHS.

¹⁷ Purple, "The Colden Family," 166 and 179. New York, *Laws of the State,* II, 579-80.

¹⁸ Cadwallader Colden to Henry Outhout and Jeremiah Van Renslor [sic] Esqs., April 22, 1788, Manuscript Letters Collection, 6920-29.100. 3255, Museum of the City of New York. Cadwallader Colden to Aaron Burr, May 8, 1787, Aaron Burr Papers, NYHS. New York, *Laws of the State,* III, 610.
    The Cadwallader named in the law of 1787 was not David's son, Cadwallader D.; he did not become trustee until he succeeded his uncle in 1795, per Catherine Snell Crary, "Forfeited Loyalist Land in the Western District of New York - Albany and Tryon Counties," *New York History,* XXXV (1954), 253.

¹⁹ Goldsbrow Banyar to unknown addressee, Miscellaneous Manuscripts B, NYHS. This letter describes a complicated land transaction involving Colden and his charges' holdings, but does not comprehend the complete arrangement. Internal evidence suggests it was written soon after March 15, 1785.
    Alexander Hamilton to Col. Cadwallader Colden, May 26, 1790, Colden Family Papers, Library of Congress. This letter was not actually sent to Cadwallader II, even though it was addressed to him. Hamilton refers to Cadwallader II in the third person, even suggesting the "Dear Sir" to whom the letter was sent did not regularly see the squire. Therefore, it is not likely that the recipient was his son, Cadwallader III. He would probably have seen his father more often than for Hamilton to have asked, "do you ever see Honest worthy Col. Colden?" Also Hamilton extends regards, "to all your family, in which Mrs. Hamilton joins." Cadwallader III was not of the social strata to socialize with the family of Philip Schuyler's daughter.
    The recipient was probably Cadwallader D., who at this time was studying law under Peter Van Schaack and occasionally visiting Coldengham. This son of a

distinguished loyalist family, then reading law under a most respected member of the bar, was at that time a socially prominent bachelor, and was certainly the type of person to whom Hamilton would write. That Cadwallader II did not write directly to Hamilton is evident in the squire's first sentence of a note dated July 29, 1790. "I know not what apology to make in being so long answering your letter of the 20th of May and the inquiry of my good friend and Kindsman Coll. Hamilton." The uncle's reply was probably also to his nephew. Conjugate reply of Cadwallader Colden, July 29, 1790, Colden Family Papers, Library of Congress.

20 On both sales made before the war, Judge Cadwallader Colden II of the Ulster County court verified the transaction. New York, Ulster County Clerk's Office, Title of Record-Mortgages, II, 182-3; III, 351. Henry Van Schaack to Peter Van Schaack, March 1784, Van Schaack, *Henry Van Schaack*, 113.

21 Cadwallader Colden to James Duane, April 10, 1792, James Duane Papers, NYHS. Edward P. Alexander, *A Revolutionary Conservative: James Duane of New York* (New York: Columbia University Press, 1938), 220. The Jane Colden who sold her quarter of lot F was probably Alexander's daughter, there being no other Jane Coldens alive in this year.

The £64.9.6 in rents collected from this patent on the Wallkill is the sum mentioned in Colden's will dated August 23, 1793, Ulster County, Surrogate's Office, Kingston, New York, Title of Record-Wills, IIB (1792-1797), 441-54.

New York, *Laws of the State*, III, 390-1, 496-7; Yoshpe, *Loyalist Estates*, 83.

Notes for Chapter X

1 Cadwallader Colden to Henry Sleght, September 21 and 25, 1784, and November 2, 1786, Senate House Site. Miscellaneous Papers, Ulster County. Historical Documents Collection, Queens College, reel UC-26.

2 Cadwallader Colden, "The Memmorial of the Present Possessors of Lands . . . ," undated, Colden Family Papers, Library of Congress. Ulster Clerk's Office, Mortgages, IV, 523, 544; V, 90-2, 428. Thomas Gregory to Coenraed Elmendorph and Cadwallader Colden, Jr., Esq., November 23, 1792, Senate House Site. Cadwallader Colden to John Turner, November 19, 1791, and Cadwallader Colden to William Ellison, May 8, 1793, Ellison Family Papers, NYHS.

3 Cadwallader Colden to Aaron Burr, July 12, 1791, Aaron Burr Papers, ibid.

4 Court of Common Pleas, May 1788; May 1789; July 1791; July 1793, Historical Documents Collection, Queens College, reel UC-, frame 149; reel UC-28, frame 533; reel UC-29, frame 3; reel UC-44, frame 573. For Henrietta Maria Colden's suit to regain some of her father-in-law's property, see, ibid., reel UC-29, frame 3. She won by default.

5 Bureau of Census, *Heads of Families, 1790*, 177, left col. Cadwallader Colden to Henry Van Schaack, June 13, 1790, Peter Van Schaack Papers, Library of Congress. This mill had been built much earlier at an uncertain date. In the nineteenth century the mill would be replaced by a textile factory. Ruttenber and Clark, *Orange County*, 385.

6 Bureau of Census, *Heads of Families, 1790*, 177, center col. Cadwallader Colden to unknown cousin, April 27, 1796, Colden Papers, NYHS.

7 Cadwallader Colden to Henry Van Schaack, June 13, 1790, Peter Van Schaack Papers, Library of Congress. Jane's age has been reckoned from the inscription on her tombstone. "Inscriptions in Colden Cemetery," 34.

8 Margaret Colden Fell's birthdate is unknown. On a Coldengham cemetery tombstone is the inscription, "In memory of Margaret Colden, relict of Peter Galatian, Died 29 March 1855, in the 75th year of her age." Ibid. Purple, "The Colden Family," 177. By

subtracting 75 from 1855, one surmises she was born in 1780. Yet, her family status in 1790 is impossible for a ten-year-old girl.

Cadwallader Colden to unknown cousin, April 27, 1796, Colden Papers, NYHS; Cadwallader Colden to Henry Van Schaack, June 13, 1790, Peter Van Schaack Papers, Library of Congress; Bureau of Census, *Heads of Families, 1790,* 177, center col. Alice's age in 1771 is computed from "Inscriptions in Colden Cemetery," 32.

9 Cadwallader D. Colden to Henry Van Schaack, January 4, 1790, Van Schaack, *Henry Van Schaack,* 170; Cadwallader Colden to Mary Colden Hoffman, March 6, 1789, Huntington Library.

10 "Inscriptions in Colden Cemetery," 35.

11 Cadwallader Colden to Henry Van Schaack, June 13, 1790, Peter Van Schaack Papers, Library of Congress. Cadwallader D. Colden to Henry Van Schaack, January 4, 1790, Van Schaack, *Henry Van Schaack,* 170.

12 Cadwallader Colden, "Thoughts on the Liberties of the People," 1788, Colden Family Papers, Library of Congress.

13 Cadwallader Colden to Henry Van Schaack, June 13, 1790, Peter Van Schaack Papers, Library of Congress. "Minutes of Trustees of Glebe," are quoted in Ruttenber, *Newburgh,* 83-5 and in idem, *Orange: Newburgh,* 160-2.

14 Solomon Sleght to Peter Van Gaasbeck, Esq., April, 1792, Senate House Site. Cadwallader Colden to Peter Van Gaasbeck, June 3, 1792, Miscellaneous Papers, NYHS.

There is no single volume which fully considers the New York election of 1792. It may be studied from various points of view in: Frank Monaghan, *John Jay: Defender of Liberty* (New York: Bobbs-Merrill, 1935), chap. 16; Spaulding, *George Clinton,* chap. 15; George Dangerfield, *Chancellor Robert R. Livingston of New York, 1746-1813* (New York: Harcourt, Brace, 1960), part IV, chap. 2; De Alva Stanwood Alexander, *A Political History of the State of New York,* 4 vols. (New York: Holt, 1906-23), I, chap. 6.

15 Cadwallader Colden to John Brown, May 9, 1793, Colden Papers, NYHS.

16 Will of Cadwallader Colden II. Van Horne remained for over a decade at St. Andrew's. In 1806 he was also appointed by the churches at Goshen, New Windsor, and Newburgh, all of which agreed to contribute to his support. Van Horne ministered to all four churches until 1809 when he left for a pulpit in Ballston, New York. Ruttenber and Clark, *Orange County,* 301, 392.

17 Cadwallader Colden to unknown cousin, April 27, 1796, Colden Papers, NYHS.

18 Purple, "The Colden Family," 176, 178.

19 Cadwallader Colden to unknown cousin, April 27, 1796, Colden Papers, NYHS. Will of Cadwallader Colden II.

20 Jones, *New York,* II, 505; David Edward Maas, "The Return of the Massachusetts Loyalists," (Ph.D. dissertation, University of Wisconsin, 1972), 472 and 500; Ashton, "Loyalist Experience," 173, 177, 183, 200.

BIBLIOGRAPHY

Primary

A. Manuscript

Clements Library, Ann Arbor, Michigan
George Clinton Papers; Sir Henry Clinton Papers; Lord George Germain Papers.

Columbia University, New York City, New York
John Jay Papers; Manuscript Collection; Van Schaack Family Papers.

Huntington Library, San Marino, California
Cadwallader Colden II, Letterbook, 1776-1779; Manuscript Collection.

Library of Congress, Washington, DC
Lord Jeffrey Amherst Papers (microfilm); Colden Family Papers; Headquarters Papers of the British Army in America (microfilm); Peter Van Schaack Family Papers; George Washington Papers.

Metropolitan Museum of Art, New York City, New York
Photographs, MM15367B; MM16175B; MM20492.

Museum of the City of New York, New York
Manuscript Letters Collection.

The New-York Historical Society, New York City, New York
Aaron Burr Papers; George Clinton, Miscellaneous Manuscripts; Cadwallader Colden Papers; Cadwallader Colden II, Day Book, August 11, 1767 - November 1768; F.A. de Peyster Papers; Ellison Family Papers; John McKesson Papers; Miscellaneous Manuscripts.

The New York Public Library, New York City, New York
American Loyalists, Transcripts of the Manuscripts, Books and Papers of the Commission of Enquiry into the Losses and Services of the American Loyalists; Emmet Collection; Miscellaneous Papers; Philip Schuyler Papers.

New York State Library, Albany, New York
Warshaw Collection.

Queens College, Flushing, New York City, New York
Historical Documents Collection.

Senate House Site, Kingston, New York
Manuscript Collection.

Ulster County Clerk's Office, Kingston, New York
Title of Record - Mortgages.

Ulster County Surrogate's Office, Kingston, New York
Title of Record - Wills and Inventories.

University of California, Los Angeles, California
Society for the Propagation of the Gospel in Foreign Parts, Letters and Journals (microfilm).

Washington Headquarters, Newburgh, New York
Manuscript Collection.

B. Printed

Abstracts of Wills on File in Surrogate's Office, City of New York. The New-York Historical Society, *Collections,* XXV-XLI (1893-1913).

Barclay, Thomas. *Selections from the Correspondence of Thomas Barclay: Formerly British Counsel-General at New York.* Edited by George Lockhart Rives. New York: Harper & Brothers, 1894.

Boudinot, Elias. *The Life, Public Services, Addresses, and Letters of Elias Boudinot.* 2 vols. Edited by Jane J. Boudinot. New York: Da Capo Press, 1971, reprint.

Boynton, Major Edward C. *General Orders of George Washington . . . Issued at Newburgh on the Hudson, 1782-1783.* Harrison, NY: Harbor Hill Books, 1973, reprint.

Burr, Aaron. *Memoirs of Aaron Burr.* 2 vols. New York: Da Capo Press, 1971, reprint.

Calendar of Council Minutes, 1668-1783. University of the State of New York, *New York State Library Bulletin,* LVIII (1902).

Colden, Cadwallader. *The Colden Letter Books.* The New-York Historical Society, *Collections,* IX-X (1876-7).

_____. *The Letters and Papers of Cadwallader Colden.* The New-York Historical Society, *Collections,* L-LVI, LXVII-LXVII (1918—23, 1937).

Colden, Jane. *Botanic Manuscript.* Edited by H.W. Richett and Elizabeth C. Hall. New York [?]: Garden Club of Orange and Dutchess Counties, 1963.

Crary, Catherine Snell, editor. *The Price of Loyalty: Tory Writings From the Revolutionary Era.* New York: McGraw-Hill, 1973.

Crevecoeur, Michel-Guillaume St. Jean de. *Letters from an American Farmer.* New York: E.P. Dutton, 1957.

_____. *Sketches of Eighteenth Century America.* Edited by Henri L. Bourdin, Ralph H. Gabriel and Stanley T. Williams. New Haven: Yale University Press, 1925.

DeWitt, Simeon. "The Last Cantonment of the Continental Army, at New Windsor." Map reproduced in Peter J. Guthorn, *American Map Makers of the Revolution.* Monmouth, NJ: P. Freneau, 1966.

[Ellison, Thomas, Jr.]. "New York Pending the Revolution." *Magazine of American History,* VIII (1882), 279-86.

Force, Peter, editor. *American Archives.* 9 vols. Washington, DC: M. St. Clair Clarke and Peter Force, 1837-53.

Grant, Ann. *Memoirs of an American Lady.* Freeport, NY: Books for Libraries, 1972, reprint.

Great Britain. Historical Manuscripts Commission. *The Manuscripts of the Earl of Dartmouth.* 3 vols. London: H. M. S.O., 1887-96.

Greene, Albert G. *Recollections of the Jersey Prison Ship.* New York: Corinth, 1961, reprint.

Historical Records Survey. New York (State). *Records of the Road Commissioners of Ulster County.* 3 vols. Albany: W. P. A., Historical Records Survey Project, 1940.

Hughes, Thomas. *A Journal by Thomas Hughes.* Cambridge: Cambridge University Press, 1947.

"Inscriptions in Colden Cemetery, Coldengham, N.Y." The Historical Society of Newburgh Bay and the Highlands, *Publications,* XVI (1914), 32-5.

Jay, John. *John Jay: The Making of a Revolutionary, Unpublished Papers, 1745-1780.* Edited by Richard B. Morris. New York: Harper & Row, 1975.

Johnson, Sir William. *The Papers of Sir William Johnson.* 13 vols. Albany: University of the State of New York Press, 1921-62.

Jones, E. Alfred, editor. "Letter of David Colden, Loyalist, 1783." *American Historical Review,* XXV (1919), 79-86.

Jones, Thomas. *History of New York During the Revolutionary War*. 2 vols. Edited by Edward Floyd DeLancey. New York: The New-York Historical Society, 1879.

Klein, Milton M. editor. *The Independent Reflector*. Cambridge, MA: Belknap Press, 1963.

Lydekker, John W. *The Life and Letters of Charles Inglis*. London: Society for Promoting Christian Knowledge, 1936.

Meyers, Carol M., editor. *Early New York Census Records, 1663-1772*. 2nd ed. Gardena, CA: RAM, 1965.

Montresor, John, *Journals of Captain John Montresor*. Compiled and edited by Gideon Delaplane Scull. The New-York Historical Society, *Collections*, XV (1882).

Moore, Frank, editor. *The Diary of the American Revolution*. 2 vols. NY: Scribner, 1860.

New Records of the American Revolution: The Letters, Manuscripts and Documents Sent by Lt. General Sir Charles Stuart . . . During the Revolution, 1779-81. London: L. Kashnor, 1927.

New York (Colony). *Calendar of New York Colonial Commissions, 1680- 1770*. Abstracted by Edmund B. O'Callaghan. New York: The New-York Historical Society, 1929.

_____. Laws, Statutes, etc. *The Colonial Laws of New York*. 5 vols. Albany: J. B. Lyon, 1894.

New-York Journal and General Advertiser, 1777-1782.

New York (State). Commission for Detecting and Defeating Conspiracies, 1777-1778. *Minutes of the Committee and of the First Commission . . . .* The New-York Historical Society, *Collections*, LVII-LVIII (1924-5).

_____. Comptroller's Office. *New York in the Revolution as Colony and State*. 2 vols. Albany: J. B. Lyon, 1901-1904.

_____. Division of Archives and History. *The American Revolution in New York. Albany: University of the State of New York Press, 1926*.

_____. Governor. *Messages from the Governors*. Edited by Charles Z. Lincoln. 11 vols. Albany: J. B. Lyon, 1909.

_____. *Public Papers of George Clinton*. 10 vols. New York and Albany: State of New York, 1899-1914.

_____. Laws, Statutes, etc. *Laws of the State of New York Passed at the . . . First Seven Sessions*. 5 vols. Albany: Weed, Parsons, 1866-7.

_____. Legislature. *Journals of the Provincial Congress, Provincial Convention, Committee of Safety, and Council of Safety of the State of New York*. 2 vols. Albany: T. Weed, 1842.

_____. Assembly. *Journals*.

_____. Senate. *Journals*.

_____. Secretary of State. *Calendar of Historical Manuscripts, Relating to the War of the Revolution*. 2 vols. Albany: Weed, Parsons, 1868.

_____. *Calendar of New York Colonial Manuscripts, Indorsed Land Papers, . . . 1643-1803*. Albany: Weed, Parsons, 1864.

_____. State Historian. *Ecclesiastical Records of the State of New York*. 7 vols. Under supervision of Hugh Hastings. Albany: J. B. Lyon, 1901-16.

_____. University. *New York in the Revolution.* Edited by Berthold Fernow. Vol. XV of *Documents Relative to the Colonial History of the State of New York.* Edited by Edmund B. O'Callaghan. Albany: Weed, Parsons, 1887.

O'Callaghan, Edmund B., editor. *Documentary History of the State of New York.* 4 vols. Albany: Weed, Parsons, 1849-51.

_____. *Documents Relative to the Colonial History of the State of New York.* 15 vols. Albany: Weed, Parsons, 1856-87.

"Records of the Reformed Dutch Church of Shawangunk, New York." *Year Book of the Holland Society of New York, 1928-1929.* New York: The Society, 1931.

Rivington, James. *Rivington's New York Newspaper: Excerpts from a Loyalist Press, 1773-1783.* Compiled by Kenneth Scott. The New York Historical Society, *Collections,* LXXXIV (1973).

"Royal Charter of Incorporation of St. George's Church, Newburgh, N.Y." Historical Society of Newburgh Bay and the Highlands, *Publications,* XVI (1914), 21-24.

The Royal Gazette [of New York], 1777-1783.

Scott, Kenneth, compiler. *Calendar of New York Colonial Commissions: Book II (1770-1776).* New York: National Society of Colonial Dames in the State of New York, 1972.

_____. "Ulster County, New York Court Records, 1767- 1775." *National Genealogical Society Quarterly,* LXI (1973), 295-302.

Smith, William, Jr. *Historical Memoirs from 12 July 1776 to 25 July 1778.* Edited by William H.W. Sabine. Hollis, NY: Colburn & Tegg, 1958.

_____. *Historical Memoirs from 26 August 1778 to 12 November 1783.* Edited by William H.W. Sabine. New York: New York *Times,* 1971.

United States. Bureau of the Census. *Heads of Families at the First Census . . . 1790, New York.* Washington, DC: G. P. O., 1908.

_____. Continental Congress. *Journals of the Continental Congress.* 34 vols. Washington, DC: G. P. O., 1904-37.

Van Schaack, Henry Cruger. *The Life of Peter Van Schaack, L. L. D., Embracing Selections from His Correspondence and Other Writings . . . .* New York: Appleton, 1842.

_____. *Memoirs of the Life of Henry Van Schaack Embracing Selections from His Correspondence during the American Revolution.* Chicago: McClurg, 1892.

Watts, John. *Letterbook of John Watts, Merchant and Councillor of New York.* The New-York Historical Society, *Collections,* LXI (1928).

Secondary

Abbott, Wilbur C. *New York in the American Revolution.* New York: Scribner, 1929.

Alexander, De Alva Stanwood. *A Political History of the State of New York.* 4 vols. New York: Holt, 1906-23.

Alexander. Edward P. *A Revolutionary Conservative: James Duane of New York.* New York: Columbia University Press, 1938.

_____. "The Provincial Aristocracy and the Land." In *History of the State of New York,* III, chapter 5. Edited by Alexander C. Flick. 10 vols. New York: Columbia University Press, 1933-37.

Ammerman, David. *In the Common Cause: American Response to the Coercive Acts of 1774.* New York: Norton, 1974.

"Robert Annan." In section "Associated Reformed." *Annals of the American Pulpit,* IX, 11-18. Edited by William B. Sprague. 9 vols. New York: R. Carter and Brothers, 1857-69.

Ashton, Rick J. "The Loyalist Experience: New York, 1763-1789." Ph.D. dissertation, Northwestern University, 1973.

Barck, Dorothy C. Introduction to *Minutes of the Committee and of the First Commission . . . .* By New York (State). Commission for Detecting and Defeating Conspiracies, 1777-1778. 2 vols. The New-York Historical Society, *Collections,* LVII-LVIII (1924-25).

Barck, Oscar Theodore. *New York City During the War for Independence.* Port Washington, NY: I.J. Friedman, 1966, reprint.

Becker, Carl L. *The History of Political Parties in the Province of New York.* Madison: University of Wisconsin Press, 1960, reprint.

————. "Nominations in Colonial New York," *American Historical Review,* VI (1900-01), 260-75.

Benton, William. *Whig-Loyalism.* Rutherford, NJ: Fairleigh Dickinson University Press, 1969.

Bonomi, Patricia U. *A Factious People: Politics and Society in Colonial New York.* New York: Columbia University Press, 1971.

————. "Local Government in Colonial New York: A Base for Republicanism." In *Aspects of Early New York Society and Politics,* 29-50. Edited by Jacob Judd and Irwin H. Polishook. Tarrytown, NY: Sleepy Hollow Restorations, 1974.

Bowler, R. Arthur. *Logistics and the Failure of the British Army in America, 1775-1783.* Princeton: Princeton University Press, 1975.

Bragdon, Joseph. "Cadwallader Colden, Second: An Ulster County Tory," *New York History,* XIV (1933), 411-21.

Bridenbaugh, Carl. *Mitre and Sceptre.* New York: Oxford University Press, 1962.

Brown, Wallace. *The Good Americans.* New York: William Morrow, 1969.

Burrows, Edwin G. and Wallace, Michael. "The American Revolution: The Ideology and Psychology of National Liberation." *Perspectives in American History,* VI (1972), 167-306.

Champagne, Roger. "Family Politics versus Constitutional Principles: The New York Assembly Elections of 1768 and 1769," *William and Mary Quarterly,* Third Series, XX (1963), 57-79.

Clearwater, Alphonso T., editor. *The History of Ulster County, New York.* Kingston, NY: Van Deusen, 1907.

Cole, Arthur Harrison. *Wholesale Prices in the United States, 1700-1861.* Cambridge, MA: Harvard University Press, 1938.

Connolly, Vincent. "Colden House Recalls Area's Heritage." *The Evening News,* [Newburgh] December 16, 1968.

Corning, A. Elwood. *Washington at Temple Hill.* Newburgh: Lanmere, 1932.

Crary, Catherine Snell. "Cadwallader Colden II: True Lover of his Country or Enemy of the State?" *Journal of Long Island History,* X (1973), 7-13.

————. "Forfeited Loyalist Lands in the Western District of New York - Albany and Tryon Counties." *New York History,* XXXV (1954), 239-58.

Dangerfield, George. *Chancellor Robert R. Livingston of New York, 1746-1813.* New York: Harcourt, Brace, 1960.

deFreitas, Gladys. "Colden Mansion: Sturdy Relic of Pre-Revolutionary Days." *Middletown Times Herald* [New York], May 14, 1938.

deJong, Gerald. *The Dutch in America.* Boston: Twayne, 1974.

dePeyster, John Watts. Introduction to *The Life and Misfortunes and the Military Career of Brigadier-General Sir John Johnson, Bart.* New York: C.H. Ludwig, 1882.

Dillon, Dorothy Rita. *The New York Triumvirate.* New York: Columbia University Press, 1949.

Eager, John. "An Early Canal." *Historical Magazine,* VIII (1864), 114-15.

Eager, Samuel W. *An Outline History of Orange County.* Newburgh: S.T. Callahan, 1846-47.

Eberlein, Harold Donaldson. *The Manors and Historic Homes of the Hudson Valley.* Philadelphia: Lippincott, 1924.

"Colonel Thomas Ellison." The Historical Society of Newburgh Bay and the Highlands, *Publications,* XVIII (1919), 9-12.

Fingerhut, Eugene R. "Assimilation of Immigrants on the Frontier of New York, 1764-1776." Ph.D. dissertation, Columbia University, 1962.

Flick, Alexander C. *Loyalism in New York During the American Revolution.* New York: Columbia University Press, 1901.

Flick, Hugh M. "The Rise of the Revolutionary Committee System." In *History of the State of New York,* III, chapter 7. Edited by Alexander C. Flick, 10 vols. New York: Columbia University Press, 1933-37.

French, J.H. *Gazetteer of the State of New York.* Syracuse: R.P. Smith, 1860.

Friedman, Bernard. "The New York Assembly Elections of 1768 and 1769." *New York History,* XLVI (1965), 3-24.

Gerlach, Larry R. *Prologue to Independence: New Jersey in the Coming of the American Revolution.* New Brunswick: Rutgers University Press, 1976.

Greene, Evarts B. and Harrington, Virginia D. *American Population Before the Federal Census of 1790.* New York: Columbia University Press, 1932.

Greven, Philip. *The Protestant Temperament: Patterns of Child-Rearing, Religious Experience, and the Self in Early America.* New York: Knopf, 1977.

Gross, Robert A. *The Minutemen and their World.* New York: Hill & Wang, 1976.

Halsey, R.T.H. and Cornelius, Charles O. *Handbook of the American Wing.* 7th ed. New York: Metropolitan Museum of Art, 1942.

Harris, Reginald V. *Charles Inglis, Missionary, Loyalist, Bishop (1734-1816).* Toronto: General Board of Religious Education, 1937.

Headley, Russel, editor. *The History of Orange County, New York.* Middletown: Van Deusen & Elms, 1908.

Henretta, James A. "Economic Development and Social Structure in Colonial Boston." *William and Mary Quarterly.* Third Series, XXII (1965), 75-92.

_____. *The Evolution of American Society, 1700-1815: An Interdisciplinary Analysis.* Lexington, MA: Heath, 1973.

_____. Families and Farms: Mentalité in Pre-Industrial America." *William and Mary Quarterly.* Third Series, XXXV (1978), 3-32.

Higgins, Ruth L. *Expansion in New York: With Special Reference to the Eighteenth Century.* Columbus: Ohio State University Press, 1931.

Hindle, Brooke. "A Colonial Governor's Family: The Coldens of Coldengham." *New-York Historical Society Quarterly,* XLV (1961), 233-50.

Hull, N.E.H., Hull, Peter C. and Allen, Steven L. "Choosing Sides: A Quantitative Study of the Personality Determinants of Loyalist and Revolutionary Political Affiliation in New York," *Journal of American History,* LXV (1978), 344-66.

Jordan, Helen. "Colonel Elias Boudinot in New York City, February, 1778." *Pennsylvania Magazine of History and Biography,* XXIV (1900), 453-66.

Jordan, Jean Paul. "The Anglican Establishment in Colonial New York, 1693-1783." Ph.D. dissertation, Columbia University, 1971.

Jordan, Winthrop D. "Familial Politics: Thomas Paine and the Killing of the King, 1776." *The Journal of American History,* LX (1973), 294-308.

Kammen, Michael. "The American Revolution as a *Crisé de Conscience:* The Case of New York." In *Society, Freedom and Conscience,* 125-89. Edited by Richard M. Jellison. New York: Norton, 1976.

_____. *Colonial New York - A History.* New York: Scribner, 1975.

Katcher, Philip R.N. *Encyclopedia of British, Provincial and German Army Units, 1775-1783.* Harrisburgh, PA: Stackpole, 1973.

Kenney, Alice. "Albany Dutch: Loyalists and Patriots." *New York History,* XLII (1961), 331-50.

_____. *Stubborn for Liberty: The Dutch in New York.* Syracuse: Syracuse University Press, 1975.

Keys, Alice Mapelsden. *Cadwallader Colden, A Representative Eighteenth Century Official.* New York: Columbia University Press, 1906.

Kim, Sung Bok. *Landlord and Tenant in Colonial New York: Manorial Society, 1664-1775.* Chapel Hill: University of North Carolina Press, 1978.

_____. "A New Look at the Great Landlords of Eighteenth Century New York." *William and Mary Quarterly.* Third Series, XXVII (1970), 581-614.

Klein, Milton M. "Democracy and Politics in Colonial New York." *New York History,* XL (1959), 221-46.

Kullikoff, Allan. "The Progress of Inequality in Revolutionary Boston." *William and Mary Quarterly.* Third Series, XXVII (1971), 375-412.

Lamb, Martha. *History of the City of New York.* 3 vols. New York: A.S. Barnes, 1877-96.

LaPotin, Armand. "The Minisink Grant: Partners, Patents and Processing Fees in Eighteenth Century New York." *New York History,* LVI (1975), 29-50.

LeFevre, Ralph. *History of New Paltz, New York and Its Old Families (From 1678 to 1820).* 2nd ed. Baltimore: Genealogical Publishing Co., 1973, reprint.

Lemon, James T. *The Best Poor Man's Country: A Geographical Study of Southeastern Pennsylvania.* New York: Norton, 1972.

Lynn, Kenneth S. *A Divided People.* Westport, CT: Greenwood, 1977.

Mackesy, Piers. *The War for America, 1775-1783.* Cambridge, MA: Harvard University Press, 1964.

McManus, Edgar J. *A History of Negro Slavery in New York.* Syracuse: Syracuse University Press, 1966.

Maas, David Edward. "The Return of the Massachusetts Loyalists." Ph.D. dissertation, University of Wisconsin Press, 1972.

Main, Jackson Turner. *Political Parties Before the Constitution.* Chapel Hill: University of North Carolina Press, 1973.

_____. *Social Structure of Revolutionary America.* Princeton: Princeton University Press, 1965.

Metzger, Charles H. *The Prisoner in the American Revolution.* Chicago: Loyola University Press, 1971.

Moffat, Almet S. *Orange County, New York.* Washingtonville, NY: n. p., 1928.

Monaghan, Frank. *John Jay: Defender of Liberty.* New York: Bobbs-Merrill, 1935.

Morris, Richard B. *The Peace-Makers.* New York: Harper & Row, 1965.

_____. *Seven Who Shaped Our Destiny.* New York: Harper & Row, 1973.

Nash, Willis G. "The Burning of Kingston." *Proceedings of the Ulster County Historical Society for 1933-34,* 51-60.

Nelson, William. *The American Tory.* Oxford: Oxford University Press, 1961.

Norton, Mary Beth. *The British-Americans: The Loyalist Exiles in England, 1774-1789.* Boston: Little, Brown, 1972.

Nutt, John J. *Newburgh, Her Institutions, Industries and Leading Citizens.* Newburgh: Ritchie & Hull, 1891.

Old Ulster, I-V (1905-09).

Paltsits, Victor H. *Introduction to Minutes of the Commissioners . . . Albany County Sessions.* By New York (State). Commission for Detecting and Defeating Conspiracies, 1777-1778. 3 vols. Albany: J. B. Lyon, 1909-10.

Pearson, Michael. *The Revolutionary War.* New York: Capricorn, 1973.

Pound, Arthur. "Charles Clinton, the First of the American Clintons." *New York State Historical Association Journal,* XII (1931), 375-89.

Purple, Edwin. "Notes Biographical and Genealogical of the Colden Family, and Some of Its Collateral Branches in America." *The New York Genealogical and Biographical Record,* IV (1873), 161-83.

Ritcheson, Charles. *Aftermath of Revolution.* New York: Norton, 1971.

Ruttenber, Edward M. *History of the County of Orange: With a History of Newburgh.* Newburgh: E. M. Ruttenber, 1875.

_____. *History of the Town of Newburgh.* Newburgh: E. M. Ruttenber, 1859.

_____. *Obstructions to the Navigation of Hudson's River.* Albany: J. Munsell, 1860.

_____ and Clark, L. H. *History of Orange County, New York.* Philadelphia: Evarts & Peck, 1881.

Schoonmaker, Marius. *The History of Kingston, New York.* New York: Burr Printing House, 1888.

Seese, Mildred Parker. *Old Orange Houses.* 2 vols. Middletown: The Author, 1941-43.

Smith, Paul H. "The American Loyalists: Notes on their Organization and Numerical Strength." *William and Mary Quarterly.* Third Series, XXV (1968), 259-77.

_____. *Loyalists and Redcoats: A Study in British Revolutionary Policy.* New York: Norton, 1972.

"Some Facts and Traditions in Regard to the 'Knox Headquarters' in the Town of New Windsor . . . ." Historical Society of Newburgh Bay and the Highlands, *Publications,* XVIII (1919), 13-9.

Spaulding, E. Wilder. *His Excellency George Clinton: Critic of the Constitution.* New York: Macmillan, 1938.

————. *New York in the Critical Period.* New York: Columbia University Press, 1932.

Stokes, I. N. Phelps. *The Iconography of Manhattan Island, 1498-1909.* 6 vols. New York: Arno, 1967, reprint.

Stowe, Gerald C. and Weller, Jac. "Revolutionary West Point: 'Key to the Continent'." In *Military Analysis of the Revolutionary War,* 154-71. Edited by editors of *Military Affairs.* Milwood, NJ: KTO, 1977.

Sutherland, Stella. *Population Distribution in Colonial America.* New York: Columbia University Press, 1936.

Sylvester, Nathaniel Bartlett. *History of Ulster County, N. Y.* 2 vols. Philadelphia: Evarts & Peck, 1880.

U.S. Congress. House. *Biographical Directory of the American Congress, 1774-1961.* House Document 442. 85th Cong., 2nd session, 1961.

Varga, Nicholas. "Election Procedures and Practices in Colonial New York." *New York History,* XLI (1960), 249-77.

Wallace, Margaret V. S. "'Big' Little Britain: Cadwallader Colden and His Canal." *Orange County Post,* February 20, 1960.

————. "'Big' Little Britain: The Rev. Robert Annan." *Orange County Post,* December 1, 1966.

Ward, Christopher. *The War of the Revolution.* 2 vols. New York: Macmillan, 1952.

Waters, John J., Jr. *The Otis Family in Provincial and Revolutionary Massachusetts.* Chapel Hill: University of North Carolina Press, 1968.

Wells, Robert V. *The Population of the British Colonies in America Before 1776.* Princeton: Princeton University Press, 1975.

Wertenbaker, Thomas Jefferson. *Father Knickerbocker Rebels.* New York: Scribner, 1948.

Willcox, William B. *Portrait of a General: Sir Henry Clinton in the War of Independence.* New York: Knopf, 1964.

Woolsey, C. M. *History of the Town of Marlborough, Ulster County, New York.* Albany: J. B. Lyon, 1908.

Yoshpe, Harry B. *The Disposition of Loyalist Estates in the Southern District of the State of New York.* New York: Columbia University Press, 1939.

Zeichner, Oscar. "The Loyalist Problem in New York After the Revolution." *New York History,* XXI (1940), 284-302.

INDEX

Adams, Samuel and loyalists: 150
Albany: 2, 4, 7, 9, 13-14, 63, 93
Amherst, Lord Jeffrey: 101, 106, 109-10
André, Major John: 103, 110
Anglicans (See Church of England)
Annan, Rev. Robert: 3; inspires anti-Colden sentiment: 4; inspiries support for revolution: 48; CC2 opposes: 58-59, 61;
Antill, Alice Colden (daughter of CC2): 124, 137, 138, 148
Antill, Alice (granddaughter of CC2): 138, 148
Antill, Elizabeth (see Van Horne, Elizabeth Antill)
Associated Reformed Presbyterian Church (see Seceder Church)
Association of the Continental Congress: 41-42, 44, 48, 53, 54
Auchmuty, Rev. Samuel: 31, 35

Banishment Act: 93-95, 106
Barclay, Susan DeLancey: 63, 127
Battle of Lexington: 34, 44
Battle of Saratoga: 79, 80, 82
Benson, Egbert: 66, 88, 91, 94, 95, 150
"Black Market" activities: 108, 110, 119
Boston: 48, 58, 59, 60
Boudinot, Elias: 113
Boyd, Robert, Jr.: 33, 120; and CC2: 52-55
Brant, Joseph: 92, 93, 120
Burgoyne, Gen. Sir John: 71, 73, 76, 78, 79, 80, 82, 83, 111
Burr, Aaron: 97, 128, 129, 136

Campbell family: 47
Canada: 51, 60, 62, 78
Carleton, Gen. Sir Guy: 60, 116, 117, 127
Church of England: 3, 29-30, 65, 148; linked to loyalism: 31, 43, 44; weakness in southern Ulster: 31, 35-38; dissenters control St. George's: 142-43; members control St. Andrew's: 145-46
Clinton, Charles: friendship with CC, Sr: 4; and CC2: 19, 32, 52; Lt. Col. in militia: 19; and revolutionary committees: 42, 45, 52
Clinton, George (royal gov. of NY): 13, 15
Clinton, George (state gov. of NY): 1, 4, 27, 48, 52, 78, 95, 115, 134; CC2's lawyer: 27, 33; and Assembly elections: 30, 32; court clerk: 33; in Prov. Cong.: 44, 46; orders CC2's arrest: 67-68; elected governor: 73; seeks public opinion of CC2: 79; defeated in Highlands: 80; sends CC2 to Council of Safety: 83; CC2 seeks help from: 84, 88, 90, 123-24; advises CC2: 88, 90; and Elizabeth Colden's trips to NYC: 106-08, 109; and election of 1792: 143-45
Clinton, Gen. Sir Henry: 106, 108, 111, 122; raids up Hudson Valley: 79-80, 82, 83; CC2 seeks appointment from: 101, 102, 110, 114; appoints CC2 to office: 113; removed from command: 116
Clinton, Gen. James: 4; and New Paltz meeting: 45; and Thomas Colden: 46; and Iroquois: 120
Coetus (see Dutch)
Colden (family): 3; divisions among members: 46, 48, 102, 103; avoids problems with NYS: 119; 121-23, 149

Colden, Alexander (brother of CC2): 2, 7, 13, 146, 148; as colonial official: 8; dominates Newburgh: 8, 17, 35; death: 8

Colden, Alexander (son of CC2): 61, 78, 137, 141; born: 24; gets estate property: 138; inherits from father: 147-48

Colden, Alice (mother of CC2): 2, 13, 14, 146; and education of children: 12; and CC2: 12, 18, 19; death: 23

Colden, Alice (sister of CC2—see Willet, Alice Colden)

Colden, Alice (daughter of CC2—see Antill, Alice Colden)

Colden, Ann (wife of brother David): 128, 129

Colden, Ann Willett (wife of Thomas): 136, 137, 146

Colden, Betsy (daughter of brother David): 128

Colden, Catherine (sister of CC2): 2, 7

Colden, Catherine (daughter of David): 129

Colden, Cadwallader, Sr.: 146; and Charles Clinton: 4; slaveowner: 5; and offices held: 6; and land deals: 6, 7; and nepotism: 7-10, 13-15, 17-18, 19-20, 148, 149; and education 11; in NY politics: 15, 96; in NYC and Springhill: 23; and protestors: 27-28; on political factions: 31; and St. George's: 37; death and will: 41, 57

Colden, Cadwallader II: moves to Coldenghams: 2, 11; and poor tax: 5; and slaves: 6; as landowner: 7, 16, 131-32, 135; love of farming: 12-13; relations with mother: 12, 18, 19; relations with father: 12, 13, 14, 15, 17, 18, 19-21, 29; as surveyor and deputy surveyor: 13, 17; and King George's War: 13-14; marriage: 15-16; prewar economic status: 16, 17, 18, 24-25, 27, 149; precinct supervisor: 17; as lawyer: 17, 18; and brother Alexander: 17, 18; and French and Indian War: 19-21; in Ulster militia: 19-21, 35; becomes master of Coldenham: 23-24; as merchant 25-26; as litigant: 26-27; and Assembly elections: 28-32; writing style: 30; and Anglicans as tories: 31; and Charles Clinton: 32; judge of Ulster court: 32-35; Justice of Peace: 34; vestryman and warden: 35-38; and St. George's: 35, 37; and St. Andrew's: 35, 37; derides dissenters: 36; and father's death: 41, 57; protests election to Provincial Congress: 44; signs Association: 44-45; and Thomas as sheriff: 45-46; and Dr. John Hill: 52; and Robert Boyd, Jr.: 52-55; first arrest and hearing: 52-55; subject of rumors: 54; in Kingston jail: 55-56, 71-72; paroled: 56, 64, 73-74, 77-78, 91-92; wants pass to NYC: 57, 66; raises granddaughters: 57; Convention hearing: 58-62, 64; and King George III: 58, 61, 65, 85, 94-95, 109, 124; and neighbors: 59-60, 68, 71, 72, 77, 78, 79, 82, 83, 84, 128, 149; Convention ignores: 60, 62, 66; a political annoyance: 62, 87, 92, 149; arrested by Dumond: 64; rejects oath: 65, 94-95; public neutral and secret loyalist: 65, 66, 103, 149; banished to NYC: 66, 95-97; gives estate to CC3: 67; arrested on orders of George Clinton: 67; imprisoned for his benefit: 68, 71, 72, 77, 78; and Rosa-Midagh episode: 68, 73; and prison fleet off Kingston: 72-73, 75-78, 80-81; considered avowed loyalist: 75; refuses to escape: 78; not sent to Connecticut: 81-82; agrees with Elizabeth to leave home: 82; sent to Council of Safety by George Clinton: 84; rejects NY legitimacy: 84-85; treated mildly by state: 87-89; at Nine Partners: 87-90; not treated consistently by NY: 89-90, 91, 95; and Banishment Act: 93-95; wants oath refusal filed: 95; and William Smith, Jr.: 96-97, 101, 115-116; ignored by Henry Clinton: 101; and new loyalists: 101, 111; visits Springhill: 101, 103, 109, 128; appeals for office: 101-102, 110, 112-13; asserts steadfast loyalism: 102, 103; insinuates family is loyal: 102, 103; offers advice on military strategy: 102, 109-12; on dole: 104; president of "Loyal Refugees": 105-06; arranges wife's visit: 107; and Thomas Ellison's will: 107-08; as commissary of prisoners: 113-14, 116-17; residence in NYC: 113; and Crevecoeur: 114-15; and William Peartree Smith: 115-16; readmitted to NY: 123-26; critic of American independence and society: 124-25, 140-42;

problems on return to Coldengham: 128;   postwar status of family: 128-29, 136-39, 146-47;   executor for relatives: 129, 130;   excutor for father: 129-32;   postwar economic conditions of: 131, 134-36;   gives land to sons: 137-38;   emotional condition: 139-40; and control of St. George's: 142-43;   election of 1792: 143-45;   and NY Chamber of Commerce: 145, 150;   and control of St. Andrew's: 145-46;   death and will: 147-48; life's significance: 148-52

Colden, Cadwallader III (son of CC2): 61, 78, 141;   born: 24;   marriage to Elizabeth Fell: 45, 46;   and militia: 45, 46;   passive revolutionary: 46;   and parole of father: 56; controls Coldengham: 67, 84;   helps father during imprisonment: 77;   and father as nuisance: 83;   writes to father in exile: 109;   lack of success: 137, 147;   and second marriage: 137;   and father's will: 147-48

Colden, Cadwallader IV (son of CC3): 148

Colden Cadwallader D. (son of David): fifteen years old in London: 127;   and the law: 129:   and CC2: 130, 139;   marriage and success: 146, 147

Colden, David (brother of CC2): 6, 13, 23, 77, 97, 107;   born: 2;   scientific interests: 9, 11;   as surveyor general: 9;   affection for father: 11-12;   investments with CC2: 16, 101;   loyalist activities: 40;   inherits Springhill: 41; denied readmission to NY: 125, 126, 127;   death: 127, 129

Colden, David (son of CC2): 24, 61, 74, 82, 83, 137, 141;   in NYC with father: 123;   gets estate property: 138;   inherits from father: 147-48

Colden, Elizabeth (sister of CC2—see DeLancey, Elizabeth Colden)

Colden, Elizabeth (wife of CC2): 61, 77, 78, 83, 122, 136;   condition in old age: 1, 139, 147;   marriage and births: 15, 16, 24;   and John Jay: 74; advises CC2: 82;   visits CC2: 90, 106-09;   appeals to John Morin Scott: 90;   in father's will: 107;   good relations with revolutionaries: 109, 121-23;   inherits from husband: 147, 148

Colden, Elizabeth (daughter of David): 129, 137, 138

Colden, Elizabeth Fell (wife of CC3): 45

Colden, Henrietta Maria (wife of Richard Nicholls Colden): 127, 129, 146

Colden, Jane (sister of CC2): 2, 7, 9

Colden, Jane (daughter of CC2): 24, 61, 137, 147-48

Colden, Jane (daughter of Alexander): 132

Colden, John (brother of CC2): 2, 13, 14

Colden, John (son of CC2): 24, 61, 64, 102, 108, 110

Colden, Margaret (daughter of CC2—see Fell, Margaret Colden)

Colden, Mary (daughter of David—see Hoffman, Mary Colden)

Colden, Richard Nicholls (son of Alexander): 146;   appointed to office: 9;   loyalist: 41

Colden, Thomas (son of CC2): 108, 138, 141, 146;   born: 24;   as sheriff: 15, 45, 46;   and British army: 61, 102;   sneaks home: 63, 64;   ill: 110, 127;   in Nova Scotia: 129;   return to Coldengham: 136, 137;   inherits from father: 147-48

Coldengham: 2, 13, 60, 64, 77, 85;   settle on: 1, 2;   slaves and masters on: 5, 6;   means of purchase: 7;   Coldens develop: 11;   family life at: 23-24;   remote from Kingston: 30;   meeting for St. George's charter at: 37;   CC2 paroled to: 56;   an emotional retreat for CC2: 61-62, 67, 79, 82;   Thomas sneaks to: 63;   given to CC3: 67;   strategic location of: 97;   Elizabeth's father dies at: 107;   wartime taxes on: 122;   farms given to children by CC2: 137-38

Coldengham store: 8, 25-26

Conferentie (see Dutch)

"Confession of Faith": 29-30

Congress, Continental: 40, 44

Cornwallis, Gen. Lord Charles: 111

Cruger family: 47

de Crevecoeur, Michel-Guillaume St. Jean: 93, 114-15
Cruikshank, Alexander: 63, 71, 73-74
Cumming, John: 90;   and British in NYC: 63;   in Kingston: 71, 72, 73-74;   escapes from prison fleet: 78;   appeal denied: 91;   in Great Britain: 111, 129

DeLancey (family): 2, 126;   faction in politics: 30, 31
DeLancey, Elizabeth Colden (sister of CC2): 2, 63:   land in her name: 7;   marries Peter DeLancey: 9;   and CC2's financial problems: 18;   son wins Assembly seat: 30;   and father's will: 41;   postwar problems: 127, 129;   death: 146
DeLancey, James: 9
DeLancey, John: 9
DeLancey, Oliver: 1, 127
DeLancey, Stephen: 127
Denning, William: 66, 108;   seeks help for CC2: 64, 92
DeWitt, Charles: 78;   wins Assembly election: 30, 32;   in Provincial Congress: 44, 46
Dissenters and Presbyterians: 3, 4, 31, 35-37, 142-43
Duane, James: denigrates CC2: 18, 66-67
DuBois, Peter: 114, 130, 146;   customer of CC2: 25;   appointed to county court: 32;   protests election to Provincial Congress: 44;   letters to CC2 from NYC: 61;   police magistrate: 100, 115;   American army occupies property of: 122
DuBois, Walter: 44, 126
Dumond, Egbert: 15, 45;   arrests CC2 in 1777: 64;   in charge of prisoners: 72
Dutch: 4;   in Ulster County: 3;   Conferentie and Coetus: 29, 81
Dutchess County: 2, 31, 49, 71

Election of 1777: 73;   of 1768: 28-30;   of 1769: 30-32;   of 1792: 143-45
Elliot, Andrew: 100
Ellison (family): 16, 26, 43, 45, 47, 63
Ellison, John, Sr. (grandfather of Elizabeth Colden): 3
Ellison, John (brother of Elizabeth Colden): 37, 107;   in army: 47;   officers use home of: 121
Ellison, Thomas (father of Elizabeth Colden): 4, 8, 16;   in French and Indian War: 19-20;   offers to pay bail of CC2: 54;   survives panic in New Windsor: 80;   Washington uses home of: 107, 121;   death and will: 107 -08
Ellison, Thomas, Jr. (brother of Elizabeth Colden): 137;   vestryman of Trinity Church: 47;   in father's will: 107;   CC2 owes money to: 109, 128
Ellison, William: 37, 107, 119
Eltinge, Roeliff: met CC2 in court: 27;   life to the Revolution: 81;   with CC2 in Kingston: 81-82;   in Nine Partners: 87-90;   banished with CC2: 97;   rejected by Senate: 125;   readmitted to NY: 126;   owes CC2 money: 136
Eltinge, Mrs.: 90, 108, 136

Fell, Judge John: 45, 122
Fell, Margaret Colden (daughter of CC2): 137-38;   born: 24;   marries: 122;   widow: 148;   inherits from father: 148
Fell, Peter: 122, 137, 138
Fishkill: 57, 60, 62, 63, 92
Flushing: 23, 40, 63
Fort Clinton: 2
Fort Montgomery: 2, 67
Fort Ticonderoga: 35, 76

Franklin, William: 105, 106
French and Indian War: 19;   in Ulster County: 19-21

Germain, Lord George: 111-13
Germans (Palatines): 3, 41
Goodwill Church: 3
Great Britain: post-1763 colonial policy: 27;   army: 41, 60;   army around NYC: 61, 99-
    100, 121;   army and sovereignty: 84-85, 96;   field strategy: 102, 109-112;   and Euro-
    pean powers: 112
Gyles, Charles: 72

Hamilton, Alexander: 130;   and Rutgers vs. Waddington: 131
Hanover Precinct: formed 3;   poor tax: 5;   middle class in: 4, 5;   committee of: 39, 40,
    42, 45, 46, 52, 54;   militia in: 39
Hardenburgh, Jacobus: 81, 83, 85
Harpur, Robert: 88, 89, 90
Harrison, Richard: 125, 126, 127, 128
Heath, Gen. William: 108
Highlands: 2, 80, 82
Hoffman, Josiah Ogden: 128, 138
Hoffman, Mary Colden (daughter of David): 121-22, 128, 129, 138, 148
Howe, Gen. Sir William: 78, 79, 111
Hudson, Valley: 3;   geography of: 2;   no anti-British prewar activities in: 28;   elections
    of 1768 and 1769 in: 28-32;   loyalists in: 49, 52, 71;   area of NY control limited to: 78;
    British raids in: 80, 121
Hugeuenots: 3
Hurley: 81, 82, 83;   committee of: 41;   CC2 paroled in: 77, 78

Indians: 2, 19-20;   in Revolution: 92-93, 120-21
Inglis, Rev. Charles: 37, 61, 106

Jay, John: 1, 50;   and brother James: 47;   and Kingston jail: 56;   and committee for
    conspiracies: 58;   and CC2: 74, 77, 83;   and election of 1792: 143-45
Jersey: 87, 113
Johnson, Sir John: 62, 63, 104
Johnson, Lady Mary Watts ("Polly"): 62-63, 103
Johnson, Sir William: 6, 7, 61
Jones, Dr. John: 64, 76, 126
Jones, Thomas: 100, 106

Kingston: 2, 3, 41, 64, 68, 81, 83;   jail: 56, 72;   destroyed: 83-84

Law of May 12, 1784: 126
Little Britain: 3, 7;   anti-CC2 sentiment in: 4;   de facto state capital: 83, 92, 122
Livinston (family): 2, 4;   political faction: 15;   members on committee for conspiracies:
    58;   manor: 73, 84, 93
Livinston, Robert R.: 27, 81, 132
Logan, Samuel: 54, 67, 107
Loring, Joshua: 113, 114
Loyalists: and Church of England: 31;   in Ulster: 31, 39-40, 120-21;   in Shawangunk:
    42-43;   rely on government for protection: 43;   CC2 distributes materials for: 44;   in

Newburgh: 44, 45, 53; families split: 46-48; strength throughout NY: 51; oath for: 64; many want passes to NYC: 66; imprisoned without charges: 71; sent to Connecticut: 81-82; sufferings: 87; attack from West with Indians: 92-93, 120-21; and William Smith, Jr.: 101, 106, 115-16; military organizations: 104; factions among: 104, 111; political organizations: 105; British criticisms of: 105-06; on length of war: 109, 110, 111; leave U.S. after war: 117, 127; as political issue in NY: 123; Loyalist Commission: 124, 129, 146; readmitted: 126
"Loyal Refugees": 105

McClaughrey, Col. James: 35, 107
Matthews, David: 100, 114, 116
Midagh, Jacob: 68, 73, 102, 107
Minisink: 18
Mohawk Valley: 6, 63
Morris, Gouverneur: 56, 58, 60, 64, 72, 78, 83, 150
Morris, Col. Roger: 104, 109, 110, 114

Neely family: 130
Neutrality: 51, 64-65, 92, 94-95, 102; CC2 claims: 53, 59-62, 84-85, 89
Newburgh: 2, 3, 4, 7, 8, 25, 26, 79, 92; poor tax: 5; and Rev. Sayre: 31, 36-37; St. George's charter: 37; committee: 42, 45; and loyalists: 44,45, 53; Gen. Washington in: 121; postwar religious strife in: 142-43
Newburgh-New Windsor joint committee: 52-54
New Paltz: 43, 44, 45, 81
New Windsor: 2, 3, 8, 25, 26, 79, 92; poor tax: 5; slaves in: 5; committee: 41, 43, 45, 54; panic in: 80; crowd action in: 119; Gen. Washington in: 121
New York City: 2, 7, 8, 11, 31, 36, 37; colonial Assembly in: 27, 28; protest committees in: 39; and British military: 41, 61; anti-tory riot and plot to capture Washington in: 48; military and loyalists: 51; ravage by fire: 99; and military corruption: 100; NY state tax on: 135
New York (Colony) Assembly: 9, 15, 20, 21; rural conservatives in: 28; elections of 1768 and 1769: 28-32; loyalists support of: 43
New York (Colony), local government: 27-32
New York (State): and loyalists: 39; treats loyalists inconsistently: 62, 87-89, 95; first state election: 73; de facto capital in Little Britain: 83, 92, 122; officals treat CC2 mildly: 87-89; currency: 120; land bounty regiments: 123; and ex-loyalists: 123; Law of May 12, 1784: 126; distribution of political power in: 133-34; election of 1792: 143-45
New York (State) Assembly: and ex-loyalists: 125
New York (State) Commission for Detecting and Defeating Conspiracies: 40; CC2 assigned to: 66, 91-93; removes CC2 from deportation list: 82; banishes CC2: 97
New York (State) Committee for Detecting and Defeating Conspiracies: 62; created: 40, 57; restraint of: 58; and CC2: 57, 59, 60
New York (State) Convention: 63, 66, 71, 76; and CC2: 60-61; and loyalist oath: 64-65; and prison fleet: 72-73, 80-81
New York (State) Council of Safety: 76, 119; sends prisoners to prison fleet: 74; and CC2 75, 83, 85, 87-89; sends prisoners to Connecticut: 80-81
New York (State) Provincial Congress: 39, 42, 44, 46, 48; and revolutionary committees: 39, 40, 45, 46; and loyalists: 39, 40
New York (State) Senate: 90; and ex-loyalists: 126
Nicholson, John: 79, 82, 83

Nine Partners: 87-90

"Oblong Patent": 7
Orange County: 7, 21, 24, 49, 72, 120

Palatines (see Germans)
Palmer, Thomas: 33, 120;   and CC2: 54, 65, 128
Park, Arthur: 135;   his store: 4, 5, 42;   begins public career: 45;   state senator: 73, 88, 91, 93
Pawling, Levi: 32, 35, 44, 46, 88, 90, 91
Poughkeepsie: 88, 91
Presbyterians (see Dissenters)
Property, distribution of: 4, 5

Quakers: 76
Quebec Act: 42
Queens County: 40, 41, 49

Religion as cause of the Revolution: 31-32, 42
Rosa, Jacobus: 68, 73, 102, 107

St. Andrew's Church (Wallkill): 35, 36, 37, 46;   CC2 dominates: 145-46
St. David's Church (Otter Kill): 35, 37
St. George's Church (Newburgh): 35-37;   trustee fights: 142-43
Sayre, Rev. John: 31, 36-37
Schoonmaker, Cornelius: 90
Schuyler, Philip: 73, 125
Scott, John Morin: 73;   and CC2: 83, 84, 88, 90;   and Elizabeth Colden: 90
Seabury, Rev. Samuel: 41
Seceder Church: 3, 48, 59
Shawangunk: 5, 25;   committee of: 42, 63;   loyalist meet at: 43
Skinner, Abraham: 113, 114
Sleght, Henry: 82;   on county court: 32;   in charge of CC2's parole: 73-74, 75, 77-78;   debt of CC2 to: 134, 136;   lawyer for CC2: 136
Smith, William, Jr.: 1, 106, 150;   and CC2: 96, 97, 101, 115-16;   and Crevecoeur: 115;   and old loyalists: 115-16
Smith, William Peartree: 115-16
Society for the Propagation of the Gospel in Foreign Parts (SPG): 29-30, 31, 35-37.
Spierin, Rev. George: 142-43
Springhill: 23, 63, 101, 103, 104, 108, 129
Swarthout, Jacobus: 66, 91

Treaty of 1783: 123, 131
Trimble, Alexander: 45
Trinity Church: 31, 35
Tryon, Gov. William: 41, 48;   political power, 100;   and "Provincial Corps": 104

Ulster County: 1;   population and ethnic divisions: 2, 3, 25, 31;   local government in: 3, 27-29;   roads in 4;   county court: 8, 26-27, 32-35;   Assembly elections in: 28-32;   keeping peace in: 33-35, 49;   Second Regiment: 46, 48, 123;   committee: 52, 54, 56;   economic problems in: 119

Van Deusen, John: 77, 78, 82, 83
Van Horne, Elizabeth Antill (granddaughter of CC2): 138, 145-46, 148
Van Horne, Rev. Frederick: 145-46
Van Schaack, Henry: 71, 106, 125, 126, 131, 137
Van Schaack, Peter: 106, 150
Vaughan, Gen. John: 82, 83-84, 105, 106

Walkill: 2, 3, 4, 16, 21, 42, 121, 122, 150;   poor tax: 5
Washington, Gen. George: 48, 107, 110, 112, 119, 121
Watkins, Rev. Hezekiah: 35, 36
Westchester County: 2, 121
Willet, Gilbert Colden (nephew of CC2): 10, 147
Willet, Isaac: 9, 10
Willett, Alice Colden (sister of CC2): 2, 7, 127, 146
Woodhull, Jesse: 73, 79, 91

Yorktown: 112, 116